World Mission Studies

CHRISTIANS OF THE COPPERBELT

CHRISTIANS OF THE COPPERBELT

The Growth of the Church in Northern Rhodesia

JOHN V. TAYLOR and
DOROTHEA A. LEHMANN

SCM PRESS LTD
BLOOMSBURY STREET LONDON

FIRST PUBLISHED 1961

PRINTED IN GREAT BRITAIN BY
CHARLES BIRCHALL AND SONS LTD
LIVERPOOL AND LONDON

CONTENTS

ABBREVIATIONS

AME	African Methodist Episcopal Church
ANC	African National Congress
CCAR	Church of Central Africa in Rhodesia
DRC	Dutch Reformed Church
IRM	International Review of Missions
LMS	London Missionary Society
MMS	Methodist Missionary Society
RST	Rhodesia Selection Trust
UCCAR	United Church of Central Africa in Rhodesia
UMCA	Universities' Mission to Central Africa
UMCB	United Missions in the Copperbelt
UNIP	United National Independence Party of Northern Rhodesia
USCL	United Society for Christian Literature

AUTHORS' PREFACE

THE objective of this study was to reach a deeper understanding both of the factors affecting the growth of the Christian Church in the Copperbelt towns of Northern Rhodesia, and of the Church's response to the pressures and demands of that cultural melting-pot. Though generalization is to be eschewed, it was hoped that some insight might be gained also into the nature of the Church's encounter with the urbanization that is taking place in so many parts of Africa.

In accordance with all the studies in this series the field-work, which lasted for eight and a half months in 1958, was concentrated upon one or two selected situations, and no over-all survey was attempted. After the initial preparations our attention was focussed for the first three months upon the African Township of the Nchanga Mine at Chingola. In addition, during the same period, one of us lived for thirty-eight days intermittently in Kansuswa, an African Township with its own board of management, six miles from Mufulira. For the next two and a half months we turned our attention to the rural background. First a journey in the Northern Province enabled us to spend a few days at several centres of the Bemba tribe, to interview Chief Chitimukulu, Chief Makasa, Chief Chikwanda, and officers of the Administration at Mpika, Chinsali and Kasama, and to visit the Church of Scotland Mission at Chitambo, the White Fathers' Mission at Ilondola, and Alice Lenshina's village headquarters at Kasomo. Then for six weeks we lived at Nsensema's among the Lunda people of the Luapula valley, three miles south of Chief Kazembe's capital and nine miles from the large station of the London Missionary Society at Mbereshi. The last two months were spent at Chingola again, with a good deal of interviewing in the other towns of the Copperbelt.

It should, perhaps, be explained that many African place-names, e.g. Kazembe, Mporokoso, are, strictly speaking, the hereditary title of the chief or the village headman who resides there. Sometimes, especially in the smaller villages, this fact is more clearly indicated by the use of an apostrophe; so 'Nsensema's' is the name of the village whose headman is always called Nsensema.

In both town and village our introduction was necessarily effected through the authorities—the Mine Company at Nchanga, the District Commissioner at Kansuswa, and both the Mission and the Administration at Nsensema's. No other way in was available and we are most indebted to these sponsors; but as soon as possible we did what we could to minimize our evident connection with authority in any form. At Nchanga we made our initial approach to church leaders, school teachers and welfare officers, first in groups and afterwards singly; we also tried to win the recognition and co-operation of the branch officials of the African Mineworkers' Union and the African National Congress. Then, under the auspices of one or other of these groups of leaders, we began to develop our contacts with ordinary workers and their families. The bulk of the material we collected consists of transcripts of personal conversations or group discussions; as often as possible we followed up the more promising conversations with second and third interviews.

We have to confess to a considerable dissatisfaction with the results we achieved. Our failure was due, we believe, to two things. In the first place the size and complexity of our field of research was too much for the time which we allowed. The number of different tribes, of different denominations, and of different social and political factors was so great that we should certainly have been wiser to lengthen the duration of the field work and, perhaps, to narrow its scope.

The second factor in our defeat was the atmosphere of suspicion which permeated Northern Rhodesia at the time of the study. We launched at Nchanga Mine a questionnaire that would have provided statistics of church membership and religious observance; but the rumour that we were collecting signatures to prove that there were Africans who favoured federation produced such a general refusal to co-operate that the findings were of no statistical value. A later attempt to discover how many elders and deacons of the congregations were also leaders in secular spheres broke down because these men were afraid of being regarded by their people as informers. Even at Nsensema's such fears made it unwise to pursue our plan to map the family relations of the various homesteads.

We offer this report, therefore, regretfully conscious that in many respects it is shallow and inconclusive, yet hoping that it may in some measure contribute towards a deeper understanding of the Church which is called to stand and make its response in the midst of this complexity and fear.

In preparing this book, though we have exchanged comments and suggestions, we have divided the material, and neither is responsible for the opinions or conclusions of the other. Dr Lehmann has written sections II and IV, and Mr Taylor sections I, III, and V. The draft of every chapter as it was written has been submitted for correction and advice to a panel consisting of the Rev. T. A. Beetham, the Rev. Neil Bernard, Canon George Hewitt, the Rev. Kenneth MacKenzie, Mr Henry Makulu, the Rev. David Ramushu, and Dr A. I. Richards. Though we do not hold them responsible for any of the shortcomings which may have escaped their notice or defeated their ingenuity, we must express our gratitude for their careful help. We wish also to thank particularly Mr. A. D. Short, the Personnel Manager, and Mr. R. G. Gabbitas, the African Personnel Manager, at the Nchanga Mine, together with all those in their departments who gave such ready assistance; Messrs G. Bentley, O.B.E., R. R. Stokes, H. H. Thompson, M.B.E., and D. G. Clough, the then District Commissioners at Chingola, Mufulira, Kawambwa and Chinsali respectively; the Copperbelt Christian Service Council which helped us with transport during the first three months; the many missionaries on the Copperbelt and at Mbereshi who endured out inquisitiveness with unfailing grace; the African clergy who co-operated so generously and in particular the Rev. Gideon Chinula and the Rev. Warren Simyembe at Nchanga; Mr Francis Mukuka who accompanied us on our journey through Bemba country and who, with the other members of his board of Management, allowed one of us to reside at Kansuswa; Chief Kazembe and David Nsensema who provided a village home for us.

Most of all we would acknowledge our debt to the Christian men and women of both races on the Copperbelt, so many of whom gave us their confidence. Numbers of them are quoted in the pages that follow, sometimes, for their own sake, under a pseudonym. Without their friendship this book could not have been written; without their faith there would be no Church to write about.

J.V.T.
D.A.L.

STUDIES IN THE LIFE AND GROWTH OF THE YOUNGER CHURCHES

UNDER this general title a series of studies is at present being undertaken by the Missionary Studies Department of the International Missionary Council and the World Council of Churches—with special reference to those churches which have come into being in Asia, Africa and Latin America during the last two centuries. The intention is, not to present a general survey of the churches, but rather, in a number of clearly delimited, selected situations, to make studies 'in depth'. This is a search to understand, at a deeper level than a general survey can attempt, what it means for individual Christians or local churches to stand at a particular point of time in a given situation; how do they respond to the different factors in this environment and what influences and determines this response? What, in fact, does it mean to be the Church—in this situation at this time? To this end the central element of this investigation consists of a number of carefully selected 'situation studies' in different parts of the world. This volume presents the second such study, undertaken from February to October, 1958, in the Copperbelt region of Northern Rhodesia.

We are greatly indebted to the Rev. John V. Taylor, M.A., and to Miss Dorothea A. Lehmann, Ph.D., for jointly carrying through this piece of research, and to all those, in Northern Rhodesia and elsewhere, who have rendered valuable help in the process. We are especially grateful to the Church Missionary Society and the London Missionary Society respectively for making the services of Mr Taylor and Dr Lehmann available to us for this study.

VICTOR E. W. HOWARD

London

I

HISTORY

I

The Converging Forces

THE place where David Livingstone died, and where his heart still lies buried, appears in a strange way to be the middle of Africa. Equally remote from Zanzibar, Mozambique and the Limpopo, the various lines of advance into the interior seem to have converged towards this centre. The desolate swamps of Bangweulu and the arid northern plateau have acted, as it were, like a vacuum drawing inwards towards this ultimate median point the migrant tribes, the missionary pioneers, the commercial adventurers and the political powers. This is the end of the trek, for this is the place of meeting.

The awkwardly shaped territory of Northern Rhodesia has been likened to a lop-sided butterfly.[1] As it flaps across the continent towards the north-west, its western 'wing' is enclosed by the watershed between the Congo and the Zambezi basins and the first great curve of the S-shaped Zambezi river; the eastern 'wing' is bounded roughly by the Luapula valley and the crescent formed by Lake Mweru, the lowest tip of Lake Tanganyika and Lake Nyasa. These wings are divided by the artificial inlet of the Congo Pedicle running down to the butterfly's head. On the eastern side of this head is Ilala where Livingstone died, and on the western side lies the Copperbelt.

The distribution and inter-relation of the many tribes of the territory is complicated; but for a cursory description one might say that there are four dominant invader tribes and more than a dozen others. Two of the invaders came in from the Congo early in the eighteenth century; these were the Bemba, a matrilineal tribe of hunters and cultivators, who settled in the centre of the butterfly's eastern wing, and the Lunda who have heavily populated the Luapula valley along the western edge of the same wing. The Bemba never traded with their neighbours, perhaps because they found their plateau soil too poor to produce any surplus; so, under their paramount chief, or Chitimukulu, they raided their neighbours and enslaved their captives, selling most of them in later times to the Arab and Swahili traders from Zanzibar who had penetrated as far as their borders. They also incorporated conquered districts by sending lesser chiefs to rule over them and such areas can still be found on the borders of Bembaland today.[2] The Lunda also raided and sold their neighbours, under their chief, or Kazembe, who held a monopoly as middle-man in the ivory trade. These Lunda, however, were more closely linked than the Bemba with the original Luba stock in the Congo. More recently they had been brought into vassalage to Msidi, the powerful Nyamwezi adventurer who dominated Katanga, and even as late as 1886 the Kazembe who had been Livingstone's somewhat uncivil host for six months was summoned to Bunkeya Mukulu and executed at the request of one of 'king' Msidi's wives.[3]

The other two dominant tribes are to be found along the lower and outer edge of each of the two 'wings'. On the east are the Ngoni who came from Natal. Fleeing from the tyrant Chaka in the 1820s they struck north in a series of thrusts, one of which settled on the Rhodesian side of Lake Nyasa. The Ngoni were a patrilineal, cattle-herding people with a highly disciplined military organization. They lived partly by raiding their neighbours, but they preferred to incorporate their captives into the tribe rather than selling them as slaves. On the west, along the fertile Zambezi valley, the fourth of these dominant tribes, the Lozi or Barotse, also owe their position to a military horde invading from the south. In 1838 these overran the Lozi people and set up a dynasty which established the tribe's supremacy over its neighbours. But after a quarter of a century a Lozi chieftain, who had once been Livingstone's cook, decimated all the males of the foreign dynasty and set himself up as king. He and his successors retained the language of their invaders and the strong centralized structure they had introduced, and extended their dominance still further, reaching eastwards and inwards beyond the Kafue river.

The Converging Circle of Missionary Advance, 1880—1890

Livingstone's death in 1873 gave an immense impetus to several different missionary societies. By common counsel the Church Missionary Society, the London Missionary Society and the Scottish Presbyterian Churches launched into a strategy of penetration from the east coast. The Universities' Mission to Central Africa did likewise, and three years later the White Fathers followed suit. By the end of 1881, seven different missions were established within striking distance of what is now

Northern Rhodesia. In the east the Free Church of Scotland, six years after their arrival in Nyasaland, had just moved their headquarters to Bandawe, half way up the eastern shore of the Lake; the Church of Scotland, though it had run into a deal of trouble, had managed to maintain its station at Blantyre, south of the Lake; and the Livingstonia Central Africa Trading Company, later known as the African Lakes Company, which was founded in order to provide transport for these two Missions, having spread a network of trading ports up the Lake, was starting to cut the 'Stevenson Road' as a link with Lake Tanganyika. The Universities' Mission to Central Africa also had just begun work at Likoma on the eastern shore of Lake Nyasa. In the north the London Missionary Society, after three successive expeditions had taken a heavy toll of life, was turning its eyes from the centre of Lake Tanganyika towards the southern end; so also were the White Fathers, whose pioneer headquarters had for two years been established facing that of the London Missionary Society on the further shore of the Lake. South of the Zambezi the Jesuit Mission was recovering from its first abortive attempt in the previous year to open work among the Southern Tonga across the river. And François Coillard and his wife of the Paris Evangelical Mission, having in 1878 won an invitation from King Lewanika to enter Barotseland, would already have been on their way there had they not been detained in Basutoland by the outbreak of the Gun War.

Yet it was none of these seven missions that first provided the man who followed Livingstone into Northern Rhodesia with the Gospel. That honour was reserved for Fred Arnot, a fellow countryman of the great Scottish explorer and in many respects his true spiritual successor. Arnot belonged to no official organization; for he was a member of the Plymouth Brethren whose 'Christian Missions in Many Lands' are individually autonomous, while keeping in touch with a central office in Bath. After spending three months with the Christian Chief Khama of Bechuanaland, in June 1882 Arnot set out to cross the northern desert, taking, besides his ox-waggon and three donkeys, 'one suit of clothes, one knife, fork and spoon, one plate, cup, some soap, beads, calico, wheat-meal, tea, sugar, coffee, a little powder and lead, and all packed comfortably into six sailor bolster bags'.[4] In December 1882 he reached King Lewanika's capital and obtained permission to remain there until the Coillards should arrive. He stayed for almost a year and a half. During that time he opened a school for the sons of the chiefs, in which the future King Yeta III and his Chief Minister, both outstanding Christians in later years, first learned the rudiments of the Faith. He was also instrumental in dissuading King Lewanika from joining Lobengula of Matabeleland in an attack upon the advancing white man. In 1884, believing that Coillard was about to arrive, Arnot sought permission to advance up to the headwaters of the Zambezi and start work among the Western Lunda. This Lewanika would not allow, so Arnot went through Portuguese West Africa to the coast.

Now some of the seven missions that encircled Northern Rhodesia were preparing to advance closer. The Jesuits made a second attempt to cross the Zambezi, this time into Barotseland, but once again they were compelled to retreat. The Coillards, after yet another year's delay, at last entered the country and set up their first station at Sesheke on 24 September 1885, advancing to a second station at Sefula near the capital in January 1887. Building on the foundation Arnot had laid, they were able to concentrate their work upon the royal enclosure and the aristocracy of the tribe, very much as the Anglican and Roman missions had been doing in Uganda and with similar results.

In 1890 yet another mission, that of the Primitive Methodists, sent forward two missionaries and their wives to cross the Zambezi, and open up work among the Ila people to the east of Barotseland. Lewanika, however, detained them for three years in his territory before allowing them to proceed to their first station on the Nkala River. In the north east the Free Church of Scotland had sent an African evangelist, William Koyi, to work among the Ngoni on the Rhodesian side of Lake Nyasa but had not yet been able to follow this up with its own missionaries. But in 1888 the Rev. Andrew Murray and the Rev. T. C. B. Vlek, of the Dutch Reformed Church of Cape Province, South Africa, came to Nyasaland to work under the Scottish Mission and, in the following year, started their own independent mission among the Ngoni at Mvera.

The Bemba were still out of reach, but the Rev. Picton Jones and the Rev. Stewart Wright of the London Missionary Society established two stations to the north of them at the southern tip of Lake Tanganyika—at Fwambo (later moved to Kawimbe) in 1887 and at Niamkolo in 1889. The White Fathers had moved their headquarters further down Lake Tanganyika to Karema and were sending exploratory parties to the south of the Lake; in 1890 they opened a station at Mambwe at the northern edge of Bemba country.

The Lunda in the Luapula valley were also untouched. But their chief Kazembe, as we have seen, was in some degree a vassal of King Msidi, whose capital was at Bunkeya, 120 miles to the west, and there the remarkable Fred Arnot, having returned from the West Coast had een living since February 1886. After working there for two years on is own he left the station in charge of two other missionaries.

So by the end of 1890 Northern Rhodesia was ringed on every side but ie south east with mission stations, five of which were actually within ie modern borders of the territory. But by this time another circle was eing drawn, the ring of concession hunters, prospectors and Company .gents, who were opening up Africa to European rule.

The Converging Circle of Imperial Advance, 1889—1900

The scramble for Africa was in full swing. None of the European owers could afford the gamble of taking over, administering and exloiting the vast areas of the African interior, yet they dared not allow thers to get there first. The answer to their dilemma was the revival f chartered companies whereby private investors ran the big risks for ie high stakes, while the State achieved its spheres of influence and xercised an indirect diplomatic and military power. It was a system hich the British Prime Minister, Lord Salisbury, that canny and conliatory expansionist, was glad to use *faute de mieux;* but he had no itention of allowing any Company to do more than serve the interests f his own brand of enlightened imperialism.

The great powers were becoming concerned not merely to acquire olated spheres of interest, but to link together their territories in order control unbroken lines of communication across the continent of frica. In the year before Salisbury came into office, the Boers of the 'ransvaal Republic had considered joining hands with German South Vest Africa, to form such a trans-continental link from east to west. 'his would have isolated the British Cape Colony from the rest of Africa, nd the danger had only been overcome by annexing Bechuanaland. Iow a similar threat appeared in the preparations that Portugal was iaking to join her Eastern and Western territories. Salisbury was insely concerned to prevent this. In 1888 he allowed the High Comiissioner at the Cape to negotiate the first of a series of treaties with obengula, the paramount Chief of the Matabele, in what is now outhern Rhodesia; he then went on to consider ways whereby he could xtend the British sphere of influence to include the areas where the iissionaries had settled around the shores of Lake Nyasa and Lake 'anganyika. His first step towards this, at the beginning of 1889, was appoint Mr (later Sir) Harry Johnston as British Consul at Mozamique, with power to penetrate up the Zambezi and to make treaties on ehalf of the Imperial Government with any independent tribes lying beyond the sphere of Portuguese control. Unfortunately the British Treasury was unwilling to meet the expenses of so undefined a charge.

It was at this moment that Cecil Rhodes came into the picture. In the previous year he had acquired a monopoly of the diamond industry and was anxious to harness his immense wealth to a scheme of northward expansion. Having just amalgamated with the rival Beit and Rudd interests to form the British South Africa Company, he was in London in May 1889 to petition for a Royal Charter to assume powers of government as far north as the Zambezi. At the same time he was negotiating a merger with the African Lakes Company, which had run into financial difficulties through its continual fighting with the Arab traders, in the hopes of extending his control, through their agency, over what is now Northern Rhodesia and Nyasaland. At a literary party in the middle of May Rhodes met Johnston, talked with him through the night and in the early dawn offered to finance Johnston's treaty-making expedition on the understanding that the new territories would be included within the sphere of the Company's charter.[5] When this proposal was put to Lord Salisbury later that day he accepted it with one significant modification. 'It would be preferable,' he declared, 'that the Foreign Office should pay your travelling and treaty-making expenses in Nyasaland, as we do not want to commit ourselves to handing over that region to a Chartered Company. Outside its limits I see no objection to Mr Rhodes paying your expenses and meeting the cost of negotiations.'[6] Salisbury did not at this juncture specify what was the western frontier of Nyasaland, but neither did he indicate, in the Charter granted to Rhodes five months later, what were the northern limits of the Company's field of operations. Northern Rhodesia still remained the vacuum, and upon it were converging not only British, but also Portuguese, Belgian and German interests.

Johnston's arrival at the south of Lake Nyasa in August 1889 baulked the advance of Portugal into that territory, and a protectorate was declared over Southern Nyasaland. He then proceeded with the assistance of Alfred Sharpe to draw a ring of concession-treaties around the vacuum. Before the end of the year Johnston made treaties with African chiefs and Arab despots right up the western shore of Lake Nyasa, northwest to Abercorn, which he bought and named as the district headquarters, and on to the two stations of the London Missionary Society at Fwambo and Niamkolo. At the same time Sharpe had procured treaties from the southern end of Lake Nyasa westwards as far as Petauke, and the next year he retraced Johnston's steps along the northern circuit and continued through the Lunda tribe, where Kazembe signed, to Katanga where Msidi, warned by Fred Arnot's two colleagues, rebuffed him.

During 1890 Rhodes also was sending his own agents north of the Zambezi to obtain similar concessions on behalf of the Company. Mr F. Lochner succeeded, through the help of François Coillard, in obtaining the first of a series of treaties, with King Lewanika of the Lozi; and Joseph Thompson arrived at the south of Lake Nyasa, much to Alfred Sharpe's surprise, and almost completed the circle of concessions by obtaining treaties as far west as the edge of what is now the Copperbelt.[7]

Meanwhile Johnston was back in England trying to get a clear answer to two questions that had not yet been honestly faced: whose servant was he, Rhodes' or Lord Salisbury's? And who was to be master north of the Zambezi, the British South Africa Company or the Imperial Government? Rhodes had set his mind on extending his Company's claim over the whole sphere of British influence north of the Zambezi. He was more interested in securing the rights to exploit the land and minerals than in administration as such. This was a necessary chore that he was prepared to pay other people to look after. He regarded Johnston as his administrator, but hoped to delegate the Company's responsibilities in this field to the African Lakes Company. He had acquired an important share and for a year he had been negotiating to secure control over all their interests.

Johnston was at this time indifferent as to whether the British sphere north of the Zambezi was placed under the Company's charter or declared a Protectorate, provided only that the administration were committed to himself as the servant of the Imperial Government. He had already formed, however, a very poor opinion of the capacities of the African Lakes Company, and flatly refused to act under their authority.[8]

The Imperial Government for their part needed the financial backing that Rhodes was prepared to give, but throughout this decade, for a variety of reasons, both the Conservative and Liberal Governments were most reluctant to give the British South Africa Company a free hand north of the Zambezi. For one thing they feared lest the Company's maladroit and bludgeoning way with foreign neighbours, whether Boer or Portuguese or German, might run them into serious diplomatic trouble—a fear that was several times justified. Secondly they were concerned to protect African interests and mitigate the worst evils of commercial exploitation.

A decision was delayed throughout the summer of 1890, while agreement was negotiated first with Germany and then with Portugal over their frontiers in Central Africa. But by the end of that year a compromise was reached by partition of the area. 'The countries adjoining Lake Nyasa' were to be administered directly by the Imperial Government as the 'British Central Africa Protectorate', while the Company was to extend its Charter to include the whole of what is now Northern Rhodesia. Administrative power over both areas was to be vested in Johnston, as the Imperial Commissioner and Consul-General, subsidized to the tune of £10,000 annually by the Company in consideration of the extension of their chartered sphere and the delegation to Johnston of their administrative responsibilities. This settlement was a bitter disappointment to Rhodes; so when, after two years' pacification in the Protectorate, Johnston was compelled to ask for an increase of the subsidy, Rhodes tried again to bargain for such an extension of the Company's land and mineral rights in Nyasaland as would virtually have brought the Protectorate into the Chartered sphere. Again, however, the Imperial Government intervened, and, after further prolonged negotiations, a new settlement was reached at the end of 1894 whereby the Company assumed independent responsibility for administering its own sphere.

Yet the tension between Company rule and the Colonial Office continued from time to time to be revived. Only six months after Major Forbes had taken up his post as Administrator of the Company's northern territories, Rhodes' most trusted henchman, Dr Jameson, launched his hare-brained attack on the Transvaal. The Company was fortunate to retain its Charter. As it was, the Colonial Office refused to extend the Matabeleland Order in Council north of the Zambezi, as had been intended, but divided the northern territory into two separate administrative units, called North-West and North-East Rhodesia.[9] Later, in 1899, when there was a fresh danger that the Company might fall foul of Portuguese West Africa, the Colonial Office put North-West Rhodesia in the charge of the High Commissioner at the Cape. The Colonial Office also appeared early in its role of guardian of African interests. In 1898 when the Legislative Council of Southern Rhodesia was formed, it was prevented from assuming legislative powers north of the Zambezi, because Lord Milner, the High Commissioner, and the Colonial Secretary believed that the northern territories were destined to become a tropical dependency rather than a white settlers' country. On these grounds the Colonial Office was opposed to any considerable alienation of land to Europeans across the Zambezi.[10] When hut-tax was first introduced by the Company in North-West and North-East Rhodesia, the Colonial Office compelled them to reduce it from £1 per hut to Shs. 10, and rejected the imposition of a poll-tax on every woman.[11] It also brought constant pressure to bear to prevent the Company's Administration itself from recruiting African labour for the mines in the south.

Naturally such a history, beginning with the dissidence between Johnston and Rhodes and continuing in tension between the British South Africa Company and the Imperial Government, has set up in Central Africa a strong sentiment of antipathy towards 'Colonial Office interference' on the one side, and mistrust of the 'man on the spot' on the other side, which continues to cause repercussions in the present.

Developments under Company Rule, 1900—1924

The first task confronting the new Administrators and their agents was the subjugation of the dominant slave-raiding tribes and the introduction of the *Pax Britannica.* Since Johnston had destroyed the Arabs' strongholds in Nyasaland and the Germans were doing the same in Tanganyika, the main routes of the trade from Northern Rhodesia were already closed. The Coillards had already turned King Lewanika into a redoubtable opponent of slavery among the Lozis; the White Fathers, as we shall see, had similarly disposed the Bemba to accept the administration, and they finally surrendered to an expedition in 1899. The Ngoni under Chief Mpeseni were more unyielding but were eventually crushed in 1898, and in the following year Kazembe of the Lunda also submitted. By the turn of the century the Administrator of North-Eastern Rhodesia had moved his headquarters from Nyasaland to Fort Jameson, on the site of the vanquished Mpeseni's old capital, and the pacification of the territory was complete.

Meanwhile the prospectors were out on behalf of the auxiliary bodies of the British South Africa Company, hunting for the copper deposits which they knew the Africans had already been working for many generations. Between 1899 and 1902 lead and zinc had been found at Broken Hill, and copper at Kansanshi, Luanshya, Bwana Mkubwa (named after a local Native Commissioner who had earned the title of 'Great Master'), and Chambishi.[12] But the full wealth of these deposits lay far below the surface, and more obviously profitable finds were made in the Katanga area in the Belgian Congo. Those monopolized the attention of investors for many years and delayed the development of the great Rhodesian deposits. Nevertheless a number of small mines were opened in the great bend of the River Kafue and at Kansanshi, and even by 1906 copper and zinc exports from Northern Rhodesia were worth £81,000. This figure was enormously exceeded when the mines at Broken Hill and Bwana Mkubwa came into operation in 1910 and 1913 respectively.

Meanwhile communications, by which Rhodes set such store, were being thrust northwards. The telegraph link with Tanganyika was one of his early dreams. By the beginning of the century it was already crossing Bemba country, and the construction of the line brought a wave of social change and advance to that remote people, only to leave them disturbed and dispirited two years later when, the work completed, cash and commerce receded as suddenly as they had arrived. Immediately afterwards the railway also began probing towards the north. The Victoria Falls Bridge opened the way across the Zambezi in 1903; the line reached Broken Hill in 1906 and had linked up with the Belgian Congo system by the beginning of 1910. The railway was not only a physical artery from Africa south of the Zambezi, but also an ideological one. It introduced a new type of European immigrant; all the way up the line from the Cape the railway workers belonged to a common fraternity, and when they organized themselves, as they were the first to do, their solidarity embodied the principles that were operative in the south. Over the border in the Congo there might be African engine drivers, but here they were in league to prevent Africans from receiving industrial training or competing with them in skilled jobs.[13]

The railway also brought a fresh invasion of white farmers. Hitherto there had been much speculation in real estate but very little settlement, apart from the area around Fort Jameson where the fertile lands of the defeated Ngoni had attracted a considerable number of immigrant farmers during the slump that followed the South African war. Now, with markets opening in the Congo mines, more holdings were taken up along the line of rail, the Company selling land at unbelievably cheap rates. A few years later absentee landlords in Britain began to buy up enormous estates to be farmed by their agents. So gradually, in spite of the intentions of the early High Commissioners that the country north of the Zambezi should not be alienated on any large scale to Europeans, the Company found itself driven by financial necessity to realize its assets in land, and from 1913 onwards African farmers were being confined to Native Reserves, as they had been already in Southern Rhodesia. In 1917 the Company proposed reducing the Native Reserves in North-East Rhodesia by one million out of a total of twenty million acres. The missionaries both in Southern and Northern Rhodesia made several moving appeals against the policy of alienating further tracts of land and confining African farmers to inadequate Reserves. For example, the Northern Rhodesia Missionary Council of 1924 passed a resolution that 'since large portions of the country have already been alienated and ceded to European owners the Conference is of the opinion that almost all the balance will be needed to meet the requirements of the native population.... The Conference suggests that all unalienated lands be regarded as held in trust for the native peoples.'[14]

But the sale of its vast land property at cheap rates could not provide the Company with an income adequate to cover the costs of administering the territory, building communications, developing the resources and paying a dividend to its shareholders. Mines and railways swallowed a lot of capital before giving back any returns. Moreover mines, railways and farms were all dependent upon one supreme asset—abundant cheap labour. But the labour did not arrive automatically; and the Imperial Government set its face intractably against the obvious forms of compulsory recruitment. The dilemma could be resolved in one way only—taxation of Africans. Taxation effectively provided the two most urgent requirements of the Company; it provided an immediate income, and it compelled Africans to work for Europeans far more certainly than any system of forced labour could have done.

So at the beginning of the century a hut-tax was introduced, and also a poll-tax on every adult male and on every wife except the first. What this was worth to the Company can be seen from the fact that in the year 1910-11, out of a total income of £95,000 in Northern Rhodesia, African taxation had brought in £57,000.[15] It was worth even more as a device to bring in labour without the normal necessity of offering a competitive wage or attractive conditions. For taxation could be manipulated as the need arose. So, for example, when it was found that Africans living in the neighbourhood of the mines were still farming in their own villages, the tax in that area was raised from Shs. 5 to Shs. 10. Similarly when such Africans were earning the tax-money by selling their surplus produce to the mineworkers, the Mine Companies started to import grain from a distance at much higher prices, simply in order to rob the local men of their market and bring them into the labour supply.[16] The tax, therefore, was set as high as possible; within a few years it was fixed at Shs. 10 per annum in North-West Rhodesia, and in the North-East, where the influence of Nyasaland and the Colonial Office had been strong, at Shs. 5. Very soon missionaries and District Commissioners were remarking on the devastating effect upon tribal life of this enforced migration of the men folk. Yet the pressure was kept up and, at the end of the first World War, in a desperate effort to reduce its deficits, the Company put up the tax to Shs. 10 in the North-East also. This produced an outcry from the Missionaries' Conference.

> 'This great annual exodus of tax-paying males,' they said, 'strikes at the whole fabric of tribal life. . . . We venture earnestly to press for a general reduction of taxation. . . . We also strongly urge that as a matter of justice and with a view to the uplift of the people and the prevention of discontent, a fair proportion of the proceeds of Native taxation, direct and indirect, should be devoted to the immediate benefit of the Native population.'[17]

Others endorsed the missionaries' judgment. The Colonial Office Administration which took over from the Company in 1924 reported that 'from an administrative point of view the decision taken five years ago to increase the tax payable by natives living in the Eastern Districts from five shillings to ten shillings was a deplorable mistake', and it was decided to reduce it in 1925 to Shs. 7/6.[18] Yet even in 1938, after the opening of the Copperbelt had greatly increased the Africans' earning power, the Commission appointed to enquire into financial and economic conditions in Northern Rhodesia reported that Shs. 7/6 was too high for the greater portion of the Territory to support.

From 1920 onwards the Company was having to exercise such rigid economy that district administration was reduced to even greater inefficiency. The European settlers and miners, moreover, were growing impatient with Company rule and demanding their own responsible government. This raised for the first time since 1895 the issue of the political status of the territory, an issue which resolved itself into two questions. Should the Rhodesias form part of the Union of South Africa? And, if not, should they be amalgamated as a single colony? To the first question both the Rhodesias answered 'No', not because they rejected the South African Native policy but because they feared Afrikaner nationalism. The question of amalgamation also received a 'No'. Here the matter of native policy was more determinative. The Southern Rhodesians expressed their fears of the 'Black North' and objected to the employment of skilled Africans in mines and administration north of the Zambezi. Northern Rhodesians for their part opposed amalgamation on two quite different grounds: farmers and industrialists resented the demands of Southern Rhodesia upon their native labour forces; the Missions disliked the restrictive native policy and land alienation which had recently been carried so much further in the South. So the Anglican Bishop May presided over the meeting of settlers which voted against the appointment of a common Administrator in 1921.[19] The die had been cast. Southern Rhodesia was granted Responsible Government in 1923, and the following year Northern Rhodesia was declared a protectorate with its own Legislative Council, and Company rule was superseded by the Colonial Administration.

Thirty years of Christian Penetration, 1894-1924

Having set the scene, we must take up again the story of the Missions. At the beginning of 1894 the Christian forces were deployed just beyond the borders of Northern Rhodesia; a few Missions had actually established bridgeheads in the territory itself. In the Lozi kingdom Coillard had three stations, and the Methodists had at last been allowed to start work among the Ila, the vassal tribe on King Lewanika's eastern border. In the far north the London Missionary Society, after heroic sacrifices, had secured two stations, and the White Fathers a third, among another subject people, the Lungu, who provided the happy hunting ground of the slave-raiding Bemba.

The winning of Bembaland became a major objective for the Missions in the north, as it was, in another sense, for the consuls of the British South Africa Company. The Bemba tribe is organized under the paramount Chief, whose title is Chitimukulu. His own sons may never succeed him but they often hold one or other of the important chieftainships under which the tribe is sub-divided. One of these, Chungu, had been visited by Dr Carson of the London Missionary Society from Kawimbe in 1893. The next year he tried to get through to another chief, Ponda, and to Chitimukulu himself, but they refused to receive him. At the same time a third mission station was opened at Kambole, some fifty miles to the west, from which it was hoped a new approach might be made. However, in 1895 fighting broke out between the Bemba and the Lungu all around Kambole, which quickly turned into a refugee camp for the Lungu fugitives. Then, just as the Bemba seemed ready to open up, death and ill-health removed all but two of the London Missionary Society's men, who were only just able to keep their three stations going because a colleague was sent to them from the Free Church of Scotland Mission.

In the meantime this Mission was making its own attempt to move in towards 'the centre', having in 1895 sent the Rev. Alexander Dewar from Fort Hill in Nyasaland to Mwenzo, outside the north-eastern fringe of Bemba country. However, events proved that in establishing

Mwenzo the Scottish Mission had almost over-reached its strength and it was not until the great Dr James Chisholm started his hospital there in 1900 that effective contact with the Bemba was established.

In the same year as Mwenzo station was opened by the Scottish Mission, the White Fathers won a foothold in Bembaland itself. The hero of this story was the astonishing Père Joseph Dupont. In 1894 the head of their station at Mambwe, assisted by an agent of the British South Africa Company, had visited Chief Makasa, the senior 'son' of the Chitimukulu. They had been rebuffed, but the next year Dupont succeeded in winning Makasa's permission to set up work at Kayambi, close to the Chief's enclosure. He at once sent for reinforcements and within a year had already established a school with five hundred boarders. Makasa was now so devoted to Dupont that he defied Chitimukulu, who promptly prepared to attack, but died suddenly, leaving a weakling to succeed him. The most powerful sub-chief, Mwamba, was now the virtual ruler of Bembaland. Deciding that his best interests lay in treating with the Company's agents, he summoned Dupont to act as his intermediary. Once again this extraordinary French peasant priest charmed his way into the confidence of a cruel and wayward chief, though after some months Arab traders prevailed upon Mwamba to drive Dupont from his district. In 1898 the weak young Chitimukulu called the Company's agents to make a treaty. The other chiefs, including Mwamba and Ponda, were prepared to fight. But Mwamba fell sick and calling Dupont to return, nominated him as his successor. The Frenchman, who by this time had been enthroned as Vicar Apostolic for Northern Rhodesia and Nyasaland, accepted the chieftainship temporarily in order to avoid the usual bloodshed that accompanied the appointment of a new chief. He also used his position to make terms with the Company. The Administration established itself at Kasama, Ponda was defeated and Bemba resistance crumpled up. From this time the White Fathers spread out through Bembaland. Many of the important chiefs became supporters and adherents, though Chitimukulu, on account of his ritual position, has never been very closely committed to the Church. In 1899 stations were opened at Luombe, Chilubula and Malole, and at Chilonga beyond the southern borders of the Bemba.

While the Bemba were becoming predominantly Roman Catholic, the other dominant tribes were also opening their door to other Missions. The London Missionary Society began to look westwards towards the Lunda in the Luapula valley. A. D. Purves made friends with Chief Kazembe, who had just submitted to the Company's consul, and in 1900 was invited to open a new station at Mbereshi, a few miles from the Chief's enclosure. Mporokoso, halfway from their earlier field of operations, was opened as a sub-station with an African evangelist in residence. The Luapula valley was also entered at this time by the Plymouth Brethren, who had already established themselves on the Congo side of Lake Mweru. In 1898 they first set up work in Northern Rhodesia at Johnston Falls, nearly one hundred miles to the south.

In the south-east the resistance of the Ngoni had just been crushed, and the defeated Chief Mpeseni called the missionaries of the Dutch Reformed Church to come westwards from their station in Nyasaland and set up work at Magwero, his capital. From this point they expanded steadily westwards, following the route that the Nyasaland labourers took on their way to the railway and the mines.

Coillard's work among the Lozi was beginning to bear fruit, and in 1898 the crown prince, who had sat in Fred Arnot's school fifteen years before, was baptized. Four years later Dr Reuter opened the first hospital at Sesheke. The Methodist work among the Ila people had been augmented by a second station, and in 1901 they sent their first missionary into the neighbouring tribe of Southern Tonga. The following year the young Edwin Smith arrived as a new recruit and started his study of the Ila language.

All the non-Roman missions that had borne the burden and heat of the day were stretched almost to breaking point and were showing serious signs of exhaustion. Coillard's death in 1904 was a heavy blow from which the Paris Mission took some years to recover. The northern mission fields were even more hard-pressed, for they never enjoyed the boost which the coming of the railway gave in innumerable ways. In the stations of the London Missionary Society, 'the discouragement and tragic losses of many years, together with the burden of overwork and ill-health that for so long dogged the survivors, had resulted among missionaries in strained relationships and cross purposes more grave and persistent than in any other of the Society's fields.'[20] With great moral courage they had invited Dr Laws and Dr Chisholm from the neighbouring Scottish mission field to survey their work and report on the causes of their weakness. The Scotsmen did not mince their words, but they saw that the trouble sprang from the shortage of men. 'Its present condition,' they wrote of the Mission, 'is very unsatisfactory and it must have been so for a considerable time . . . the cumulative effort has been disastrous. . . . Chief among these causes is . . . lack of continuity in the service of the agents and in the policy of the Mission.'[21] But the Scottish Mission also, though spiritually less exhausted, had reached the limit of its resources. From 1901 to 1913 they discussed again and again the crying need for a westward advance, but always had to abandon the scheme for lack of funds and man power. When the Administration invited them to open a station at Chitambo, near the place of Livingstone's death, a special appeal in Scotland enabled them to send Mr and Mrs Malcolm Moffat and Dr Alexander Brown to start work there in 1906. But that almost proved to be the last straw. In 1909 the General Secretary of the London Missionary Society enquired privately whether the Free Church of Scotland Board of Missions would annex the whole of their work in Northern Rhodesia, only to be told that the Scottish Mission had already drafted a proposal to request the London Missionary Society to take over their station and hospital at Mwenzo.[22]

It is sadly ironical, therefore, that just at this time many new missionaries should have arrived in the country under the auspices of other societies and denominations. In 1905 Mr Philips of the Nyasa Industrial Mission (Baptist) opened work at Kafulafuta near Bwana Mkubwa; the Jesuits at last made a successful entry up the new railway line to Broken Hill, followed immediately by the Seventh Day Adventists and the Brethren in Christ. In 1906 Fred Arnot's brother-in-law, Dr Walter Fisher, who had been working across the Angola border, moved to Kalene Hill and started a new field for the Plymouth Brethren among the Rhodesian section of the Western Lunda.

In 1910 the Anglican Bishop, J. E. Hine, arrived at Livingstone with the first party of the Universities' Mission to Central Africa. The bishop himself fully realized that they were entering a field in which others had been at work for twenty-five years. He wrote at the time, 'There are large tracts of country untouched by any of these societies; it will be our aim to work as far as may be possible in a spirit of brotherly co-operation with all those who have already done so much and have been the pioneers of Christianity in this land.' It was not the fault of the pioneer party that the official history of the Society, slipping into the narrow focus that affects all missionary propaganda from time to time, recorded that they 'set out to evangelize an area about two and a half times the size of the whole of the British Isles'.[23] The sites which Bishop Hine selected during four years of tireless marching were certainly scattered over a vast area. From Livingstone the Rev. John Barber and Mr MacLennan opened up Mapanza and Shakashina among the Southern Tonga, while from Fort Jameson in the south-east, Msoro station was established fifty miles away, in the charge of an African priest from Nyasaland, the Rev. Leonard Kamungu. His ministry, with other Nyasa teachers, bore immediate fruit in the two short years before his death, probably by poison, in February 1913. The third area chosen by Bishop Hine was in the Luapula valley where William Deerr set up the station which he moved, after two years, to Chipili. After starting with this flourish the Anglican Mission did not attempt to open its fourth district until six years had passed, when Deerr, the indefatigable pioneer and now a priest, set off again to start work at Mkushi, the centre of the Lala tribe north-east of Broken Hill. Eighteen months later he had died, and work in the Lala district ceased until in 1924 it was started again at Fiwila by the Rev. George Hewitt.

It is not possible to speak of the Anglican Mission, even in its pioneer stage, without referring to work among Europeans as well as Africans. In the year following its first arrival the white population of Northern Rhodesia numbered about 1,500, of whom a considerable proportion would no doubt have styled themselves as members of the Church of England. From that time to the present, when nearly 40 per cent of the white population of the Federation are Anglicans, the white membership of the Anglican Church in the territory has always been greater, or very little less, than the African, and this is true of no other denomination. This has inevitably produced a subtle difference of emphasis. Moreover it has been peculiarly the mark of the Anglican work, springing as it has from the background of the English Establishment, that it has regarded itself not simply as a mission but as the Church of a diocese, and has therefore confronted from the very beginning the problems of a multi-racial Church. The European residents in Livingstone had already raised the money for a church, and almost the first problem that Bishop Hine had to deal with in Northern Rhodesia was the desire of some of them to exclude Africans from the new building; before the church was dedicated he had won his point, and an early morning Eucharist for Africans normally preceded the other Sunday services. In Fort Jameson the first Anglican church had been consecrated for the settler community four years earlier, and had been served for a short time by a Chaplain provided by the Society for the Propagation of the Gospel, and paid by the British South Africa Company. Now, soon after the arrival of the first priest-in-charge, a separate church for Africans was built and from this dual centre he ministered both to the scattered planters and to the African population in the Ngoni country round about.

Before the outbreak of the First World War, three more Societies entered the Territory. In 1910 Fred Arnot, still as great a strategist as ever, brought Mr Bailey of the South Africa General Mission to start work at Mutanda close to the Kansanshi mine. Two years later the Wesleyan Methodists opened a station at Chipembi, near Broken Hill. And in 1913, shortly before his own death, Arnot made his last contribution to Northern Rhodesia in persuading the Rev. J. J. Doke, of the South African Baptists, to extend the work already started by Mr Philips, among the Lamba tribe, in whose midst the Copperbelt was destined to arise. Doke himself lost his life on his first journey of reconnaissance, but he was followed by others, including his son and daughter.

A meeting of missionaries and Africans in 1913 to examine Edwin Smith's Ila translation of the New Testament led to the calling of the Missionary Conference of North-West Rhodesia in 1914, which was attended by representatives of the Paris Mission, the two Methodist Missions, the Jesuits, the Plymouth Brethren and the Anglicans. This was the first of a series of conferences, held every three or four years, which achieved an unusual degree of missionary co-operation. Between 1922, when it was first constituted as the General Missionary Conference of Northern Rhodesia, and 1932, it contained at one time or another every missionary body in the territory, including the four Roman Catholic Societies.[24]

These conferences revealed an astonishing similarity of experience in all the missions during the pre-Copperbelt era. All were facing the practical difficulties of evangelizing huge areas with a small force of workers. In the river valleys the population was fairly concentrated, but over the rest of the territory it was spread very sparsely, and in many areas of arid soil the slash-and-burn system of cultivation produced a semi-nomadic community. Besides this constant moving-on of family groups, which was traditional, the labour migration of modern times, as we have seen, was already drawing away a high proportion of men. Added to this the tsetse fly ruled unchallenged in many districts, and from time to time districts were temporarily depopulated on account of sleeping sickness—part of Bembaland in 1902, Lake Mweru in 1905, around Fort Rosebery in 1912. In such circumstances it was difficult to build up anywhere a coherent Christian group.

Among the Lozi and the Bemba, where the work had been built upon a preliminary alliance with important chiefs, this was more easily achieved; elsewhere, if the chief was hostile or unaffected, it seemed impossible to establish anything like a local church until some missionary, by dint of long service *in one place*, had become such a figure in the scene as to function, at least psychologically, as a kind of substitute chief. It was their permanence even more than their remarkable gifts which made men like Robert Laws and François Coillard so precious to the local church. Fortunately for the Christian cause, after the rapid turnover of the pioneer years, other missions began to produce father-figures of a comparable longevity—men such as James Chisholm of Mwenzo (1900-1935) who, starting from scratch, left nearly 1,400 full church members and 28,000 annual outpatients at his hospital; Mr Malcolm Moffat who, with his wife, helped to open the station at Chitambo in 1906 and remained there until 1930; the Rosses of Kambole (1904-1939); Walter Draper of Kawimbe (1902-1927), who earned the title of 'the best-loved man in Central Africa'; and Walter Fisher of Kalene Hill (1906-1935), who gathered around him in the work such a clan of relatives that a young grand-daughter once asked him, 'Why is everyone in the world called Fisher?' And some there are who 'remain until now'; these it would be invidious to name.

But the Missions could not rely only on the long-term influence of great personalities to create a coherent local church in a constantly shifting population. Most of them, therefore, adopted the method of assembling around the mission station a settled and largely dependent community of adherents. The opportunities of working in this way were irresistible when fugitive slaves and the victims of raids sought refuge with the missionaries.

We can see this happening as we read the Annual Reports of the London Missionary Society. After their first arrival at Fwambo in 1887, Picton Jones' second letter home records only the isolation. 'There is no life here. We are only two Europeans. Two boys came here yesterday morning and said they were going to remain. Last night they returned to their village and never came back again. The quietness and solitude of this place damps their ardour.' Six months later the country was disturbed by Arab raiding. Chief Fwambo moved his village nearer to the mission station for protection. The first African to be baptized was a ransomed slave. In 1891, after the station had been moved to Kawimbe, sixteen families had settled in the neighbourhood. By 1892 the Mission had purchased nine square miles of land and there were eighty houses surrounding the station. The same pattern was reproduced at Niamkolo and Kambole. Then the Bemba attacks on the Lungu brought a new inrush of fugitives, and by 1899 the Directors were reporting that their Central African Mission was 'gathering round it the scattered remains of the native tribes of a once populous district'.[25] This was taking place in other Missions also. When Thompson and Crawford of the Plymouth Brethren moved from Katanga to the western shore of Lake Mweru in 1894, they took a concourse of Christian adherents with them. Eleven years later, when sleeping sickness compelled them to move again, the dispersion moved off in two great parties, one to Lake Bangweulu, the other to Kaleba. Similarly when the Anglican station was moved from Ngomba to Chipili in 1914, 70 men, women and children moved with Deerr to form the nucleus of the new station.

The effect of this pattern was, unfortunately, to create a congregation of dependants that was to a considerable extent cut off from the tribal community and the jurisdiction of the local chiefs. The missionaries found themselves, for the most part reluctantly, compelled to act as unofficial magistrates. One member of the London Missionary Society, transferred in 1898 to Central Africa from Madagascar, wrote in dismay, 'We are known and feared just as the Natives know and fear the Company's agents, and that chiefly because we use, and threaten continually to use, the same mode of punishment.'[26] This early authoritarianism has left a memory that has proved hard to eradicate.

In spite of the enclosed and self-sufficient nature of these 'residential' mission stations, as Dr Roland Oliver has called them, the missionaries did everything they could to look outward and to use the station merely as the centre from which to serve the district beyond. But increasingly specialized work on the station—medical, educational or industrial—whittled down the time available for itineration. Dr Chisholm at Mwenzo was feeling this dilemma as early as 1908. 'As the people departed on the Monday, after Thanksgiving Service, one felt more poignantly than ever . . . that they were scattering as sheep without a shepherd. Many of them are two or three days' journey away and cannot be seen by us for six months at earliest.'[27] For many years he did, in fact, itinerate not only in the area around Mwenzo but also in the Chinsali District a hundred miles to the south, attempting to hold it against encroachment by the White Fathers until at last in 1913 a station was opened there. But every week spent on itineration damaged the work of his hospital at Mwenzo.

The obvious solution to this dilemma is to employ African assistants in the evangelistic and pastoral outreach, who will in time become the indigenous ministers of the young Church. On this point it is interesting to compare Nyasaland and Northern Rhodesia. The former is a compact country with a fairly concentrated population. Not only are mission stations closer together, but each station has all its sub-stations within easy reach. An African could be put in sole charge of a sub-station without being left isolated and unsupervised for months at a time. So from the beginning both the Scottish and Anglican Missions in Nyasaland were accustomed to give considerable responsibility to their African agents, and such men were ordained to the ministry quite early in the history of these Missions. Since large numbers could be served pastorally from one centre, it was feasible and more economical to employ a small body of clergy rather than a large number of unordained catechists. In somewhat the same way, since in this compact society most children can attend day school from their own houses, the school teachers are well integrated with the life of the villages and play their part as leaders of the community. The minister and the Christian teacher, therefore, are the main agents of the local church, which is thus blessed with a leadership of comparatively high professional competence and social standing. This has led naturally to a comparatively rapid advance towards responsible participation by Africans on the Councils of their Church.

In Northern Rhodesia, on the other hand, the mission stations were scattered over such vast and such empty spaces that they had to make use of large numbers of unordained itinerant workers. Because it was impossible to supervise sub-stations from a great distance, the missionaries felt they could only give these men greater responsibilities by bringing them into the central station, and this in itself retarded their development towards real self-reliance. Teachers, as elsewhere, were trained at almost every mission station in the early days to be the agents of the Church for evangelism as well as education, and many of them gave faithful service. But because of the enormous distances, pupils in Northern Rhodesia were very often boarders, living away from their own homes. The whole school community, therefore, was something external to the life of the village. So, however keen teachers may have been as individual Christians—and almost all candidates for the ministry have come from their ranks—they have tended to play a smaller part in the life of the local congregations and to concentrate more upon their purely professional tasks.

Understandably, therefore, the Missions in Northern Rhodesia were comparatively slow to develop an indigenous African ministry. Dr Laws, in his report on the London Missionary Society's work in 1905, commented on their failure to provide any systematic training of pastors or teachers. Yet it was not until 1934 that they opened at Mbereshi a Bible training school, which produced in 1938 their first three indigenous ministers since work began in 1877.

For a long time those Missions which had work also in Nyasaland or Southern Rhodesia were able to conceal to some extent their lack of a strong indigenous leadership by importing many of their best African colleagues. When Alexander Dewar opened the station at Mwenzo in 1895 he was supported by John Banda, a Tonga from Nyasaland, who remained there until he was killed in the First World War. The Anglicans enjoyed the comradeship of such men as Leonard Kamungu at Msoro, and Matthew Azizi who worked at their Mapanza printing press from its beginning in 1914 until it was closed down in 1929, both of whom came from Nyasaland. Similarly the Methodists were strengthened by some outstanding men from Southern Rhodesia. Strangely enough, so far from inhibiting the sense of responsibility in the Northern Rhodesian Church, the presence of such men seems, by example, to have stimulated vocations among the indigenous church members. It was the Anglican Church, after only twenty years in the country which most quickly accepted Africans of Northern Rhodesia to be trained for the ministry.

Meanwhile the increasing demands of specialized work at the mission stations and the growing burden of administration allowed the missionaries less time for itineration. The First World War brought the recruitment of new workers to a standstill until the early 1920s; and the advent of motor cars ushered in an era of more superficial contacts and more emphasis on 'efficiency'. This was particularly marked in the sphere of education. The Phelps-Stokes Commission was investigating. The new Colonial Office Administration was proposing a far closer partnership with the Missions. At the General Missionary Conference in 1924, five out of the sixteen papers were read by Government Officers. A Department of Education was about to be set up with an Advisory Board consisting mainly of missionaries. Grants in aid and the salaries of certificated African teachers were to be given to approved centres of education, and the emphasis was to be laid on boarding schools and a less 'bookish' syllabus.

The following table shows the position of the Missions at the end of this period, as indicated by figures in the Government Reports on Native Affairs and Education. The non-Roman Missions are able to include some of the wives of missionaries in their totals of teachers; those with technical qualifications may also be numbered among the teachers of literary subjects. Already the high proportion of missionaries engaged in

Mission	Date of first Station	Administrative District (1958 demarcation)	Mission-aries (1924)	Stations' (1924)	Schools (1925)	Missionary teachers Literary Subjects	Missionary teachers Technical
Paris Evangelical	1885	Barotseland, Livingstone	27	7	49	16	3
London Missionary Society	1887	Northern, Luapula	14	5	249	10	1
White Fathers	1890	Northern, Luapula, Eastern	32	12	542	32	3
Primitive Methodists	1893	Southern	11	5	59	12	0
United Free Church of Scotland	1895	Northern, Central	12	5	307	11	1
Plymouth Brethren	1898	Luapula, Northwestern, Barotseland	19	7	55	24	1
Dutch Reformed	1899	Eastern	20	9	464	14	9
Baptists	1905	Western	3	1	7	3	3
Jesuit Fathers	1905	Southern, Eastern	20	5	86	17	9
Seventh Day Adventists	1905	Southern, Eastern, Luapula	11	4	36	7	1
Brethren in Christ	1906	Southern	4	2	8	2	1
Universities' Mission to Central Africa	1910	Southern, Eastern, Luapula Central	17	6	62	9	1
South Africa General	1910	Northwestern, Barotseland	11	4	14	7	0
Wesleyan Methodists	1912	Central	2	1	37	2	0
Church of Christ	1923	Southern	2	1	2	3	2

education is remarkable. Schools, of course, may mean anything from a boarding school on a mission station to a bush school where an untrained catechist gives irregular religious instruction; their number is, however, some indication of the spread of congregations and shows, for example, the great advance of the Dutch Reformed Mission.

The Beginnings of Prophet Movements

Yet in spite of the new drive for efficiency and specialization, perhaps at no time was the pastoral ministry more urgently needed. Tribal life, more than ever before, was showing the effects of the many changes and tensions of the past thirty years, culminating in the First World War. A new type of young man, initiated in the mission elementary school and graduating in the mine compounds, was beginning to make his presence felt. Already in 1924 the first 'Native Association' had been formed in the Mwenzo district. The chiefs still wielded great authority, but they neither earned it in the manner of the old regime nor deserved it by the new standards of 'Indirect Rule'.

> 'The chief is no longer the fountain of justice and the law giver, the leader in battle and the distributor of the spoil. The heir to a chieftainship does not as in the past have to fight for his place. . . . Different qualities are required, and they are qualities which do not make the same appeal to the people as in the olden days.' 'The chief has mystical but no longer absolute power and the young educated have also to be considered. Chiefs cannot be by-passed but cannot be used for much administrative responsibility.'[28]

In growing numbers Africans were searching for direction, and distrustful of those who might have given it. At such a time the exotic and confused gospels of prophet movements and 'Ethiopian' sects had a particular appeal. These had already made their appearance in Barotseland and, to a much more serious extent, in Nyasaland. In 1900 a youth of the Nyasaland Tonga tribe called Kenan Chirwa Kamwana, who had been educated by the Church of Scotland at Bandawe, attached himself to the free-lance missionary, Joseph Booth, who, after a variegated spiritual history, had recently become associated with the Jehovah's Witnesses. Two years later Kamwana was baptized with the name of Elliot. After some years in Johannesburg Kamwana spent six months of the year 1907 with Joseph Booth at Capetown. He returned to the neighbourhood of Bandawe in 1908, and began preaching the doctrines of the Jehovah's Witnesses, with the enthusiastic approval of the Johannesburg branch. Very soon about ten thousand had been baptized by him. The Scottish Mission was naturally disturbed, and the Government of Nyasaland considered that the promise of Christ's return in 1914 and the teaching that all human governments are doomed to destruction were sufficiently dangerous to warrant Kamwana's arrest. He cannot, however, have been guilty of serious subversion, for he was offered the option of reporting at regular intervals to the District Resident or of removing himself beyond Nyasaland. He chose to go back to Cape Colony, after which no more was heard of him for many years.[29]

In recent times, however, the name of Elliot Kamwana has appeared again upon the stage after a long absence—whether enforced or not does not appear to be clear. A not very influential group, the Bamulonda, or People of the Watchman, hails him as its prophet and founder, the seventh 'angel' in the history of the Christian Church. This movement seems to have originated in Nyasaland, but there are concentrations of followers near Solwezi, in some of the Copperbelt towns, and in the Luapula valley, where we came across them during our stay at Nsensema's (see pp. 238ff).

A far more serious and tragic event occurred in Nyasaland in 1915. The Rev. John Chilembwe, a pupil and close associate of Joseph Booth, whom he had accompanied to America, later set up his own independent all-African Mission Station near Blantyre. From his church he launched an abortive insurrection in which several tea planters were murdered. The rising was quickly put down and Chilembwe was shot while trying to escape capture. Yet even today his name is recalled by Africans as that of a hero.[30] Chilembwe appears to have had no direct link with the Jehovah's Witnesses other than his friendship with Joseph Booth. Yet that was enough to establish the connection in many people's minds.[31]

During the First World War the Jehovah's Witnesses were proscribed in Nyasaland and Northern Rhodesia, because they advocated passive resistance to the Army's requisitioning of porters on the Tanganyika front and because their luridly illustrated pamphlets were regarded as a threat to morale.[32] This drove the Movement underground. Since there was no headquarters in the territory, the teaching was propagated entirely by African open-air preachers and the distribution of tracts. So it became merely one ingredient in a hotch-potch of ideas, contributing its millennial expectations and its condemnation of governments to an amalgam of biblical symbolism, speaking with tongues, pagan practice, licentious dancing and anti-European propaganda.[33] In the early 1920s groups appeared in various parts of Northern Rhodesia and won large numbers of adherents, especially in the unreached or only partly evangelized districts.[34] The CID reported that they failed to find any direct political significance in it and the Government wisely adopted a policy of toleration.[35]

In the autumn of 1925 one Tomo Nyirenda, who had some smattering of the 'Watchtower' doctrines, appeared in the backward Mkushi district as a prophet and witch-finder, calling himself, as many pagan prophets had done before, '*Mwanalesa*', God's child. It is significant that he was an educated Nyasa, for in another outbreak of witch-hunting nine years later it was observed that the practitioners were well-dressed young men from Nyasaland, which was regarded as the home of education and high wages.[36] Nyirenda adapted the rite of baptismal immersion to the ancient craft of witch-finding. He became the protégé of Chief Shaiwila who used him as his instrument to get rid of his personal enemies. In the course of a short campaign among the Lala and Lamba people, more than thirty were done to death as witches. In the course of our study we spoke with one educated African who remembered these events taking place.

'Tom Mwanalesa,' he said, 'and the other African missionaries of Watchtower arrived with their big Bibles, saying, "Something is coming." Every villager turned out for them; even the pagans went to listen. The movement sprang up in very big numbers. Thousands were baptized in the river, including myself. Another reason for their success was that they seemed to be destroying witchcraft. Mwanalesa got the co-operation of the chief by saying that his baptism could disclose anyone who was a witch, for witches did not go down deep into the water. It was usually frightened old people who were marked out in this way. Such victims were ordered by the chief to be killed, or their relatives had to redeem them by paying sums to him. Mwanalesa also preached that Europeans and all leaders of the organized Churches were snakes.'

For a short time Nyirenda also crossed the frontier into the Belgian Congo. At the beginning of 1926 he, Chief Shaiwila and one other were tried and executed.

It is worth recording these facts, drawn from the official reports of the Native Affairs Department, because subsequently a recurrent legend has grown up about 'Mwanalesa', which confuses him with an entirely different outbreak of murderous witch-hunting that occurred a little later on the western border of the territory, and also connects him more closely than is warranted with the true Watchtower Movement. The Native Affairs Department stated at the time that 'the "Watchtower Movement" cannot be charged with direct responsibility for these murders but it does appear to have provided the first germ of "Mwana Lesa's" idea and then the prepared soil in which it grew'.[37] It appears now that after the disturbances on the Copperbelt in 1935 the Commission of Enquiry certainly laid too much responsibility at the door of the Watchtower Movement and accepted many serious allegations on very slender evidence. But on the strength of its report the literature of the Jehovah's Witnesses was banned. In a few districts, especially in the Luapula valley where a big influx from the Congo had followed the Belgian Government's proscription of the Movement in 1934, the chiefs carried out a vigorous campaign of suppression, burning down the Watchtower meeting enclosures, so that in some places the members hived off and built their own villages.[38] This persecution did something to purge the Movement of its less reputable 'hangers-on' and led the 'missionaries' of the Jehovah's Witnesses to tighten up their administrative control in Northern Rhodesia.

NOTES

1. Kenneth Bradley, *Copper Venture,* Mufulira Copper Mines Ltd, 1952, p. 15.
2. I am indebted to Dr A. I. Richards for this information.
3. F. S. Arnot, *Missionary Travels in Central Africa,* 'Echoes of Service,' Bath, 1914, pp. 84, 99.
4. *Ibid.*, p. 5.
5. Roland Oliver, *Sir Harry Johnston and the Scramble for Africa* Chatto and Windus, 1957, pp. 152-5.
6. H. H. Johnston, *The Story of My Life,* p. 238 (quoted by R. Oliver, *op. cit.*, p. 155).
7. L. H. Gann, *The Birth of a Plural Society,* Manchester University Press, 1958, pp. 56 f.
8. Oliver, *op. cit.*, pp. 182-4.
9. Gann, *op. cit.*, p. 62.
10. *Ibid.*, pp. 62 f., 137.
11. *Ibid.*, p. 80.
12. For the whole story, now part of the mythology of Northern Rhodesia, see Bradley, *op. cit.*
13. Gann, *op. cit.*, pp. 130-132.
14. *Proceedings of the General Missionary Conference of Northern Rhodesia*, Lovedale Press, 1924, p. 24. See also A. S. Cripps in *IRM* X, 1921, pp. 99-109.
15. Gann. *op cit.*, p. 83.
16. *Ibid.*, pp. 122, 124.
17. *Proceedings of the GMC . . .*, pp. 16 f.
18. *Report of the Native Affairs Department, Northern Rhodesia,* 1924-5.

19. Gann, *op. cit.*, p. 172.
20. Norman Goodall, *History of the London Missionary Society, OUP*, 1954, p. 274.
21. *Ibid.*, p. 296.
22. Church of Scotland Missions Archives. Daly to Wardlow Thompson, 21.vii.1909; Daly to Laws, 3.viii.1909.
23. A. G. Blood, *History of the Universities' Mission to Central Africa* II, UMCA, 1957, p. 6.
24. C. P. Groves, *The Planting of Christianity in Africa* IV, Lutterworth, 1958, p. 137.
25. *London Missionary Chronicle:* 1888 (pp. 338, 412, 470); 1891 (p. 190); 1892 (p. 147); 1893 (p. 15); 1897 (p. 224). *Annual Report* 1899.
26. Goodall, *op. cit.*, p. 272.
27. *Livingstonia News* II, 1909, p. 4.
28. *Report of the Native Affairs Department, Northern Rhodesia,* 1924-5, 1926.
29. *Livingstonia News* II, 1909, pp. 23 f., 72-5. *The Watchtower* July 1909.
30. *The Report of the Nyasaland Commission of Inquiry* (Devlin Report) July 1959, § 16.
31. The whole story is brilliantly recounted in G. Shepperson and T. Price, *Independent African,* Edinburgh University Press, 1958.
32. R. L. Buell, *The Native Problem in Africa*, Macmillan, New York, 1928.
33. D. Fraser in *IRM* X, 1921, p. 114; Griffith Quick in *IRM* XXIX, 1940, p. 216.
34. Blood, *op. cit.*, p. 196.
35. *Report of the Native Affairs Department, Northern Rhodesia,* 1924-5.
36. *Ibid.* Cf. Audrey Richards in *Africa* VIII, 1935, p. 448.
37. *Report of the Native Affairs Department*, 1925, 1926.
38. Griffith Quick, *op. cit.*

2

The Opening of the Copperbelt

HITHERTO the more obvious wealth of the Katanga deposits and the delays of the War had retarded the further investigation of Collier's claims on the Rhodesian side of the frontier. Now fresh discoveries of ore at Nchanga and Mufulira in 1923 stimulated a serious development of this area and in a remarkably short time the Rhodesian Copperbelt, the second richest copper deposit yet known in the world, sprang into activity. In 1924 the Bwana Mkubwa Company bought the claim at Nkana, where the Native Commissioner of Ndola had found copper fourteen years before. Drilling began at several places in 1925. In 1927 the Roan Antelope Copper Mines Company was formed and was actually mining underground by 1928, and in that year fresh drilling started at Mufulira and at Chambishi (since closed). Meanwhile from the railway link with the Katanga a branch line was sent out which reached Luanshya in 1929 and Mufulira in 1932.

Anticipating the result of these years of development, we may describe the Copperbelt today as a constellation of seven towns, arranged somewhat like the Great Bear. At the corners of a rough rectangle stand Ndola, Luanshya, Kitwe and Mufulira, and the tail, curling west and northwest from Kitwe, consists of Kalulushi, Chingola and, latest of all, Bancroft. Some of these have had a checkered and spasmodic history; the big five to-day are Ndola, which, though close to Bwana Mkubwa, has no mining but is the commercial clearing centre; Luanshya, adjoining the Roan Antelope Mine; Kitwe, by the Nkana mine; Mufulira; and Chingola by the Nchanga Mine. The Roan Antelope and Mufulira Mines and the Chibuluma mine adjoining Kalulushi are controlled by the Rhodesian Selection Trust with a considerable American influence; the Nkana, Nchanga and Bancroft Mines are controlled by the Oppenheimer interests in South Africa through the misleadingly styled Anglo-American Corporation.

It will be noticed that four of the towns have names different from those of the mines which adjoin them; this is signficant of the organization of the Copperbelt. In every place there are really two towns, one called the municipality, where live all who are not employed by the Mine Company, and the other called the Mine. For the word 'Mine' covers not merely the industrial plant, but the houses, roads, markets, hospitals, cemeteries, schools, canteens and recreational centres of the employees. All the necessities and most of the amenities of life from the cradle to the grave have gradually been taken on as the responsibility of the Mining Companies, with the omni-competent paternalism of modern industry. Commerce for the most part, however, retains its independence and the shopping centre in several places stands as a kind of bridge between the Mine and the municipality.

There is a second line of division in each town: both the municipality and the mine are bisected into European and African residential areas and members of one race are forbidden to reside in the Township allocated to the other. The Municipal European 'Township' is administered directly by its own elected Mayor and Council; the African Housing Area, lying within the boundary of the Municipality, is governed by the African Affairs Committee of its parent Municipal Council. This Committee can delegate certain powers to an Area Housing Board to which the African residents elect representatives and so participate in a modicum of local government. In 1958 these African Housing Areas were commonly, though erroneously, called Municipal African Townships, and that term is used in this book.

The Mine European 'Township' is the responsibility of the Personnel Manager of the Company and the Mine African 'Township' is governed by the African Personnel Manager. Commerce again shows a certain independence of these divisions; although there are a first-class and a second-class trading area which cater in general for the Europeans and African needs respectively, persons of either race are now admitted into shops in both areas—though this has not always been so—and private traders, both black and white, also do business in the Mine African Township, in shops rented from the company.

At this point it will be well to mention an additional feature of the scene which has appeared in quite recent years. A few miles away from each of the five big towns, except Kitwe, is an African freehold Township, governed, under the chairmanship of the District Commissioner, by its own nominated Management Board of Africans, with a salaried Board Secretary. Here Africans may build and own their houses and manage their affairs. Most of the men in these Townships are in some line of private business, many of them having retired from mine work or domestic service; so these are the only places in the Copperbelt where it is common to find grandparents as well as parents and children. A home-ownership scheme for white mineworkers was introduced in 1957, enabling them to live in their own freehold property if they wish. But so far no African who is still in mine employment is allowed to reside anywhere but in a company house on a Mine African Township.

The present population (1958) of the whole Copperbelt including women and children is allocated as follows:

	Africans	*Non-Africans*
In the Mine Townships	132,110	20,918
In the Municipal Townships (including 'freehold' Townships)	75,756	10,530
Total	207,866	31,448

Small numbers of Asians, mainly traders, are found in the municipal Townships.

But this present-day picture is a digression and we must return to the mid-1920s. At that time organization was rough and ready; problems were solved in a hand-to-mouth manner as they arose. Clearing the surface, drilling and constructing the pilot plant required a great deal of cheap labour. Huge camps sprang up in the open bush of the Lamba country. Living conditions were crude enough for the white supervisors and technicians; for the unskilled African labourers, wages, rations and housing were of a standard which is hard to imagine today,[1] and beyond these bare necessities there were almost no amenities. It was typical of this period that a commission appointed by the Government in 1926 commended a scheme of Welfare Work to be undertaken in the lead mine of Broken Hill by the Mine Company and the Government jointly. But the proposal met with disfavour and nothing came of it. In its early years the Copperbelt fared no better.[2] During the 1930s the cover-design of the annual reports of the United Missions in the Copperbelt included a grim-looking row of barrel-vaulted blocks, reminiscent of the Nissen huts of a war-time camp. Half-way through the series, this item in the design was omitted in silent recognition that the era of the 'compound' was beginning to give place to that of the 'African Township'—the name which to-day is everywhere *de rigeur*. Prior to 1930, however, the African housing scarcely deserved even the name of compound, and the whole lay-out of a mine was still described as a 'camp'.

Yet enormous numbers of men were concentrated in these camps. The steep rise in the numbers of Africans employed on the Copperbelt during these first seven years gives some idea of the speed of development:

1924	1,300 Africans employed
1925	4,000
1926	10,000
1927	10,946
1928	16,073
1929	22,341
1930	30,000

The influx of white labour was just as startling. Only 260 white immigrants had come into the territory during 1923; during 1930 the intake was 3,651. Between 1925 and 1931 the white population trebled its size. The ratio of African to white inhabitants of Northern Rhodesia was radically changed. In 1911 there had been 548 Africans in the territory to every white person; in 1921 the figure had dropped to 270, and in 1931 it was only 96. In those early years, between sixty and seventy per cent of the white labour force on the Copperbelt came from the Union of South African (in 1958 it was about 39 per cent). From the beginning the Copperbelt has had to compete with the Rand in attracting white labour; wages, bonuses and conditions of service have always, therefore, been boosted to an abnormal level, resulting in an artificial standard of living. In such a situation any drop in wages produces a quick exodus, so throughout the history the impermanence of the white population of the Copperbelt has been almost as great as that of the Africans. This is an important factor which can too easily be forgotten, but the following figures underline it emphatically:

Length of service of the Copperbelt labour force
31st December, 1958[3]

	Percentage of all white employees	Percentage of all African employees
Men having served less than 3 years	45·5	42·4
Men having served over 3 but under 6 years	22·1	25·8
Men having served over 10 years	16·2	12·2

Average length of service—White : 5·4 years; African : 4·9 years

Among the African mineworkers there has been a slow but steady growth in stability, but in those early days the turnover was very rapid. There was an immediate demand for men from Nyasaland. These had

had a longer contact with Europeans, many of them were mission-trained and, moreover, had already done minework in South Africa or Southern Rhodesia. Fairly early the Roan Antelope Company set up an agency to redirect Nyasalanders from Southern Rhodesia to the Copperbelt. Later, as men of other tribes became more competent, the Nyasalanders provided a corps of instructors and were the first to qualify as clerks. So from the start the workers from Nyasaland won a position of leadership which has had significant results in society and in the Church.

The disruption of tribal society by this great concentration of wage earners has been described too often to need repetition at this point. The optimistic expectation of the Department for Native Affairs that the development of Mines nearer home would give labourers more time in their villages was naturally doomed to disappointment.[4] Rural life was still further impoverished and the breakdown of family disciplines was accelerated. Yet the liberating as well as the destructive effects of these developments should be taken into account. Industrialization, by loosening the old ties that often inhibited responsible individual decisions, provided the great opportunity for the emergence of a new type of African leadership, already latent and chafing against the old authorities which the British policy of Indirect Rule sought to perpetuate. As we have seen, the Reports on Native Affairs for these years draw attention to this source of conflict (see p. 26 above), That tension between the mystical appeal of the tribal head and the new powers of the 'young educated', which was to play so great a part in the Copperbelt story, was already apparent. The Mines provided the crucible in which the leadership of the future was inevitably to be refined and moulded; unfortunately it has taken authority too long to recognize that, as Julius Lewin pointed out in 1940, 'Indirect rule cannot be applied in urban and industrial conditions.'

The Union Church of the Copperbelt, 1925—1935

The sphere in which this emancipated leadership was first able to expend its energy was the Church. Most of the more capable Nyasalanders, as we have seen, had received their education in a mission school and many were practising Christians of the second generation. Now, faced with an unprecedented situation and with no guidance from their missionaries, who were hundreds of miles away, these men made their own responsible answer to the call of God. This was the moment of response, comparable to the years of persecution and revolt in the history of Buganda, when the Church in Northern Rhodesia came into its own.

The only missionaries within a day's journey of the Copperbelt at this time were Professor C. M. Doke and Miss O. C. Doke, later to be joined by the Rev. A. J. Cross; all were of the South African Baptist Mission to Lambaland, with their headquarters at Kafulafuta. They first became aware of what, in 1925, these African Christians were doing in the compound at Ndola. 'The phenomenal development of the work at Ndola is the outstanding feature of the year. The secret of its success lies largely in the fact that it is a spontaneous native movement.'[5] That year an autonomous African congregation had elected its own board of elders to organize the work of the Church, attend to discipline and recommend candidates for baptism. Sixty-four baptisms had taken place. A considerable fund had been raised, out of which the congregation was supporting its own evangelist. A successful school had been opened and, in their spare time, the Christian miners evangelized not only in the compound but in the Lamba villages round about. Two years later they set about building their own church at Ndola. 'Clerks, store assistants and others employed in many other capacities during the day would still be ready to turn their hands on Saturday to brick-making, water carrying, or anything else that was needed at the time, after their day's work.'[6]

Ndola was not the only place on the Copperbelt where this spontaneous church life had sprung into being. The Rev. R. J. B. Moore, recounting what he had been told of these beginnings which preceded his own arrival on the field, wrote:

> 'Passing through a compound after dark on almost any night, you could find little groups of people gathered round the light of an underground worker's acetylene lamp, singing Christian hymns. At last someone struck the bright idea of building a church, and this they did with their own hands, calling it the Union Church of the Copperbelt.'[7]

At the Roan Antelope Mine the congregation spent many Sundays making sun-dried bricks and they eventually built a church which the Mine Company replaced with a better one three years later. They also supported their own full-time evangelist. At Nchanga an evangelist from Nyasaland, Adamson by name, was supported by the Ndola congregation for several years. Here also a church was built before any missionary had visited the compound, and in one year thirty villagers from the surrounding district were baptized as a result of evangelism by Christian mineworkers. At Mufulira was another active congregation, many of whose members had previously been employed in the Katanga Mines and consequently revealed the influence of the methodist Episcopal Mission which was at work there. Strangely enough no congregation had as yet appeared at Nkana; there the work was initiated by Cross.

By 1929 Cross was able to report on the situation in the whole Copperbelt that

> 'a self-supporting, self-governing native Church has grown up and it is daily gaining in strength and experience. A very vigorous evangelistic work is carried on by the Church on its own initiative and responsibility, not only among the mining employees but also in the unevangelized villages of the circumjacent native district. A body of elders ably governs the Church; these elders arrange the Church's evangelistic programme and the instruction of converts besides the ordinary services of the Church. In the pastoral work they are particularly successful, and one has often been struck with the spiritual sagacity they have displayed in dealing with difficult cases of discipline or in the restoration of erring members. . . . Natives of widely varying tribes, speaking different languages, whose ancestors were once hereditary enemies, are making the grand experiment of working and worshipping in closest unity and co-operation. Not only are these natives drawn from varying tribes but their spiritual history is associated with Missions of various denominational connections; but they give objective proof of their one-ness in Christ Jesus.'[8]

When eventually this African Church appealed to him for help, Cross, with great wisdom, decided that nothing should be done to undermine either their autonomy or their financial independence. He visited the separate congregations to give advice and to sell books but abrogated to himself no special authority over them, and gave no monetary support. He also acted as the local correspondent of the various Missions from which these Christian Africans had come to the mines. Eventually the London Missionary Society, the Scottish Mission and the Plymouth Brethren came to regard Cross and the Union Church as being responsible for their African adherents while they were on the Copperbelt. It is extremely difficult to determine how far Christians from other denominations also participated in the life of this Union Church. It seems most probable that those from the areas of the Dutch Reformed Mission, the Methodist Mission and the Paris Mission would have done so without question. The Anglican chaplain at Bwana Mkubwa, who began spasmodic visitation of the African compounds in 1930, reported that year that beside the African compound of the Roan Antelope Mine there was a church with nearly a hundred Christians, mostly Nyasas. It is unlikely that in that year there was an exclusively Anglican church and congregation of such a size, for in February 1931 only 45 attended his Mass there, so this may mean that African Anglicans were also sharing in the life of the Union Church at that stage.

However that may be, until after the slump of 1931-2 Cross remained the only missionary on the scene. Father Wilfrid Ellis, the Anglican chaplain to the European community at Broken Hill since 1927, who had been paying monthly visits to Bwana Mkubwa and Ndola, took up residence in 1930 at the former town, where his flock had already built a church. In keeping with the Anglican emphasis he was primarily concerned with the six European congregations on the Copperbelt, who soon made themselves responsible for his support; not much could be done for the scattered groups of African communicants. The Roman Catholics contented themselves with sending priests on pastoral visitations from the White Fathers' station at Chilabula in the Bemba country or from the Jesuit Mission at Broken Hill until 1931, when the Franciscans began permanent work on the Copperbelt, setting up stations at Bwana Mkubwa, Luanshya and Kitwe. From Broken Hill also the Dutch Reformed Church sent a man regularly to take services in Afrikaans and to visit the African Christians who had come from the Dutch Reformed Mission areas. The London Missionary Society, the Church of Scotland Mission and the Plymouth Brethren, as we have seen, relied on the Union Church to shepherd their African flocks, and sent no missionary into this field; but there was a Congregationalist minister looking after Europeans at Luanshya, a Wesleyan minister doing the same at Nchanga, and after 1931 H. C. Nutter, a retired missionary of the London Missionary Society, who had become welfare officer at the Nkana Mine, took services for Europeans and Africans at Kitwe.

In retrospect it seems extraordinary that the Missions, with the exception of individuals such as W. P. Young of Nyasaland, were generally so slow to recognize the centrality of the Copperbelt to the territory as a whole and to the life of the Church in it. For years the Anglican Mission refused to accept the Mines as an area of evangelistic responsibility, on the grounds that a man's residence in the Copperbelt was so temporary that it was impossible to guarantee a sufficient continuity of instruction. The acting priest in charge stated in 1931 that he considered that it was not necessary for a missionary to take more than ten days at a time off his usual work in order to deal with the Copperbelt; and in 1936 the Anglicans still preferred that all baptisms should be performed on the rural mission stations rather than on the Mines.[9] Even as late as

1940 the official Anglican reluctance to accept the reality of urbanization was noted by the Forster Commission, which reported that—

> 'There are in the territory two schools of thought, the missionaries stationed in the mining area tending to favour the establishment of a stabilized urban community, while others with perhaps a wider outlook, as for instance the Bishop of Northern Rhodesia and certain Government officials, foresaw possible difficulties inherent in such a policy'[10]

—and this in spite of the fact, confirmed by evidence brought to the Commission, that two-thirds of the children in Copperbelt schools had been born in the Mines and knew nothing of tribal life. Other Missions also, while not making it a matter of principle, have been almost as resistant to the demands of the new situation. Within the orbit of the Roman Catholic Church and the UCCAR there are still some rural mission stations with a larger staff of missionaries than the whole of the Copperbelt, and it has always been a struggle to get African ministers and evangelists posted to the Mines.

And yet, reading over the history of those years, one is left with the uneasy suspicion that, perhaps, the slowness of the Missions to enter into the Copperbelt was not wholly to the disadvantage of the African Church there, greatly though it needed guidance and support. For at least, during those seven or eight years, the African congregations were allowed to be the Church, making their own discoveries of God through having to make their own decisions and their own mistakes; and when the Missions did come into the field it was, in some cases, to separate that which had been united.

The United Missions in the Copperbelt, 1936—1955

At the end of 1931 a serious slump hit the Copperbelt, forcing several mines to close down entirely. The African labour was reduced from 30,000 to less than 7,000 and this gave rise to a new sense of insecurity.

In 1932 the Department of Social and Industrial Research of the International Missionary Council commissioned a group of experts, under the chairmanship of Mr J. Merle Davis, to enquire into 'the effect of the Copper mines of Central Africa upon native society and the work of Christian missions'. Their report appeared in the following year under the title '*Modern Industry and the African*'. With regard to the actual up-building of the local African Church they recommended that the work of the Protestant Free Churches should be united in the Copperbelt under the direction of one missionary society, or, at most, two societies dealing with the two main language groups; they suggested also that the General Missionary Conference of Northern Rhodesia should create an Inter-Mission and Inter-Church Council for the Copperbelt and the Railway zone. In February 1934 representatives of British missionary societies concerned with the Copperbelt met in London to draw up a memorandum suggesting the lines along which a co-operative venture might develop; and three months later, when Dr John R. Mott met a special conference of missionaries in Northern Rhodesia, this was discussed.

Prior to this the London Missionary Society, anticipating a co-operative move, sent out in the autumn of 1933 as their share a young recruit, the Rev. R. J. B. Moore, who had had special training for this kind of work. After six months' language study he began to make contacts with the African Union Church, and with the authorities of the Mines, and to make plans against the coming of reinforcements. His first year was spent mainly in the selection and development of a headquarters station at Mindolo, a site adjoining one of the African compounds two miles north-west of Kitwe. Following the conference with Dr Mott, he was invited to draw up a scheme of work for future co-operation on the Copperbelt. Moore also initiated a quarterly fraternal to provide opportunities of contact between missionaries of the Free Churches and the Roman Catholics and Anglicans. Meanwhile he found time to attend to what he regarded always as his primary task, the strengthening of the African Church and the evangelization of the masses in the compounds. He started open-air preaching, the performance of Gospel plays and the distribution of Christian literature. Finding that the local congregations were isolated from one another he made plans to call the elders together into regular conference at Mindolo in order to create a greater sense of unity. He introduced a uniform course of instruction for catechumens, and trained leading laymen in each congregation to undertake systematic visiting in the compounds. It was unfortunate that for this first year in the field he was more single-handed than he need have been, because it had not been made clear enough to other missionaries that he had been appointed for a co-operative project.

Meanwhile the Rev. G. R. Fraser, a Scottish missionary, on his way home for his first furlough, visited the Copperbelt, and was greatly impressed with the opportunity there. In England he met the Home Boards of the Societies who had been considering action on the Merle Davis Report. His sense of urgency and his personal charm gave the spur to the Societies in Britain. With the secretaries of the various boards he worked out the details of the scheme, and the concept of the Copperbelt Team came largely from him.

In 1935, as a result of the sudden imposition of increased taxation, rioting occurred in several compounds, particularly at Roan Antelope. This served to bring home to the General Missionary Conference of that year the urgent needs of the Copperbelt and to give a special relevance and point to their discussion of Moore's report.

So simultaneous discussions in Britain and Northern Rhodesia brought matters forward, and a plan was made for a new venture which would not be another Mission, but a collaboration of missions. The title 'United Missions in the Copper Belt' (shortened to UMCB) was intended to show this, but the 's' was only too easily omitted. The Societies concerned were to second men and women to the Copperbelt who would work together as a team on a concerted programme of educational and welfare work, the missionaries of the non-Anglican missions building up also the Union Church of the Copperbelt and the Anglicans in this respect going their separate way. The participating members, as shown in the annual reports, were the London Missionary Society, the South African Baptist Mission, the Church of Scotland Mission, the Methodist Missionary Society, the Universities' Mission to Central Africa (Anglican), the United Society for Christian Literature and the South African Presbyterian Church. The last named had no men to spare for the North but, through Dr Wark's recognition of the importance of this venture, gave a regular grant.

On the face of it this showed more co-operation than might have been expected. Unfortunately a great many questions had been left unasked and the inherent ambiguities provided breeding grounds for the germs of disunity. The South African Baptist Mission was included, inasmuch as their missionary Cross was the Team-leader, and one of their evangelists accompanied him. But they were a small society and could not afford to take on new commitments. When Cross, putting the claims of the United Missions first, moved to Mindolo a crisis was precipitated. The South African Baptist Mission replaced him with another man at Fiwale Hill and discontinued their support of him, his salary being thereafter subscribed by the mining companies. The strength of the United Missions lay not in the unity of the participating societies, which was more apparent than real, but in the quality of the individuals who made up the Team. Arthur Cross, the first Team-leader, Mike Moore and George Fraser; his mother, Dr Agnes Fraser, and Miss Graham-Harrison; David Greig, Bernard Icely and Frank Bedford; and, magnificently supporting them behind the scenes, Bishop Alston May and J. G. Soulsby, the leader of the Methodist Mission—such people and others who worked with them knew that they belonged to one another, and from that alone sprang the vitality of the United Missions in the Copperbelt. The fact that more than one of them was ultimately broken by the intractability of Christian disunity does not diminish the inspiration of their high-hearted initiative.

Cross, Moore and Fraser were in their several ways the architects of the United Missions in the Copperbelt, each one bringing a different type of courage to the inspiration of the common enterprise. Cross had the gentle strength of the saint. The courage of faith by which he, before all others, had dared to believe in the potentialities of the African congregations on the Copperbelt and to be so self-effacing in his nurture of them, enabled him also, when he felt it necessary, to take an independent stand in deviation from his supporting Mission. First in the field, he was the natural choice for leadership and he often proved this capacity through his power to inspire co-operation. Moore's prophetic intensity and questing, creative imagination often carried him ahead of his colleagues and contemporaries in realizing the scope of Christ's redemption and the range of Christian responsibility. It was he who recognized the significance of the great church he built at Mindolo, of the tri-lingual hymn book he worked on, of the African co-operatives he helped to initiate. This passionate adventuring not only aroused the suspicion and hostility of the Mine authorities but sometimes isolated him from his fellow-workers. If Moore was something of a lone wolf, Fraser was the unswerving advocate of the Christian team. He had learned under Dr George Macleod in Govan the strength of Christian community in action, and this experience informed his whole conception of the Church. Suffering keenly the shame and pain of disunity, his faith in the reconciling power of a completely self-giving and committed group endured beyond the breaking point.

At first these three enjoyed the support of colleagues who fully shared their vision. If the United Missions in the Copperbelt had been able to maintain the quality and flair of their original Team, they might have overcome all the difficulties that were to beset them. But, under the pressure of the war years, the Missions either did not have the men at their disposal or did not appreciate the necessity to select men who had the temperament for teamwork. Some of the later additions had had only the individualistic experience of a parochial charge in Britain or an equally autonomous position on a rural mission station, and were unable to adjust to the daily give and take of the United Missions. A rapid turnover of such members upset the continuity of the spirit of the Team and endangered its relations with the African congregations.

The first few years of the United Missions were marked by a virile enthusiasm. The emphasis in the reports for 1936 to 1938 was mainly on evangelism in the African compounds and the strengthening of the Union Church. Separate worship was arranged for the different tribal groups, some of which were quite small. The six African congregations were brought together under a Council of Ministers and Elders, matters of doctrine and discipline being considered by a committee of the Ministers only, European and African. The second annual report remarked that 'the African members of the Joint Council show a capacity for wise debate'.[11] The Union Church, in addition to the upkeep and erection of its own buildings was pledged to contribute £126 yearly to the common effort. The Missions in the rural areas responded well by sending ten evangelists, though these were untrained, and from Nyasaland a second pastor was sent for a short time to support the Rev. Isaac Gondwe who was already on the Copperbelt; but already it had become evident that clergy and evangelists needed a special training for the conditions of urban life. Nevertheless, during these first two years, evangelism was undertaken on a scale never to be repeated. A lorry load of sixteen elders and evangelists lent from the Chitambo mission station travelled from place to place for several weeks; where they went into action, camp fire meetings were to be seen all over the compound. A series of such campaigns took place during those years. In 1937 the London Missionary Society sent an additional team of evangelists from their Bemba field to assist in a campaign of visiting. This brought to light the fact that already there were comparatively few Africans in the Copperbelt who had not had some previous contact with the Gospel; Roman Catholics were at least equal in number to all non-Roman adherents combined; and the Watchtower Movement still had a strong following.

In the next two years, 1938-1940, the Union Church showed an increase in membership of 60 per cent, with congregations of up to 300 in every compound. Further evangelistic efforts were made, particularly in 1939 when the Plymouth Brethren sent one of the Fisher family with two picked African evangelists to conduct a campaign on behalf of the Union Church. The Anglican and the Dutch Reformed Churches also reported growing congregations and new church buildings. But the shortage of African ministers and catechists was a serious weakness. In 1939 Isaac Gondwe returned to Nyasaland and although Gideon

Chinula, a teacher, had offered himself for ordination in 1936, he was still in training at Livingstonia. The Anglicans had a few outstanding laymen to lead their congregations; at both Mufulira and Luanshya the chief African clerks were Anglicans from Nyasaland, and a class of specially picked men with experience of urban life were being trained for the Anglican priesthood at Kakwe Lesa, near Fiwila. Another drag upon the work was the rapid turnover of African personnel. For example, one small tribal congregation was established at Roan Antelope in 1938, consisting of twenty-eight members and a deacon, but within two months all but one of them had left the Copperbelt.

Perhaps the most significant development of these years was the beginning of women's organizations. Miss Graham-Harrison and Dr Agnes Fraser, an honorary Team-member, living often in conditions of extreme discomfort, achieved a remarkable *approchement* to illiterate African women, Christians or pagans alike, and earned the admiration and support of Mines' staff and Government officials, when these were still suspicious of other members of the Team. Their devotion was contagious and, after a few years, numbers of European women began offering voluntary part-time help in the work. Women's classes were started in every compound with a total roll of 470 in 1939, and the next year saw the first African Christian Women's Conference at Kafue. (Judging by the history of the Church in West Africa and the Union of South Africa this is likely to prove to have been a most important milestone.) Innumerable meetings and clubs for women and girls occupied them almost incessently. The complete harmony of these two, the Anglican and the Presbyterian, in the work of evangelism and the edification of the Church was equalled only by their sympathy with the convictions of others who held different views as to how far co-operation in church work should extend. Their gay partnership remained unbroken for five years. Thereafter 'Monty' Graham-Harrison continued to throw herself into this work until years of self-neglect and overwork caused a breakdown.

During the war years the African leadership in the churches grew stronger. By 1945 there were on the Copperbelt four African ministers of the Church of Central Africa in Rhodesia (into which the Union Church was now incorporated) and two African Anglican priests. But the United Missions had lost some of their outstanding members, and those who carried on were more than ever stretched by the multiplicity of the tasks that fell to them. Mike Moore was withdrawn from the Team at the end of 1939 and died in 1943; and A. J. Cross died suddenly at the end of 1945. At the end of the war almost all missionaries were due for furlough. The rural mission stations, faced with acute shortage of staff, had to recall some of those whom they had seconded to the Copperbelt. Appeals for reinforcement for the United Missions were unanswered.

From the beginning the United Missions had envisaged a total Christian approach to the life of the Copperbelt which accepted responsibility for developing educational and welfare work. In the draft programme which Moore drew up in 1934, he had embraced three spheres of need with which he believed the Team was called to deal—the up-building and extension of the Church, which we have already partly described; the development of education, including adult education and a more creative use of the recreation centres provided by the Mine Companies; and the fostering of African co-operatives and associations, not only to benefit the mine workers but to secure a stable standard of life in the rural areas.

With regard to this third field Moore hoped always for the arrival of an expert colleague; failing that, little could be done, for the Team had neither the qualifications nor the time to take up thoroughly these Christian responsibilities in the economic sphere. Nevertheless he and George Fraser played a great part in guiding and fostering the growth of the African Welfare Societies, the progenitors of the African National Congress, and Moore's active concern for the creation of an African Trade Union was one of the reasons for his withdrawal from the Copperbelt. After he had left, the Rev. Bernard Icely took over this special concern for industrial relations.

In the field of education and welfare, however, the United Missions exercised a responsibility and influence out of all proportion to their numbers. In their first year of activity the United Missions had schools at Mindolo near Kitwe, Luanshya, Mufulira and on Nchanga Mine, with sixteen African men teachers and one woman. In the second year there were 1,200 pupils in the United Mission's schools, a teachers' refresher course was held, and in every place local education councils had been set up with a large African representation. The United Missions began seriously to consider establishing a teacher-training centre at Mindolo. The Government had accepted the principle of financial responsibility for education in the Copperbelt and had put up new or enlarged school buildings on every mine. The Director of Education, in his five-year plan, had estimated for enrolment of 2,000 children on the Copperbelt in 1941 but this figure had already been passed in 1938-9. It became necessary for the United Missions to appoint George Fraser to special duties as their education secretary and, supported by the newly-formed Education Sub-Committee, he faced an ever-growing task. The rural mission stations sent certified teachers to augment the staffs for a two-year period while new teachers and pupil-teachers were being trained for the Copperbelt schools. The Government had set its face against denominational schools, and refused a request of the Roman Catholic Bishops in Northern Rhodesia to be allowed to inaugurate 'United Roman Catholic Missions' schools. The Team responded in 1939 by inviting the Roman Catholics to take a full share in the staffing and control of their schools. The same offer was made to the Dutch Reformed Mission, and to the end the fullest co-operation with both these bodies was enjoyed in the Education Sub-Committee. There was a steady improvement in the quality and number of the Roman Catholic teachers in these schools, rising eventually to about one third of the total staffs.

The Team might have done well to limit its concern to the United Missions' four schools with their thirty teachers and their enrolment of over 2,000 pupils. But Government policy was now clarified. It wished to use the United Missions' Team as its agent in the whole educational field, and in 1940 entrusted to it the management of all schools in the Copperbelt. By 1942 this meant the supervision of eight schools, taking 6,000 children in two daily sessions, a girls' and boys' boarding school, and refresher courses for all the teachers. In its General Development Plan, which the Government issued at the end of the war, schools in four mining towns were up-graded to Standard VI, feeding schemes were launched and put under the supervision of the United Missions, and it was proposed to introduce compulsory primary education throughout the Copperbelt by 1948. But after the death of A. J. Cross, George Fraser was nominated as Team-leader and the appointment of a full-time education secretary became urgent. In 1947 a man was recruited for this post, but his resignation after little more than one strenuous year, coupled with the loss of other of its educationists, compelled the hard pressed Team to devolve on some other body the responsibility for the Copperbelt African schools. As had been foreseen, the Ordinance for compulsory education produced a vast increase in the school population, yet at the same moment the cutting of the cost-of-living bonus from their salaries caused a serious shortage of teachers. Overwhelmed by their administrative burden the United Missions advocated the establishment of local governing boards and begged the Government to appoint, from their expanding educational staff, African or European school managers. Once again the United Missions considered founding their own teacher-training centre at Mindolo but, as before, the appeals for additional staff met with no response. Finally, with misgivings but also a sense of infinite relief, the administration of all the schools was handed over to the Government African Education Department. The United Missions' Team insisted that the Churches, rather than Missions, should be properly represented, through lay as well as clerical delegates, on the Local Education Authorities and School Councils, believing that this was at least as significant as the right of entry of clergy for Religious Instruction periods.

Meanwhile in the field of social welfare the same members of the Team had been equally active. During the first year of the United Missions, David Greig took charge of the recreational side of the work while Moore concentrated on the cultural side—lectures, discussion groups and the provision of literature. Greig's contribution was invaluable in gaining for the United Missions a recognition by the Mine Companies and a welcome into their compounds which had hitherto been only grudgingly granted. Sport greatly increased the contact of the United Missions with both the European and African communities, and the reputation of their schools was enhanced by the high standards which David Greig and, later, Frank Bedford produced in football and athletics. In 1938 the Government established a Central Advisory Committee for Native Welfare on which A. J. Cross represented the Team. For many years the United Missions were protagonists of a particular approach to welfare work. The Mine Companies at that time appear to have regarded it solely in terms of recreation, financed by the profits of the official beerhalls. The Team was working for a wider concept of welfare work, such as that advocated in the Jan Hofmeyr school in Johannesburg.

In 1939 adult schools were started; in one centre alone over 200 men were enrolled. In the same year the first Women's Centre was opened at Mindolo, and, as we have seen, women's classes were started on every mine; another Women's Centre was opened on the Nkana Mine in 1942. The need for trained welfare assistants was soon apparent. The Team undertook the first Welfare Officers' class at Nkana in 1939, and, later, short courses were run for African women leaders. After the war the United Missions encouraged European women volunteers to help in the classes for women and girls in the different mines. By 1945 their members were to be found on the Welfare Committee of every mine, and were responsible for most of the women's and girls' work. Libraries and adult schools were everywhere supervised by those members of the Team who were provided by the United Society for Christian Literature. Other members were helping in the training of African Welfare Assistants and directing a wide Adult Literacy campaign.

The following year Mr (now Sir John) Moffat put before the United Missions the Government's far-reaching General Development Plan and asked them to decide what part in it they were going to be able to play. The Team was acutely aware of the magnitude of the needs. When George Fraser went, shortly afterwards, to the United Kingdom, he put before the London Committee of the United Missions the responsibility for training and supervising Christian leaders both in education and welfare work; he spoke also of juvenile delinquency, of the lack of hostels for unmarried girls, and the urgent need for trained sociologists and educationists; he pleaded the urgency of a situation in which racial tension was rapidly intensifying. But the eleven men and eight women that were required, on his estimate, were not forthcoming, and when it became clear that the United Missions could not secure the necessary staff to meet the demands, the Government went ahead independently with its plan, and a Social Welfare Department was set up with local Welfare Councils for each town.

The besetting problem of the United Missions was chronic shortage of staff. With gallant faith they continued to cut their coat in the expectation of cloth to come, instead of according to the scraps they had. Perhaps if they had had a common mind as to what they were intending to be and do, they might have been able to refuse some parts of the load which, in accumulation, eventually broke their back. But there were two unresolved ambiguities regarding their purpose and direction which in the end proved to be a fatal weakness.

In the first place it was never clear whether the Team was to be directly concerned with the life of the Church or not. Merle Davis in 1932 had proposed a co-operative undertaking 'for the supervision of the Christian work in the Copperbelt'. The draft constitution in 1937 and again in 1946 laid down that 'the purpose of the United Missions in the Copperbelt is to make a united Christian approach to the population of the Copperbelt'. From the start, of course, it was known and reluctantly accepted that Anglican participation must not be regarded as commitment to ecclesiastical unity. Yet it is obvious from the reports of the first three years that evangelism and the care of the African congregations were a primary concern of the Team. They co-operated in evangelistic preaching and agreed to joint instruction of enquirers up to the catechumen stage. There was common daily worship in the United Missions' schools and an agreed syllabus of religious instruction. Matters affecting the Union Church were discussed in Team sessions by courtesy of the Anglican members. But after the early years there was a hardening of the definitions, coinciding with the arrival of a new group of Team members. There was an official reaffirmation of its position by the Universities' Mission to Central Africa; it was agreed that, to save time, the affairs of the Union Church should be discussed by non-Anglican members of the Team meeting in a separate sub-committee, and that the budget should be so drawn as to avoid any question of joint funds being devoted to denominational work. With the advent of more African priests, the Anglican Church was no longer content with only joint, non-denominational, religious instruction in the schools. During the war years their concentration on educational and welfare work concealed their divisions. But in March 1944, when Wilkie of the Church of Scotland made a survey of the Team's work, he commented on the need for deeper co-operation between the participating Missions; and, as the tenth annual report points out, when the Government began to take over more of the Team's educational and social work, so enabling it again to concentrate on its pastoral and evangelistic priorities, their divisions were brought to light.

The Dutch Reformed Church Mission had never participated in the United Missions. The Methodist Mission, while no members of the Team co-operated more heartily than theirs, nevertheless appeared to stand somewhat aloof from the Union Church. This was probably because comparatively few of their adherents were in the Copperbelt and because they hesitated to commit themselves to a Church of one race only. The Plymouth Brethren had entrusted their members to the Union Church while they were on the Copperbelt and contributed evangelists and teachers to the common effort until 1942. Thereafter three of their own missionaries were stationed on the Copperbelt, and their distinctive methods and principles began to make co-operation difficult, and some of their up-country missionaries were already asking for a complete separation. However the principle of co-operation with liberty to exercise different practices prevailed for four more years, particularly since they concentrated on the West-Lunda-speaking group in the Union Church. After the war, however, the break became complete. At about the same time also the death of A. J. Cross removed the nominal link with the South African Baptists; and the South African Presbyterian Church, with full understanding from the United Missions, discontinued its grant on financial grounds.

The second ambiguity concerned the scope of the Team's responsibility. Could it include the European Christians or not? From the first the priests of the Anglican Church, whether members of the Team or not, always included both Europeans and Africans in their pastoral responsibility; in practice, as we have seen, the European work tended to assume the priority. Meanwhile considerable groups of Europeans not connected with the Anglican Church were demanding pastoral care, and the Team, feeling its responsibility for all races, undertook that their non-Anglican ordained men would give such help as they could. The principle was unexceptionable but in practice the burden was too heavy for so small a staff. The annual report for 1938, conscious of this trend, stresses that 'the work is *one* but the time and attention of Team members must be more and more occupied in meeting the needs of Africans'. That year a Free Church Council for the Copperbelt was formed by the European congregations and the United Missions' Team was relieved to learn that they intended to find and support their own full-time minister. This hope however was frustrated by the war, and the Team members continued to serve the European congregations who, by 1945, besides having weekly services in every town were demanding more time and attention. The staff shortage after the war resulted in each ordained Team-member being occupied fully with the African and European congregations in his own town; there was no chance of specialization or joint projects and for a time the Team became in practice little more than a ministers' fraternal. In 1946 the new draft constitution of the United Missions redefined their aims as 'a united Christian approach to the population of the Copperbelt of Northern Rhodesia, to the African peoples in the first instance but also to the Europeans, collaborating wherever possible with all who are working for the welfare of both Africans and Europeans'. Yet two years later the European work was taking even more of the missionaries' time and becoming a source of misunderstanding in the United Missions' Team. The Free Church members were sensitive of the fact that while three white Anglican priests and a part-time fourth were working for the Europeans, only the part-time fourth was a member of the Team. The Anglicans, on their side, seeing how in every town a European Free Church congregation looked to the Team to supply its minister, were inclined to complain that the Free Churches had built up their European work with the strength of the United Missions. The position was but slightly improved when the Free Church Council made itself responsible for the support of one minister on the Team.

In March 1951 the Anglican Bishop Selby Taylor proposed the dissolution of the United Missions and suggested that responsibility for the Copperbelt should be taken over by the Christian Council of Northern Rhodesia which had come into existence in 1945. George Fraser, the Team-leader, felt profoundly the failure to maintain unity which seemed implicit in such a decision, and fought to preserve the life of the United Missions. In August 1951 his health completely broke down. But by the following May he was sufficiently recovered to issue, together with the Bishop and two other Anglicans, an agreed statement which recorded the desire of the Anglican Church to continue to participate in the United Missions in the Copperbelt, provided this became a more broadly based Christian welfare association. On this decision Fraser commented: 'To speak of "defining the field of co-operation" as (a) welfare and (b) education, opens the way to the most tragic misconception of the unity and wholeness of the Christian Mission. Would not two committees representing the Churches now function equally well?' His assessment was correct. For three years more the United Missions lingered; then they were replaced not by two, but one committee, which regularly works its way through a ponderous agenda, known as the Copperbelt Christian Service Council.

The true spiritual successor to the United Missions in the Copperbelt, however, seems to be the Mindolo Ecumenical Centre, founded in 1958. After a lapse of years the strategic potential of the Mindolo site is once again being exploited with imagination. Launched by the Christian Council of Northern Rhodesia and adopted as a project by the World Council of Churches, the Centre has been set up as an independent foundation with the threefold purpose of Leadership Training, Consultation and Research. Training was first in the field and includes a centre for residential courses in Christian home-making, a Literacy and Writing Centre designed to train authors, journalists and literacy workers from all over Africa, and a Youth Leadership centre in which the co-operation of the YMCA and the YWCA for which Mike Moore longed has come at last into action. Consultation is likely to take the form of an on-going series of conferences of various professional or specialist groups, drawing together people of opposite points of view in the social, political and industrial fields and seeking, in the manner of an 'evangelical academy', the Christian insight into the problems of Africa. These activities will, it is hoped, be supported by the work of a small research section if the personnel is available. The presence at Mindolo of the permanent secretariat of the All-Africa Church Conference should help to ensure that the Ecumenical Centre remains aware in all its activity of the wider context of the young Churches throughout the continent.

From 'Missions' to Churches

It is clear from the reports and letters of the 1930s that another source of embarrassment to the United Missions was their ambiguous attitude towards the Union Church. Cross, Moore and Fraser saw this as a real Church and hoped that it might eventually form the nucleus of a wider union embracing the congregations in the different Mission districts also. But other members of the Team, and the Missions in general beyond the Copperbelt, seemed to regard it only as an *ad hoc* economy. In neither case were the constitutional, still less the theological, issues raised by the Union Church properly faced. The transition from 'mission field' to autonomous church, therefore, has been worked out independently by each of the Missions on its own, and has been hardly at all affected by the isolated episode of the Union Church of the Copperbelt. The manner and the speed of the transition has naturally differed in the various Missions according to their theological understanding of the nature of the Church.

The process can be traced by observing two outward phenomena—the growth of the African ministry and the development of constitutional structures of church government. The relative growth of an African ministry under different Missions can be seen from the following table, dated 1959:

Mission	Date of entry into Northern Rhodesia	Date of first ordination of African of N.R. origin	No. of ordained Africans active today in N.R.	No. of ordained missionaries today in N.R.	Ratio of African ministers to baptized African adherents
LMS	1887	1938	8	6	—
RC	1890	1946	36	279	1 : 9,500
MMS	1893	1937	8	18	1 : 79
C of S	1895	1930	9	6	—
DRC	1899	1929	14	13	1 : 1,190
UMCA	1910	1932	13	26	1 : 1,770

In the last column LMS and C of S are omitted because their joint responsibility for the UCCAR confuses the figures. There are more than thirteen white ministers of the DRC, but this figure is due to their exclusion of ministers of the Dutch Reformed Church serving European congregations from the number of missionaries working for the Mission, a distinction which other denominations do not draw.

As elsewhere in Africa, the Roman Catholic Church has demanded that its African priests should undergo the same standard of training as those of any other race and has been prepared to take its time in achieving this. Even by these standards, however, an abnormally long period passed during which this Church appeared to be more mission-dominated than any;[12] then, suddenly, highly-qualified African priests appeared on the scene with a steadily growing influence in the Church. However, no African priest has yet been posted to the Copperbelt.

The Anglican Church, as has already been said, was the one which most rapidly produced an African ministry. The first four deacons were ordained in 1932, and three of these were priested in the following year—Isaya (now Canon) Mazala, Isaac Mungwa and Patrick Muyawala, all of whom are still in the service of the Church. In 1941 ten more men were ordained deacon who had been specially chosen for their previous urban experience; six of them are still serving as priests, three being in the Copperbelt. After the evident success of these two ordination classes, it is surprising to find that only two Africans have been ordained in the Anglican Church in Northern Rhodesia since 1941. At the present time the training of Anglican clergy is organized on a Provincial basis with the seminary of St John the Baptist, Lusaka, serving all the dioceses in the Central African territories.

The Church of Scotland has leaned heavily on the great traditions of the Livingstonia Mission. There has been a continuous trickle of Nyasaland clergy coming into Northern Rhodesia to serve in the four mission districts and in the Copperbelt, and these men have exercised a very profound influence upon the United Church of Central Africa in Rhodesia. The Methodist Mission, like the Church of Scotland, has relied largely on an imported African ministry, in their case from Southern Rhodesia. They have, however, eight Africans from the Northern Rhodesian field in the ministry today, though none of them is actually serving in the Copperbelt. As we have already noticed above, the London Missionary Society, was very slow to produce an African ministry from within Northern Rhodesia itself.

Yet the mere production of an African ordained ministry, symptomatic though it is, does not itself ensure that the Mission is giving place to a responsible Church. As early as 1932 Merle Davis pinpointed a weakness which later observers have found to be still present.

'A further implication of the Copperbelt,' he commented, 'is the need of giving larger responsibility to Native Church leaders. The Native returns from the mines with a new self-confidence and sense of his own capacity and with an urge to express it in the Church life, and he is often restless and dissatisfied under the old mission tutelage. We were told of the craving of evangelists, pastors and teachers for *more of a share in shaping mission policies and for the confidence and comradeship of the missionary*.'[13]

How far, during these years, had the various Missions gone towards giving to the African church leaders, in a concrete constitutional form, this share in shaping policy?

In one sense the question never arose for the Roman Catholic Church, since policy, for them, is not shaped by the local branches of the Church; the making of authoritative decisions rests with the clergy and, as we have remarked, once an African becomes a priest he commands as much, and as little, authority in the Church as any other priest. Yet the African laity has not been altogether denied opportunities for responsible leadership in the local congregations. In the late 1920s Father Jourdain had introduced a system of 'elders' in each of the larger congregations, and in 1935 this was adapted to the patterns of Catholic Action which Mgr Riberi, the new Apostolic Delegate, introduced with great enthusiasm. Today almost every local church in town and country has its group of 'Actio's', as they are called, appointed by the priest-in-charge to be answerable to him for the administration and discipline of the congregation. In the Copperbelt there is also a wide variety of organizations for the different age-groups, and the leaders of these in each congregation constitute a Church Committee which is responsible for the life of the Roman Catholic community in that place, as well as for the upkeep of the church buildings. These organizations are allowed considerable autonomy but, of course, have no constitutional position in the system of Church Government.

The Universities' Mission to Central Africa, by sending a Bishop as its pioneer missionary, was able officially to be constituted as the Anglican Church in the area from its very inception. Nevertheless Bishop May wrote in 1926 that 'the sole bond of union is the Bishop . . . and for many a long day to come the Diocese of Northern Rhodesia must continue to be, not a body, but a loose association of scattered limbs, waiting to be assembled.'[14] In the following year the first conference of priests met at Broken Hill and constituted itself as the first Diocesan Synod, but there were no Africans present, only one layman was included and deep divergences between the widely separated mission-stations were revealed. By 1948, however, the Synod had become fully representative of clergy and laity. Today every rural Mission District is sub-divided into localities. Each locality has its representative council consisting of delegates from every village congregation. These councils, which no European attends, can pass on their resolutions and send their representatives to the central Mission District Council, under the chairmanship of the Missionary-in-charge. In the towns the European and African congregations, living separately, are organized in separate parishes, though the African parishes are still called by the old name, Mission Districts. The Diocesan Synod consists of all clergy and roughly two lay representatives from every Mission District and parish in the diocese.

The story of the development of the congregations of the Church of Scotland Mission and the London Missionary Society into a fully autonomous local Church is more complicated, since their polity is such that, unlike Roman Catholics and Anglicans, they cannot assume as a matter of course that their missionaries are members of the same Church, and subject to the same constitution, as their African adherents.

In 1913 the London Missionary Society had instituted for its area an Annual General Church Council consisting of all missionaries, all African evangelists and one deacon from each church; later, as the number of local congregations grew, this representation had to be thinned out. In 1929 an additional Native Church Council was instituted, consisting wholly of Africans; this was allowed to submit its recommendations to the General Church Council, which remained, in spite of its constitution, firmly under Mission direction. In 1940 the Society's Foreign Secretary reported: 'The Church is still a mission affair. There is little sense of its belonging to the people themselves.' [The Councils] 'are a bit liable to degenerate into a kind of ministerial Trade Union for mutual defence and collective bargaining.'[15]

During the 1930s two influences were at work. The existence of the Union Church of the Copperbelt raised the question of unity between the Churches in the Northern Rhodesian fields of the London Missionary Society and the Church of Scotland; and the development of the Copperbelt diminished the ascendency of Nyasaland over the affairs of the Church in Northern Rhodesia. This happened only gradually, first in the sphere of education and later in ecclesiastical organization. The establishment of a separate theological centre at Kashinda in 1947 was an important turning point; but the psychological reorientation only appears to have taken place after 1950.

In 1945 the Scottish Mission districts in Northern Rhodesia were permitted to form a separate 'North-Eastern Presbytery in Rhodesia' of the Church of Central Africa Presbyterian, which had existed for many years in Nyasaland. At the inaugural meeting representatives of the General Church Council of the London Missionary Society's area were present and a union of the two was consummated. Rural Africans, who were not strongly represented on either of these bodies, had little say in this decision; but the Union Church of the Copperbelt, in which the African voice predominated, had unanimously craved entry into the proposed Union. In a short time the new Church was established as the 'Church of Central Africa in Rhodesia'. Work was quickly begun on a draft constitution and on the preparation of a common hymn book.

On the principle of *solvitur ambulando,* three issues were left unresolved, namely the relationship of this new body with the European 'Free Church Council' in the Copperbelt, with other Churches in the territory, and with its own missionaries. Subsequent progress can be reported as follows:

(i) For a few years the United Missions in the Copperbelt served as a link between the 'Free Church Council' and the Church of Central Africa in Rhodesia. The almost miraculous story of their eventual conjunction to form, in 1958, the 'United Church of Central Africa in Rhodesia', is told in a later chapter of this book (see pp. 200f).

(ii) Some have thought that the haste with which the enthusiasts of 1945 launched the Church of Central Africa in Rhodesia and appropriated to it the Union Church of the Copperbelt, has been a stumbling-block in the way of other Churches committing themselves to joining in. Yet as soon as they were drafted, copies of the constitutional proposals had been submitted to the sister Churches to avoid including any point, if possible, which might increase the difficulties of later union with them. And the cause of unity would probably not have been so advanced as it is today if this action had not been taken in 1945. Since the days of the United Missions in the Copperbelt, the Methodist Mission has continued to co-operate with the Church of Central Africa in Rhodesia in all the towns along the line of rail. On more than one occasion, on the Copperbelt and at Broken Hill, Africans familiar with the Congregationalist or Presbyterian tradition have threatened to break away because they failed to understand the greater autonomy claimed by a Methodist minister. Yet negotiations have gone forward and the United Church of Central Africa in Rhodesia looks forward to including the Methodists also, with an additional Southern presbytery under the one Synod to cover that area in which their work predominates. Similar discussions have been carried on since 1950 with the Church of Barotseland (together with the Paris Evangelical Mission), and the same form of incorporation is likely to be accepted in their case, with a separate Barotseland presbytery.

(iii) Gradually the missionaries of the London Missionary Society and the Church of Scotland have come to the point of integration into the constitutional structure of the Church of Central Africa in Rhodesia. In 1948 the Scottish Mission in Rhodesia had set up its own Mission Council, independent of Nyasaland. In 1955 this was dissolved, as also was the District Committee of the London Missionary Society. Instead, each of the Missions accepted a Joint Council made up of equal numbers of missionaries and representatives of the District Church Councils. This was regarded as an interim measure until, in 1958, fuller integration was achieved, and missionaries, like the ministers of both races, were put into the hands of a staffing committee of the Synod.

As the development from a Mission-pattern to a Church-pattern was taking place in the separate denominations, so also in the field of ecumenical co-operation the General Missionary Conference was moving towards becoming a Council of Churches. That has not happened yet. The Christian Council of Northern Rhodesia, which succeeded the General Missionary Council in 1945, is a heterogeneous body representing at present nine missionary societies, two other societies and six Churches. It is as yet a council in which the European and missionary voice predominates. In order to correct this bias the General Missionary Conference in 1939 called into being the African Christian Conference. In this, representative Africans met alone to discuss the needs of the Church as they saw them, and to submit recommendations to the General Missionary Conference, and later, to the Christian Council. The scope and wisdom of these recommendations from the eight African Christian Conferences that were held are most striking. But in 1955 it was decided that since the Churches could send African delegates directly to the Christian Council, there was no further need of a separate African Conference. However, the proportion of African delegates in the Council continues to be small. In 1957 the Christian Council consisted of forty Europeans and thirteen African delegates, while its Executive Committee had fourteen Europeans and two Africans; in 1959 the figures were forty Europeans and eleven Africans on the Council, nineteen Europeans and two Africans on the Executive.

Nevertheless perhaps the most hopeful feature of the present time is that the Missions throughout Northern Rhodesia appear to have begun seriously to believe in the Church—not the Church which they represent, nor even the Church Universal, but the Church which is there. It has been there, of course, for half a century; today there is evidence that its devoted servants may be prepared to let the Church be the Church.

NOTES

1. In 1924 African labourers were paid from Shs. 12-15 per month on the mines and railways, plus a food ration worth about Shs. 8. This compared favourably with the tobacco estates round Fort Jameson, where the wage was Shs. 5 per month, with a Shs. 5 food ration.
2. A. J. Cross in *World Dominion* VII, October 1929, p. 412.
3. *Yearbook of the Northern Rhodesian Chamber of Mines 1959*, Tables 20 and 33.
4. *Report of the Native Affairs Department, Northern Rhodesia*, 1926.
5. *Lambaland*, the quarterly journal of the South African Baptist Mission in Northern Rhodesia, October 1926.
6. *Ibid.*, January 1928.
7. R. J. B. Moore, *Man's Act and God's in Africa*, Livingstone Press, 1940, p. 55.
8. *World Dominion* VII, pp. 412-414.
9. The records of the Church of St Michael, Ndola (MS).
10. *Report of the Commission appointed to enquire into the Disturbances in the Copperbelt* (The Forster Commission), July 1940, p. 162.
11. For information in this and the following paragraphs, I have drawn upon the Annual Reports of the United Missions in the Copper Belt, Nos. 1-10, 1936 to 1951. I am indebted also, for many suggestions and corrections, to Miss B. D. Gibson, once London Secretary of the UMCB, the Rev. George Fraser, the Rev. A. J. Griffiths, Africa Secretary of the LMS and the Rev. J. A. R. Watt, Africa Secretary of the Church of Scotland Foreign Missions Committee.
12. Donald Attwater, *The White Fathers in Africa*, Burns Oates, 1937, p. 53.
13. J. Merle Davis, *Modern Industry and the African*, Macmillan, 1933, p. 370 (italics mine).
14. A. G. Blood, *The History of the Universities' Mission to Central Africa* II, p. 272.
15. Norman Goodall, *The History of the London Missionary Society*, p. 300.

3

Setting the Scene

BEFORE proceeding with the material which arose from the field-work itself, it is necessary to fill in a few details concerning the Nchanga Mine African Township, upon which the study was primarily focused, and the Christian congregations within that Township. We have already mentioned in the previous chapter that in 1958 the total African population on the Copperbelt was estimated as 207,866. Of these 34,256 were actual employees of the Mine Companies.

The population of Chingola in 1957 (figures are not yet available for 1958) was analysed as follows:

		Africans	Non-Africans
Nchanga Mine Townships :	Men	6,807	1,315
	Women	4,084	1,009
	Children	10,210	2,522
	Total	21,101	4,846
Municipal Townships :	Total	12,000	800

The tribal origins of the African labour force are worth noting, since it has an important bearing on the Mission origins of the Christian community. In the second quarter of 1958 the home background of the African mineworkers was as in the table on the following page.

It is natural that Chingola, lying at the north-western end of the Copperbelt, should attract a higher proportion from the north and the west and a smaller proportion from Nyasaland and the east, compared with the other towns.

It would seem to be a simple thing to discover how many of this population are Christian, but in fact it is extraordinarily difficult. The main reason for this is that the responsible leaders of the Church apply

Tribal Origin	Nchanga : per cent	Copperbelt total : per cent
Northern Province, mainly Bemba	31·9	29·3
Outside Northern Rhodesia, mainly Nyasalanders and Nyakyusa	24·9	27·5
Luapula Province, mainly Lunda	20·4	16·9
North-Western Province	9·5	6·1
Eastern Province	7·1	8·4
Barotseland	2.5	1·8
Central Province	2.1	7·7
Southern and Western Provinces	1·6	2·3

a different criterion of assessment from that of the ordinary mineworker. Ministers, elders and deacons judge in terms of full membership, church attendance and payment of dues; the ordinary layman considers that he belongs to a particular denomination simply because that was the Church or Mission exercising the predominant influence in his home village. From the one viewpoint it appears that a high proportion of the population of the African Mine Township is still pagan; but from the other viewpoint the great majority seem to regard themselves as having some link with a Christian denomination. Out of 2,067 schoolchildren questioned at Chingola, only 38 said that they were pagans; but since African traditional religion is widely associated with lack of civilization, it is natural that children should claim to belong to some Christian denomination, however tenuous the link.

Statistics relating to other towns may give some indication of the position at Nchanga. McCulloch's survey of the African Township at Livingstone found that 65.6 per cent of the adults declared themselves as followers of the African traditional religion; but of those who came from the Northern and Eastern Provinces, only 33 per cent did not claim to be Christian. This reflects fairly accurately the much greater advance of Christianity in the north and east of the Territory, and since such a high proportion of workers in the Copperbelt came from the north and the east, the same factor is likely to be operative there. This is borne out by statistics of African 'advancees' at Roan Antelope Mine, which show that 63.7 per cent of them claimed to be church-goers. One would expect that the percentage of all workers, including the non-skilled, would be considerably lower.

The baptismal register of the UCCAR at Nchanga suggests that more women than men in the Mine Township are actively Christian. Of 60

Christian mothers who presented children for baptism during 1957, 35 only had husbands who were able to register as Christian. In 1958, of 34 Christian mothers only 23 had Christian husbands.

The numbers attending church regularly are not very encouraging. On Sunday mornings the average adult attendance at the Church of Central Africa in Rhodesia at Nchanga Mine Township, from 1955 to 1957, was 152. Our very limited experience suggested that a similar number might be expected at both the enclosures of the Watchtower Movement on Sunday afternoons, and between 300 and 400 at the Roman Catholic Mass. When we attended the African Reformed Church there were 52 adults present, and in our experience, the average number of adults at the Anglican Eucharist was 35. On Easter Day it appeared that numbers at the Roman Catholic, Anglican and UCCAR services were above average, but elsewhere they were almost unaffected by the Festival. We reckoned that in all the congregations that day, including Jehovah's Witnesses and all the sects, there could not have been more than 2,200 adults present, that is to say 20 per cent of the total adult population of the African Mine Township.

From these tentative figures we may suppose that up to 25 per cent of the adult population at Nchanga maintains at least a spasmodic contact with the Christian community; probably there are at least another 25 per cent of 'lost sheep'—men and women who have been actively associated with a church at some time in the past, but have drifted away—and an even wider circle who would label themselves with the name of the Mission which was at work in their home district. The visible Christian community, however, is divided into many denominations. In the Nchanga Mine African Township in 1958 there were eight congregations under missionary influence, besides the Jehovah's Witnesses and seven sects that we knew of, including a considerable assembly of the Lumpa Church. There was also a Muslim congregation. There were five church buildings, one of them shared by several denominations, and a sixth church was being built. The remaining groups met for worship either in school classrooms, by permission, or in open-air enclosures fenced with poles or reed-work, or in private houses. The African Personnel Manager has the unenviable task of alloting building sites to any *bona fide* religious group that applies and can give evidence of its ability to erect and maintain a building. In the past it was easier to put aside one strip of land for this purpose, with the result that in some townships the church buildings stand side by side in a row. At Kansuswa, which followed this pattern, about a dozen of the faithful were in the habit of meeting daily at 6.0 a.m. to sing a hymn and pray before the day's work began; but they did so in three separate, adjacent churches. At Nchanga, however, the church buildings are distributed more widely over the Township, only three standing together as a relic of earlier days.

It would be unwise to attach too much importance to the denominational allegiance claimed by the 2,067 African schoolchildren questioned in Chingola, but it is interesting to compare it with the figures given by the 'advancee' adults at Roan Antelope.

	Children at Chingola: per cent	'Advancees' at Roan Antelope: per cent
Roman Catholic	45·3	25·6
CCAR	36·4	15·7
Watchtower	6·4	29·4
African Reformed (DRC)	2·8	9·8
Anglican	2·0	7·8
Others	7·1	11·7

The very high Roman Catholic figure reflects the extremely successful work among the schoolchildren that was being done by the missionary priest at Nchanga during 1958. This was borne out by the testimony of every one of the headmasters. The Watchtower Movement, on the other hand, has no special children's work. The percentage therefore of Christian adults at Nchanga would probably stand higher than that of the children for the Watchtower, and lower for the Roman Catholics.

Different denominations, as we have seen from the previous two chapters, tend to show a particular tribal emphasis according to the geographical distribution of the various Missions. The higher proportion of Bemba at Nchanga is reflected in the greater strength of the Roman Catholics. On this reckoning one would expect to find in the congregation of the United Church of Central Africa in Rhodesia at Nchanga more Lunda and Bemba from the London Missionary Society's field than Nyasalanders with a Church of Scotland background. This, however, is not the case. The predominance of the Christians from Nyasaland is just as marked as it is in several other congregations of the UCCAR on the Copperbelt. This can be seen in the following analysis of full church members by tribes from the records of four separate congregations.

Tribal Origin	Percentage of the congregation at: Nchanga Mine Township	Chingola Municipal Township	Mindolo, Kitwe	Buchi, Kitwe
Nyasaland	46·4	66·4	30·0	45·0
Nyakyusa	21·0	1·0	28·0	—
Eastern Province	11·6	5·5	4·0	—
Lunda	8·5	7·0	5·8	6·0
Bemba	7·0	13·1	26·4	36·0
Others	5·5	7·0	5·8	13·0

The significance of these figures becomes apparent when it is remembered that the men from Nyasaland tend, more than others, to be the white-collar workers and to belong to the emerging African middle class.

[illegible]

II

SOCIAL CHANGE

4

Old and New in Urbanized Communities

ONE of the most striking sights one notices when flying from the north to the Copperbelt is the difference between the African villages and the mining Townships. It is worth while to bear this in mind when considering social change, because the material structure and the social framework of people's lives are obviously interrelated. The villages of the northern province, the Bemba country, are hardly noticeable from the air. The thatched houses cannot be discerned amid the surrounding grass and bushland; the burnt-out cultivated patches in the clearings must first arrest our attention before we perceive the small villages, clusters of houses grouped in irregular patterns, with wide spaces between the groups. The country looks empty—and it is empty, when one compares its density of population with that of Europe. The only two bigger settlements in the north, Abercorn and Kasama, immediately show European influence; they are artificial agglomerations round Government and commercial posts.

A few straight roads, like the threads of a spider's web, seem to converge ahead of the plane, and soon we are above a big clearing in the moss-like forest. We see the head frames of the shafts, the smelters and the high cooling towers of the mining sites, and next to them vast built-up areas like concrete honeycombs, white and glaring, rectangular geometrical patterns of thousands of small houses in close proximity, divided into blocks by macadamized roads. We also see playing fields and market squares, situated on the edge of the European Township, the dull symmetrical pattern and unimaginative identical houses of which are softened by trees and colourful gardens.

This is the Copperbelt, where live nearly half of the people in employment in Northern Rhodesia—120,000 Africans and 38,000 Europeans.[1] The towns are planned, and economically built, for this labour force which produces the world's third biggest copper output.[2] The first start in the late 1920s was nearly crushed by the depression of 1931, but since then the mines have had no difficulties with the recruitment of labour. The drawing power of wages has been so strong that tribesmen from Northern Rhodesia and from the neighbouring countries of Nyasaland, Tanganyika, the Congo and Angola, have signed on in sufficient numbers in the urban labour offices. In the second quarter of 1956, 56 per cent of the African workmen in Nchanga came from the Northern Province, 22.5 per cent from outside Northern Rhodesia. There is a continuous movement in the country to and from the towns. 36 per cent of those who left employment in the copper mines had done less than a year's service but nearly 8 per cent had worked there for more than eight years, and only 42 per cent of all who stopped working in a Mine went back to their villages. In 1957 the increase of the African population in the Copperbelt was four times the rate of that in the other parts of Northern Rhodesia.

The Katanga Mines in the Belgian Congo have worked on a policy of stabilizing their labour force and, in sharp contrast to the Rand in the Union of South Africa, have encouraged their miners to bring wife and children with them to town.[3] This influenced the later development of Copperbelt policy. Since 1931 any recruited mineworker may bring his wife and young children with him, or at any time on request have them brought to him, at the Mine's expense. In 1957 about two thirds of the men had their family with them; only 15 per cent had left them in the villages, 12 per cent were single men, 5 per cent widowers or divorcees. The turnover is, of course, much bigger in the single men's group.[4] The majority of them are saving up money to go and marry 'a home girl' and then, as quickly as the in-laws allow, to return with her to the mine for the period of their working lives and longer. The towns have come to stay, and their influence on the economic, social and political life of the country is felt in the remotest small village.

The Church shares with most Rhodesians misgivings about this development and is therefore tempted to fall into one of two false attitudes, either dreaming of a past 'Golden Age' of rural, social stability, or else showing an impatient iconoclasm towards the old, uncivilized, heathen ways. *Uwibukisha fya kale alafwa*—'He who constantly remembers the past will soon die', says the proverbial philosophy of the Bemba. It is not easy to have a clear and detached view of what is happening in an 'area of rapid social change', but this challenge stands before the Christians, who have to solve the day-to-day problems which confront them and the community in which they live, on their way to a fuller, happier life in a new security.

One of the most obvious differences indicated in the two settlement patterns is the change in family structure. Each of the small clusters which form a village is the habitat of an extended family, three or even four generations living in close proximity. All the Bantu people we met on the Copperbelt came from tribal societies in which the families were linked together by common descent from an ancestor who is traced either through the male line, i.e. patrilineally (father, father's father, etc.), or through the female line, matrilineally (mother, mother's mother, etc.). The majority of the tribes have a matrilineal organisation, e.g. the Bemba and the Bemba-speaking peoples of the Northern and the Luapula provinces, the Lamba, Lala, Kaonde and many others. Husbands used to live in their wives' family, at least in the first years of engagement and married life. In matrilineal society, the mother's brother (Bemba: *nalume*) is the guardian of his sister's children, overriding the authority of the children's father. Succession and inheritance pass from the maternal uncle to his nephew.

People of patrilineal tribes come from the north east (Mambwe, Lungu) and from Nyasaland, as well as from the big group of Southern Bantu in the Union of South Africa, Portuguese East Africa and Southern Rhodesia.

In Northern Rhodesia the name of a village is often a personal one, e.g. at Musonda's (village). This name of the (possibly legendary) founder, the ancestor of the villagers, is also used as a title of each successive headman. Nsensema's village, in which we lived for a short time, was typical of one on a main road, with a good deal of traffic passing through and linking it daily with the Copperbelt. The Senior Chief and the tribal headquarters were two miles away, a Protestant and a Roman Catholic mission station within a ten-miles circle, and the Boma, the seat of Government, a few miles further. The centre of the village was the headman's big house, with his mother's next to it. She had two of her granddaughters sleeping with her, while the unmarried sons of the headman slept in a hut on the other side of the father's house, next to the village store which was kept by Nsensema and two of his sons. One of these was married and lived opposite, near the house of his eldest sister, who divided her time between this village, where her eldest daughter lived with the grandmother, and Elisabethville, the nearest town in the Belgian Congo, where her husband worked. Another daughter of Nsensema lived with her husband in her own house behind those two. Her brothers, together with her father, the headman, and her husband, were building a house next to hers for her eldest daughter, who had married in the Congo and was expected home soon for some length of time. Kunda and Champo, the two widows of the former Nsensema (who had been the maternal uncle of the present one), lived together on the outer circle of this central group of houses. Mwape, a daughter of the late headman, occupied the next cluster of houses with her husband and family and looked after her mother and her father's second wife. The next two houses on the road had been built by the sons of two sisters of Nsensema, but they were absent, working in the fish trade between Lake Mweru and the Copperbelt. The headman allocated these to us for the time of our investigations. During our stay he called the older boys and the women to a community project (*mbile*), to build a house for a young woman whose mother lived next to us. Mary had been married in the Copperbelt and, after divorcing her husband when he married a second wife, she had returned with her small baby to the village. Her father, a famous thatcher, was away working on contract with the government, but her mother's house was small and two children of Mary's sister shared it already with their grandmother. We found several such clusters of women, usually mothers, daughters and grandchildren, in Nsensema's village. Only 25 of the 70 taxable men registered in the village lived at home; 12 worked in the Congo, 18 outside the Luapula province in the territory, most probably in the Copperbelt, and 15 were at work somewhere in the province. Those who visited most frequently were either fishermen in the Luapula swamp and on Lake Mweru or engaged in the fish trade. One son of the headman was hawking dresses for his father in the district and returned, usually for the week-end, to take away the dresses that his father had sewn up during the week, but since his wife lived with her parents in Kawambwa village, his loyalty was divided and he ought probably not to be counted as one of his father's villagers though he owned and occupied a house in the village.

Four of the men whom we learned to know quite well, and who spoke rather more freely, were 'retired' from urban work and had attached themselves to Nsensema's village. The first, Luka, was married to a sister of the headman. While in the Congo, the second, Joseph, had married a woman from this village and when his mother and her brother, Kabasa (related to Nsensema's father), attached themselves to Nsensema after he had inherited the headmanship, Joseph decided to build a house there next to Kabasa. The fourth, Mubanga, who wanted to try farming after more than forty years' work with Europeans as hospital orderly, teacher and driver, asked Nsensema for a piece of land next to the village and built three houses there, for himself, his mother and his widowed sister.

The family pattern of Nsensema's village is fairly clear, though it was not possible to establish all the blood or marriage relationships of the villagers: three generations normally live together, and the closest links are between grandparents and grandchildren and brothers, sisters and their children. The middle generation is the unstable factor in the local group, with the men working in other places for long periods often joined by their wives, who have nevertheless a tendency to return frequently to their mothers or brothers, especially in the case of divorce or at their request for the grandchildren. Girls who marry in the towns are expected to bring their husbands to their mothers' village, if only for holidays. Though the statistical numbers of inhabitants, not all resident in the village (see p. 68), show a slight overbalance of the male population—78 men and 60 boy children against 72 women and 57 girls—the village presented in actual fact the picture of a settlement of women and children; many houses did not even have an old grandfather living in them, and only three able-bodied unmarried teen-age young men lived there permanently in a house of their own, fishing for the village cooking pots. They had been working with their older brother, Luka, but they were constantly having trouble over the money, so he decided to give them one of his two boats to let them work on their own. They came pleading, 'You are killing us', but he stuck to the arrangement. Luka was fully integrated into his wife's family; he had a big modern house near the small hut in which his mother-in-law, a wife of the late headman, lived, and the room between their houses was the living room, in which the women worked and cooked and sat and rested, gossiping while Luka entertained his friends on the front verandah of the house, which faced the main road and was a much more public place. In a similar way men used to sit in front of the headman's store, talking while Nsensema was working with his sewing-machine, making comments on and to the passers-by on foot, bicycle and lorry, who frequently stopped for a short rest and exchange of news and some small purchase.

The children had the whole village as their playground. Once they had left their mother's or elder sister's carry-cloth, they toddled between the houses and even into the main motor-road, either in twos or threes of their own age group or running along with older children. The mothers never appeared worried; they trusted that all adults would take equal responsibility for a child which involuntarily got into danger. When for instance the boys once discovered the spoor of a snake between the houses and pursued it to a palm tree, two men running towards them shouted sharply to the children to stand back and took on the chase themselves. This unobtrusive attention of all for the safety of the children kept the little ones from getting lost by wandering into the gardens or the nearby swamps, and even the older boys, who could not be restricted from setting snares in the bush or fishing in the waterholes of the swamp, were immediately and angrily called back by the women if they ventured near the waterholes which customarily supplied the drinking water for certain households.

The boys lived a most free and happy life in their small world. During the school holidays they could be seen together in neighbourhood groups all day, amusing themselves, playing football, quarrelling, walking along the road singing, sitting in little groups to play with spinning-tops, and once making an earth bow as a musical instrument on which they took turns to play. On the morning that school opened, an unnatural quiet lay over the village, after an unusually early excitement of waking up. Obviously nearly all of primary school age—8 to 12—had gone either to the Local Education Authority's school in the chief's village nearly two miles away, or to the Roman Catholic mission, four miles in the opposite direction. Many of the older boys and also some of the girls went to boarding schools. In our immediate neighbourhood two children were kept at home, although they obviously wished to go to school.

Sunday was a twelve-year-old boy, an orphan who lived with his maternal uncle. He probably suffered from the man's rather domineering wife who was concerned for her own only son, a possible future Nsensema, since she was 'in the right line'. Chibwe was a fifteen-year-old girl who lived with her grandmother and had finished Standard III when she reached puberty. She had to stay because her mother in the Congo had accepted a suitor for her and already received the best part of the bride-wealth.[5] The girl was unhappy about not being allowed to go back to school, but she appeared to be quite pleased with the teasing of her girl friends about her impending marriage. She divided her time between helping her grandmother with the household tasks, the age-old repetition of fetching water, collecting firewood, peeling, soaking and pounding cassava, and washing and ironing her clothes and berets, showing her uneducated friends her new skill, parading with them on the road and taking part in the activities and troubles of the Free Church choir, although she was a Roman Catholic. This choir served as a substitute for a youth club and was the daily afternoon meeting of the five marriageable girls, two or three young wives of the teen-age group whose husbands were absent from the village, and three blind young men who lived with relatives.

Another girl of that group, Malita, caused some excitement by running away from her foster-mother to her brother, when her maternal relatives accepted the initial gift of betrothal from a man whom she disliked because 'he was too young and did not earn much money in the chief's village' where he lived. She was an orphan, obviously just as self-willed as her mother's sister, who had adopted her as well as Sunday. In spite of efforts to persuade her and the strongly voiced disapproval of her disobedience in the village even among the girls of her own age-group, she did not give in nor come back till the money was returned and the marriage negotiations thus terminated.

All the young girls had at some time in their childhood been in a town and were looking forward to going there again. Nobody seemed to expect the young men to serve a trial period in their in-laws' families. The old custom of living with the family of one's wife was only preserved in the long leave periods and, in some cases already mentioned, for retirement. But the emphasis on matrilineal descent and the strong bond between brothers and sisters was very easily recognizable at Nsensema's.

It is not surprising that the young men move so easily out of the village into the towns, because even in the old days they had to leave their family group and attach themselves to their father-in-law's. The important difference in the modern situation is that they stay isolated, living as individuals not immediately integrated into a new family, but rather charged with establishing a family themselves, on an entirely different basis.

At Nchanga Mine the usual sequence is that a man signs on and is allocated a place in the single quarters of the Mine. When he has saved enough money for a ticket for a bus or railway journey for his wife, he asks the township manager for married quarters. When these are available the manager signs a form to agree that the wife may come. This is sent to the home chief who calls the wife, sends her to the Boma, the Government District headquarters, where she gets a certificate which the chief must sign. She also needs a marriage registration certificate. All these papers must be produced at the Customs Posts on the Congo-Rhodesia or Nyasaland-Rhodesia borders.

In May 1958 Nchanga African Mine Township had 4,152 houses for married men, 2,750 places in 'single quarters' and nearly 900 names on the waiting list for the 550 new houses designed for employees with three or four children, each containing two bedrooms, a living room, a kitchen, shower and lavatory.

It is easy to see how the move to the Mines breaks the old family pattern. Very rarely several members of a big village family group, a 'sib', move into the same compound at the one time. But even if they do, it is quite impossible for them to live together. The two- or three-roomed houses break each basic family of husband, wife and children out of its larger setting.

Sometimes the older wives refuse to follow their husbands, because they are reluctant to break away from their maternal sib; this ends usually in a divorce. Young girls who marry into town often return to their mothers for the birth of the first child. Very few grandmothers follow their daughters into town except for short periods. A group of three elderly women we met on their journey to the Copperbelt said, when asked why they went, 'We want to rest; there is no hard work in the towns, but plenty in the village.' Others come to see their grandchildren and often want to take one back with them to the village.

One of the most frequently heard complaints about town housing is that the houses are too small. When a family has growing children, there is no possibility of giving boys and girls separate bedrooms, and visitors have to sleep in the kitchen or in a shelter in the yard. In a discussion the members of an African women's club of the Nchanga Welfare Centre said, 'If we had bigger houses we would keep the girls here. But the grandmothers like them to go and stay in the village. Girls learn to obey in the villages but not here.' A school-teacher said, 'It is not too bad in Nchanga, but Mufulira (a neighbouring Mine) is a proper kitchen town', *i.e.* many people have erected cooking shelters in the spaces between the houses, which are usually fenced in and used as a yard, a very limited equivalent of the 'living space' of the women in the village.

The Mine Township Management recognizes only parents and children as a legitimate family, and they insist with varying degrees of strictness that only one wife can be in residence, though the Customary Native Law does not ban polygyny. Other members of a family have to ask for a visitor's permit, which normally is not granted for more than a fortnight. The authorities have, on the other hand, few means of coping with the problem of 'loafers'—visitors, mainly young men, who stay with relatives while they are unemployed, either for lack of work or through laziness. This includes the many boys who are sent from the villages to live with their uncles or elder brothers, in order either to go to school or to find their way into earning money in the many ways which are open to them only in a European settlement, *e.g.* as garden boys or newspaper boys. These loafers are sometimes felt to be an unfair drag on the economy of the small urban family, which usually depends on one wage packet, but the social training of the village is still strong enough to maintain recognition of these obligations. The teachers of a certain town school—not in a Mine compound—once asked the school manager to impose restrictions on visitors as the Mine Managements do, 'for we ourselves cannot send our brothers away, but we have not enough food left for our own children.' A Trade Union official said that the notices at the compound gates prohibiting unauthorized visitors had been 'dead' for the last two years, but with the closing of a neighbouring mine, Bancroft, a considerable number of unemployed had floated into Nchanga and the Management had revived the restrictions.

The influx of unattached women is another hardly controllable factor. We were told that the women of a certain Congo tribe managed to get past the Border control with the permit to visit their 'brother', and that as many as ten were living as visitors in one house to which they brought a lot of money earned as prostitutes. It is very difficult to verify if this is more than slander against a tribe which has a surprising number of tall, attractive-looking women who have the distinctive and rare custom of polyandry.

The relationship between husband and wife has to undergo difficult and profound adjustments to this urban situation in which they are isolated from their familiar groups and thrown together in mutual dependence of a kind which is totally different from marital relationships in a village setting. They are given freedom to build up their own life with little help or interference from their neighbours, who are more often than not of different tribes with foreign dialects and customs. Those who have grown up in town life and have some education do not usually find it difficult. A young African minister who had experienced South African town life since the age of twelve married the daughter of his superior, well educated according to Northern Rhodesia standards, and they showed after two years of married life a harmonious partnership, working together or independently as was necessary, with obvious love and respect for each other as equals. With them lived two small schoolboys, a younger brother and a nephew, 'to be educated in town.'

The wife's mother came to look after the baby and keep house for her son-in-law when her daughter fell ill and had to go into hospital. The young couple visited her parents frequently and there was obviously no kind of customary avoidance of the 'in-laws', which would have been very difficult to carry out while the father-in-law was the superintendent of the young minister's work.

Another couple with much stronger village links and less formal education had achieved a similar kind of partnership through twenty years of town life. The husband was very successful in his work on the Mine and had developed his ability of leadership in the trade union movement. During his long leaves he usually went back to Nyasaland to spend part of the time in his village and the rest with his wife's parents. He told us that some time after the birth of his first two children, when the eldest was three years old, they went to his wife's village and his mother-in-law said to him, 'Thank you for looking after my child and my grandchildren; I'll no longer look at the path (i.e. avoid you).' And so the taboo was broken in the usual way. When they returned after two months' holiday in 1955, with their seven children, they found that a strike had just begun. It was very hard for the wife to stand in the relief organization's food queues, so he went for her. When another long leave was due to them they talked over together what they should do. If they went away from the Mine, the four elder children would miss the first month of the new school year. The political and labour tensions were in such a state that another strike was pending. Therefore they decided that the husband should stay in the town looking after the children while he was free from duties and the wife went to Nyasaland with the baby to visit the grandparents.

The difficulties of adjustment to this new urban life vary of course greatly, according to the background of both marriage partners, and they are often tried to breaking point when the standards of education or the tribal customs differ.

When Chisanga had been trained and given his first job as a teacher by the Jesuit Fathers, he looked around for a bride but he could only find a girl educated to Standard II. They married in a Roman Catholic village church. His wife was not happy with him because she did not have a second child. They consulted a *ng'anga,* a native doctor, who promised them another child 'after some time'. The husband went to a town for further training, and during that time his wife had her second child by another man. Meanwhile her husband had found the understanding companionship of Ruth, an educated nurse. He divorced his first wife in a Native Urban Court and then contracted a civil marriage with Ruth, though she was of a foreign tribe. They both found work in a mining town. The man praised his second wife after seven years' married life with her for her high standard of housewifery, her participation in his interests and the problems of his job, for her loving and efficient care of their four children and her patience with his mother, who, after his father's death, had come to live with them. His wife showed also that she was devoted to her husband and her children, but she confessed that she was often very unhappy because she felt very isolated and had not found a satisfactory place in the community in which she now lived. 'I have no friend here. They blame me for speaking English. They say, "We fear people from the South." I cook what my husband likes, I serve what his friends are used to eat and in the way they like it served. But they still don't like me.' And she did not manage to get on with her husband's family. His daughter by his first wife was sent down from school because she had become pregnant. Chisanga offered to take her in because she did not like her stepfather. Ruth tried to make her feel at home, gave her a room on her own in the already overcrowded house and was grateful for her assistance. 'It is very difficult to bring up small children properly if one has no relations to help.' But the girl did not fit herself into the customary role of the eldest daughter; she ran away. Another time, since Chisanga is the only child of his widowed mother, he asked her to come from the village and live with them on the Compound. He underestimated the troubles which the language question, among other problems, would cause between the two women in his house. His mother refused to understand the broken Bemba which the normally English-speaking daughter-in-law used to communicate with her, and she resented the fact that her grandchildren were brought up speaking a 'foreign language'. Ruth with her nursing training could not help feeling worried about the grandmother's habits. 'Her standard of hygiene is very low, she does not mind sitting with her friends in the backyard next to the communal lavatory. It is difficult to teach my children proper ways when the local people have different customs.'

These three examples do not represent the average family life of the copper miner; they belong rather to the emerging middle class than to the rank and file of the labourers. But they seem to be typical of the opportunities as well as the dangers which belong to the transition from the life of the extended family to the urban basic family. This basic family is, of course, in existence in the village and can theoretically be separated from the larger unit. All the ritual connected with married life, the mystic dependence of the luck of the hunter on his wife's faithfulness, the danger to the life of the wife in childbirth if her husband has committed adultery during her pregnancy, the ablutions after intercourse to keep the kitchen fire 'clean', without poison to the food cooked on it—all this shows a strong belief in the importance of the husband-wife relationship. The women teachers of the Nchanga Women's Welfare Centre confirmed that even the educated girl accepts the small waterpot which she is given by an older woman on her wedding night and keeps it as secret in her town house as her village sister. But very few of the town girls have gone through the training of the puberty initiation. The young couples forget quickly what the old people have told them; some say: 'It is just superstition,' and stop the old custom. Others are suspicious of what their wives are doing while they are on shift work. 'Her adultery has brought me bad luck' is a frequent accusation in matrimonial cases, corresponding with the women's complaint that their husbands are unreasonably jealous. New rites to express the unity of marriage, and teaching to help stabilize this relationship, have not yet been found. Many of the women still look for support and security to their maternal uncles and their brothers rather than to their husbands. Are they unconsciously resenting the individualization and the changed status in the relation to their husbands which urban life has made inevitable?

A similar ambiguity exists in the relationship of the children to their parents' generation. Since most of the tribes in a town compound belong to the central African group of matrilineal Bantu, it is not surprising that so many nephews are found living with the basic families, especially schoolboys or at least boys of school age, and that the guardian who is registering the marriage of a town girl is more frequently the *nalume*, her mother's brother than her father. The African news magazine of Nchanga published the picture of a proud man with two small girls entered by him for the baby competition—they were his nieces! But it is now often the father who pays school fees or gives his consent for an operation on his children. The councillor of Senior Chief Kazembe expressed this trend: 'In ten years' time all these old customs of following the mother's brother will be changed—that is civilization.' And another councillor was tried and had to serve a prison sentence because he had made an 'advance payment' to himself out of public funds to enable him to pay school fees for his child and his wife's son of her former marriage. Is the father assuming a new role? In conflicting situations in town between the husband and his wife's brother (as, for example, when marriage negotiations for a girl are started), the mere fact that the maternal relations live far away shifts the responsibility to the father. But a girl who objected to the choice her mother made for her was told by her father, 'This has nothing to do with me' (*te mulandu wandi*).

The link between grandparents and grandchildren has been remarkably well preserved in the transition period. It seems to have always had a strong emotional basis. In the village the old people who stay at home when everybody goes to hunt, fish or cultivate the gardens are the natural protectors and teachers of the children, and they enjoy the small services which the growing grandchildren can give them, help in household chores as well as companionship. For this reason the grandmothers, as already indicated, often explicitly request that one or more of their town grandchildren should return to the village to live with them. They feel responsible for their well-being. Some babies wore charms round their wrists and their necks when they were baptized in Nchanga. The mothers, when asked why they did this, answered, 'The grandmothers sent them specially; we don't really mind but the old people are superstitious.' Members of one tribe in the Northern Province consult the grandparents before naming a new-born child. The name links the child in a magic way with one of his ancestors. In the village we were confused by an old lady who told us that she had that morning buried her grandmother but her grandfather was still with her—pointing to a small boy. Does this mean that the youngest generation represents the ancestors? One of our best informants denied that it was more than the recognition of the possibility that the qualities and character of a dead relation can manifest themselves in a new life. But A. Richards was told some twenty years ago that 'each dead man or woman is succeeded by a close relative of the same sex who acquires his or her name and guardian spirit (*mupashi*)'.[6] The name of a new-born child is chosen from those of the dead 'grandparents'—never one of those who are still alive—and it is 'tried out'; if the baby is content and progressing well, it has got its 'right name', but if it is sickly or cries a lot another name is substituted, and this change may happen more than once.

The children in the village seem to get attached to their grandmothers when they are weaned, i.e., in many cases when their mother expects her next child. The Copperbelt women, even when they still had quite young children of their own, pointed out their grandchildren to visitors with special pride. A woman who had borne five boys said 'I wish I had a daughter; they care for old parents better than boys.' But the actual help and care, the real security in old age, is given by the daughters' children.

The destitute old people are those who have neither daughters nor grandchildren. These are not found in the towns; the Social Survey of the Copperbelt shows in the population age pyramid of Luanshya that there are hardly any women over 45 or men over 55 living in the Mine or Municipal Townships.[7] Kansuswa has a certain number of 'retired' men living with their families, i.e., married children and grandchildren either in the same Township or one of the neighbouring Mines. The reasons for the preference of an urban rather than the usual villages retirement are given: 'My wife and I are of different tribes and we do not want to separate or to go to a place which is foreign to one of us.' Or, 'Life in a village is very hard, and we like to be where our children are.' The Kansuswa Management Board has two such grandfathers as members. One of them is chairman of the Development Committee. When his daughter had a divorce, she came to leave her children with him and his wife, and took a job in a hospital. Another pair of grandparents looked after the illegitimate children of their eldest daughter, together with their younger children. How far do the grandparents consciously see their grandchildren as a source of security? And how far does their readiness to join their grandchildren to their own households contribute to the instability of their daughters' marriages or even to the promiscuity of the town girl? Such a tendency was definitely found in the South African townships, where the patrilineal tribes developed under urban conditions extended family groups, in which the husbands of the daughters had a peripheral role comparable to the status of the young men in the initial period of their marriages in matrilineal society.[8]

The conflict between the search for security in a joint family more or less adapted to urban life and the advantages of the easy mobility and social autonomy of a small family for industrial conditions is aggravated by the tensions which exist between the food-producing, self-supporting economy and the wage-earning, money-spending new order. Listening to the leisurely, spontaneous talk of people in the towns, especially to men, one finds that most frequently the themes are money—prices, incomes, attempts to borrow, and boasting about spending. The wives complain that their husbands do not give them a fair share of their 'ticket money' (the cash paid after the completion of 30 days' work), and couples of the educated middle-class keep their individual earnings not only in separate post-office savings books, but secret from each other, as for example a school-teacher married to a nurse, told us. When asked, 'What causes more trouble, beer or money?', a group of young mothers in Nchanga said unanimously, 'Money spoils the relationship between husband and wife. A woman who earns some money on her own has to hide it carefully or her husband will take it and spend it on beer'.

Mr Dauti Yamba, a member of the Northern Rhodesian Legislative Council has written a booklet in the vernacular, *The Way of Marriage,* in which he describes a conversation between a tribal Elder and a young man. 'The love of money has in our time spoilt the marriage arrangements. In the old days the grandparents and the maternal uncle of a girl looked at her suitor and took a long time considering his character: was he energetic and courageous, patient, self-controlled and willing to accept advice? Nowadays the parents(!) ask only: how much does he earn in the job? The family demands a big initial *chisungu* gift and keeps the final *mpango* (bridewealth) small, because the latter has to be repaid in the case of divorce.' (*Chisungu* is the Bemba name for the puberty rites for girls. The bridegroom had to take part in the ceremonies and contribute towards their cost. Nowadays they are rarely practised in full, but the young man is asked to reward the older woman of his bride's family for the instruction of the girl in her womanly duties.) Both 'gifts' are nowadays usually sums of money which in 106 cases checked at Nchanga Urban Native Court varied from 2*s.* to £14 for *mpango,* and in three cases, where both *mpango* and *chisungu* gifts were registered, the proportion was 1 : 11.

The adjustments to a family budget based on money are especially difficult for the women, who in the villages produce and distribute the staple food. In the Bemba *chisungu* ceremony, the initiation of girls into their role as wives, the importance of hard work in the garden to support the family, the care of the food in store, and all the domestic duties like fetching water and cooking, are impressed in strongly emotional ritual. These are fundamental beliefs which stabilize married life.[9] The 'lazy one who smokes all day' is derided in a song as a fool, one without wits. Many of the town women try to cultivate a garden in the bush which surrounds the compound. When the hoeing season starts, all women's meetings such as welfare or church classes dwindle and every morning can be seen a general exodus of women from their homes into the bush. Some have to walk for miles to find the kind of soil they want for growing special relishes, maize and pumpkins and spinach, to supplement the staple food which is usually bought and was till a few years ago issued by the Mine as part of the wages. Others collect mushrooms, caterpillars or flying ants in season, and many use the garden or wild foodstuffs to get cash, selling them in the markets or to their neighbours. Another profitable activity which many Nchanga wives take up is charcoal-burning. But the easiest and quickest gain is made by brewing and selling beer. The restrictions on this vary in the different Copperbelt places from strict prohibition of all brewing to licensing sections of the townships in turn. Most managements try, like Nchanga, to reduce home brewing, with its after-effects of quarrels and fights, by making the beerhalls which they run and control more and more attractive. Women protest against this; the African Congress women's organization boycotted so actively that it led to rioting in some instances. Their main complaint is that the beerhalls are in unfair competition with them, that the money spent by their husbands in the beerhall should rather go through home-brewing back into their hands. The African welfare officer in an article in the African newspaper, *Nchanga Drum*, agrees with them, though with a slightly different emphasis: 'Let them buy beer but let them consume it at home. In this way beer will perform the noble duty it used to in pre-industry African days. Beer is a social cement. . . . Many unmarried girls flock to the beerhall on the trail of their spending fathers and likewise many bachelors flock to the beerhall to drink with married women. The resultant is a strange moral behaviour which leads to many divorces and plenty of domestic misunderstandings.' He ends with an appeal to the local African leaders to send their wives to welfare classes on family budgeting.

In the villages, beer drinks were in the old days either festival occasions or a reward for help with, for example, building a house. It was also a form of tribute to the chief, who in turn had to provide it for his visitors, the tribal councils and people labouring for him. 'But,' said one informant, 'young unmarried people were not allowed to drink and men and women had their beer in separate parties.' 'Nowadays a young man with money can do anything he likes.' A woman at Nsensema's who had learned brewing for sale in the Copperbelt started a 'Koko bar' in the village. (Beer for home consumption is made of ground maize which is boiled in water one day and drunk the next. But if it is to be sold, sugar is added for greater potency. It is then called Koko, we were told.) The brewer attracted quite a crowd from neighbouring villages, as well as the young people of her own. It seemed that the girls who went, in spite of the disapproval of the headman, saw this rather as an escape from the dullness of their village life. They were not consciously used as 'the ones who make beer nice'—*baciwamyo bwalwa*—young girls employed by older women brewers in the Copperbelt. The 'bar', though run as a permanent business for earning regular money, was worked rather on the lines of bartering fruit and wild or garden foodstuffs. Only when money was wanted for a certain purpose did the women think of selling something; for instance, a woman offering some eggs for sale said, 'I want a shilling,' and when told that was too much she replied, 'I need it to buy some soap; will you take a paw-paw with them?' During the six weeks in the village I can only remember two occasions in which the noise from the Koko bar told us that it was open. There was beer sold in the senior chief's township every week-end, and young people on their bicycles passing on the road shouted to each other to which village they were going for beer.

This is nothing, however, compared with the frequency with which men go to the beerhalls in the towns. A Nchanga school-teacher said, 'On the Mines nearly every man goes to the beerhall daily, as soon as his work is over. He has nothing else to do. The only time for visiting men in the Mine is Sunday morning before 10 o'clock, i.e., when the beerhall opens. Women do not drink so much; the unattached women do, but the married women very little.'[10]

The beerhall functions as a meeting place of relatives, friends, or members of the same tribe, who live miles apart in the compound and whose houses and yards are in any case small and crowded. When a group of Bemba Elders who sat together in the beerhall were asked jokingly how they could afford bottles of beer at the end of the month, they pointed out that a number of young men drinking with them had bought these as gifts of respect.[11] Even the glimpses at the drinking parties which one gets when driving along the wire-mesh fence of the beerhall reveal that amid all the noise and hilarity many groups sit in serious discussion, and African social research assistants confirm that many 'cases' of tribal members are considered at these gatherings and that the young men still listen to the moral instructions which are based on customary laws. But at the same time it is the beerhall which provides the opportunity to meet women of other tribes who wait for a 'pick-up' marriage and induce the men to break away from tribal customs. The visit to the beerhall is to be regarded as an urban leisure-time activity comparable to attendance of football matches and other sports activities, the dances and cinema shows. Work in industry means fixed timetables and definite hours with 'nothing to do', which give a chance to re-establish social relations. The villager is hardly ever isolated in his work from his social group, and the men who, for instance, return from fishing with their brothers and go to discuss with the headman what to do about some youngsters who damaged their nets, would not regard one activity as work and the next as relaxing in good company. But the compound drinking party, when greeted with *Mwabombeni*—'you are working'—laughed with the reply *Tuletusha fye*—'we are only resting.' The labour gang with its 'boss boy' is not simply the village working party with an elder as leader transferred into an urban setting, and the complaint of the Boss Boys' Committee about the lack of manners between Africans underground and more particularly the insufficient respect paid to the boss boys by their gangs[12] show clearly the difference in the moral attitudes in the two *milieux*. The division of life into work and 'off-duty' is an urban problem which has to be solved in individual ways.

The young people who are attracted by the ways of town life do not see this as a difficulty, but rather as a chance of a fuller life with a wide choice of activities: few seem to see work as more than a way to earn money and get a house. After work, the beerhall and the welfare clubs, the night school and the handicraft centre, trade unions and political parties, and all the various church groups are open to them, and from the evidence which the women of the UCCAR congregation in Nchanga gave, the decision to join one of these community activities is usually made in the first three months. The choice is, of course, to a certain extent limited by background and previous education, but also by the work group in which the newcomer finds himself: 'A man may be expected to work night-shifts as much as four to five years without change,' one informant explained, 'and I have been on Sunday work, doubly paid, for ten years and had no chance to go to church.'

Which marriages survive when the chances are so heavily loaded against them? The Nchanga Young Mothers' Club was quite emphatic: 'We want our daughters to be educated before they marry. It would be a good thing if the women of all churches came together and demanded more schools.' Many members of the Club are illiterate, and their initiative in joining the club for adult education is exceptional. As with the men, handicrafts are more popular in their obvious immediate usefulness, compared with the three R's. But the discussion of girls' education revealed that the women see the inequality of educational standards between husband and wife as a great risk. They quoted the case of one of the best-known African leaders, who had worked himself up into a position where he had to entertain frequently. At first he tried to have tea made by his 'village wife' for his educated African colleagues, but he felt ashamed of her ignorance, the way she dressed and her reluctance to sit with the men 'in a civilized way'. He asked the younger, more sophisticated women members of his organization to be hostesses for him and in the end divorced his first wife to marry a girl who had completed Standard II, then the highest level which girls of his tribe had reached. Some mothers realize that the complaint of the school-teacher, 'My wife is no companion to me' (p. 74) is well founded. A young school-teacher's wife wrote from the village, 'The thing which I desire in the Copperbelt is the Women's School. It would bring me in the way which my husband would like, though we are called primitive.'[13] The formal education of girls along with the boys up to puberty is now generally wanted by parents who live in town. According to the mothers, the schools still discriminate against the girls; while the headmasters point out that the lower classes have fairly equal numbers and the parents are to blame that so few girls remain in school after the fourth year.

A senior chief of Lubemba told us that many women asked for divorces on the ground of desertion, and said, 'I cannot count the young men who have left, but there is no help against this; we have no work for the men here. It is very difficult for the family left behind, unless they receive money from the man in town. The chief's court grants a divorce if, according to reliable witnesses, the woman has been five years without help. If the address of the man is known, he is contacted before the case is heard, but often nobody knows where he is.' The chief knew, of course, as well as the deserted wives, that those 'lost men' had uprooted themselves and found strong ties in the town by marrying for convenience a 'pick-up', a town girl who offers her services to an unattached man. By contracting an Urban Court marriage with her, the man can supply the paper necessary to get married quarters from his employer, and he can expect to find his meals cooked for him and a companion who is more knowledgeable about 'town ways' than he is. The Native Urban Courts do not regard these as anything but temporary marriages, though the marriage licence registers two formal features of a 'marriage according to customary law', the *mpango* (bridewealth) and the consent of the guardian of the woman, because under customary law the woman is a legal minor in all marriage negotiations. Till 1953 it was necessary to get the consent of the Tribal Authority if a marriage was to be registered in town, but this procedure was abandoned because it did not work. The Native Tribal Authorities often did not know their people who had perhaps been working away from home for years, and most of them were opposed to inter-tribal marriage. But the Urban Native Courts had to accept the 'town marriages' as a fact, and the Court Members' Conference in 1953 decided to register every couple which came with a guardian to testify the consent of the bride's family. An African Court social worker said that these guardians were often bribed by the couple—paid to speak for them because they either did not or could not get anybody from the girl's family. We received one confirmation for this statement in Nsensema's village when a woman told us that her daughter had married in a Congo town but she did not know her son-in-law's name or his tribe. Nevertheless she expected them both to visit her when their first child was due to be born.

Not all pick-up marriages end with a quick divorce. It would be interesting to know how many of the new urban marriages survive the shock of a definite break with tribal tradition and, in freedom of personal choice without the interference of the members of the bride's sib, create a firmer link between husband and wife and a better adjustment to the individual responsibilities of town life. Unfortunately, our attempt to make a survey of African marriages at Nchanga did not succeed. We know that many leading members of the African community see the instability of married life in the towns as one of the most deplorable features. On the other hand, nobody really knows what percentage of urban registered marriages goes through the divorce courts, and even a superficial look at the court files shows that only a few of the 'pick-up' women seem never to settle. In 169 divorce cases at Nchanga, 133 women and 35 men petitioned and in one case a couple said that they both wanted a separation. Only one women said she had never intended her marriage to last when her husband retired and wanted to go back to the country—'he is just a town man.' In three cases, the reason given was incompatibility, because of tribal differences. Five women wanted to be freed from a husband who had insulted the wife's parents and two men brought the corresponding accusation against their wives. Jealousy and cruelty (36 cases) are the most frequent accusations against the men, which in the village would hardly lead to the Court but be settled by the Elders, who have a thorough knowledge of the actual facts behind the accusations. During attendance at Senior Chief Kazembe's Court, we felt that the assessors did not rely on the evidence which was produced by the witnesses but that they took their personal knowledge of the parties into account. This may have its dangers for the proper administration of justice but it helps to guard the harmony of social relationships. Not just two quarrelling individuals but the whole setting in which the dispute occurs can be considered on the village or tribal Court level; that is *mano* (wisdom)—a word which A. Richards beautifully translates as 'social sense'.[14] The town couple cannot appeal to a group who knows them both well enough to get at the root of their quarrels and troubles. Many are reluctant to talk to their church officials or welfare workers, and the temptation to take the easy way out and get a divorce is obviously a strong one. But it might be wise to study how many marriages last in spite of the double difficulties of urban and personal adjustment, and to find the resources from which the power to persevere comes.

It seems that a marriage between two town-born people has the same stability as the union of a basic family who moved into town together. In 55 cases out of 169 the break had been caused by the tension between the 'home-girl' and the 'pick-up'. The young unmarried villager who goes to work in the town asks his family to look for a wife for him. He marries a town girl and when the frictions with her mount, he tells her that the women 'at home' have a much more obedient, less demanding bride awaiting him. Since the Mining Companies do not allow more than one wife to stay with him in the compound, she has to go. Usually the woman herself pleads for a divorce; polygyny is legal under Native Customary Law, but in town it is felt to be 'uncivilized', out of tune with the new way of life, and the housing difficulty is only one of a set of reasons for refusing to live in a polygynous family. Women are a liability, a drain on the income, and not, as in the old tribal days, a source of income through their agricultural work and of status in the community.

The married man who leaves his wife in the village while he looks for work in town has sooner or later to face the dilemma of choice between the town girl who may have established a satisfactory relationship with him, and his 'true wife'. It is a conflict between loyalty to tribal values and customs and the new order. Our very limited case numbers do not allow a firm conclusion as to how the Nchanga miner solves this problem; the 'village wife' seems to be slightly on the winning side—in 16 cases out of 27 the 'town wife' went out of the house on her arrival. But these few cases may not be at all typical, because the great majority are probably settled out of court. One should also bear in mind that the registration of marriages is entirely voluntary and that at least some employers do not ask to see the certificate but accept the African family as a *fait accompli*. Considering the circumstances, it is surprising how anxious people are to have a 'proper marriage', and to obtain the certificate from the Urban Court as a security, an outward sign that they are not promiscuous. Quite a number of 'pick-up' marriages are not immediately brought to the Registration office because the partners want to see 'if they can agree', i.e., live through a trial period, and one may wonder if this does not show a high value placed on harmonious family life rather than contempt of sanctions.

A few of the people in the top income group have 'concubines', as the educated call them. In two cases this proved to be a compromise in the conflict between the town and the village wife. The men had not dissolved their first marriages and took full responsibility for their wives and children when they found a more 'civilized' companion. They did not attempt to unite them in one household but kept them in different sections of the town. A case which caused a considerable stir in the compound was the trial of a highly respected and trusted clerk who, after twenty years' service, was found to have obtained £1,600 by false pretences out of African savings. He had two 'women friends' who ran businesses for him in the home village and in a Congo town. His 'first wife' was an educated woman who earned an income of her own, but her spending for 'prestige' for herself and her seven children was far above her own resources. Polygyny as a means of income could not be successfully played in this modern variation.

Is education the miracle drug which will cure all the social upsets of Northern Rhodesia? Those who doubt it are found in the towns as well as in the country, but they are not yet very many.

Since the children are enrolled when they are eight years old, the girls reach marriage age before their primary education has been completed. A change of government policy allows the headmaster to take girls of seven years old in preference to boys if he has any places left after enrolling the eight-year-old children. Not often is that the case in the towns—where in 1956 only 45 per cent of all the children between eight and twelve could get a place in the schools. Nchanga women formed a queue over a mile long when the headmaster started enrolling for the new school year in 1957. The teachers of that school said that in cases of transfer from one town to another, the main grumble of African Mine employees was that their children could not get places in school in the new town, and if they went to the country many villages were far away from a school. In two new Mine Townships the Education Department relaxed the rule of a maximum number of 35 in a class, to cater for children of the families transferred.

An African welfare officer met a number of working parents who did not press their children to go to school because, they said, 'There is no advantage in it. To educate a boy is only to make him a *makobo*.' This name of a species of fish is used as an insult: 'tasteless and very soft, with big mouths, but no good for eating.' It is mainly directed against white-collar workers who belong to the group of people in constant close contact with the European 'bosses' and have to mediate between the labourers and the white mine staff. They are all suspected of being 'informers'. Since the formation of the trade unions, many of the senior African staff belong to the Mines African Staffs' Association (MASA) and not to the Trade Union, and thus 'a wedge has been driven between the educated and the illiterates. Even the children of the two groups are divided and will not play together'. It is interesting to note how the division and emotional reactions of industrial work relations influence the domestic social life, and that the European is made responsible for the tension.

The educated man is the 'odd man out' in a society in which half of those employed by the mine are unskilled labourers. 'People who speak English are cowards. They are afraid of losing their jobs.'[15] But education is still the way to more money, and consequent improved standards of living, and enhanced social status. The educated man can overcome his isolation by using his income to gain a following; he has to be generous in supplying drinks for his friends 'like a chief', and as long as he does not associate too closely with Europeans he is admired for widely copying Western ways of behaviour. 'Why should our leader not have the same American car as the General Manager?'

The educated men who cannot or will not follow this kind of appeal to public favour have great difficulty in keeping the status which they originally had and still usually hold in the villages; the two most noticeable groups of these are the African ministers and the school-teachers. The turnover of teachers is a very serious handicap for the development of school education in Northern Rhodesia. In 1957 just as many teachers left the teaching service as completed their training. All the older members of the salaried African staff, welfare officers and drivers, as well as a considerable number of the traders and fish-sellers in Nchanga, finished their education with a teacher-training course, but they soon found that they could use their education far more profitably in other jobs. The 'white-collar' has still a considerable value for status in a village, but even there the young mission-trained craftsman, the carpenter and the builder, are more highly paid than the schoolmaster, and the B.A. headmaster who changed into overalls and started a transport business with fish trading as a side line was highly admired for it. Nobody seemed to consider it as a waste of his training and potential intellectual leadership.

While the clerk, the mine boss-boy and the teacher find a new social security in integrating themselves into a working group, usually under European management, in which they are limited and 'advanced' by factors which they cannot control, the business man has chosen a freedom of enterprise which carries with it considerable risks. These are often lessened by sharing them with relatives, the financial backing and the co-operation of the extended family. The best-educated member—not always the senior or the initiator of the scheme—is put in charge of the accounts and books; in a few cases the family business partners decide who must take up special training, or employ 'experts' for those duties. These modern African business men, though as yet few in number, play an important part in the link-up between the town and the country. Their headquarters are usually in a town, sometimes in several places at the end of the lines of communication, like Lusaka—Copperbelt—Lake Mweru—Kasama, the Provincial Headquarters of the Northern Province. But the most enterprising and efficient are very mobile, supervising and controlling their affairs by frequent visits. At the same time they are free to attend important family functions like funerals and wakes, call on their old people in case of illness, and preserve much closer relations with their families than the uneducated, illiterate *machona,* the 'lost men', who left their villages in search of work and have never been heard of again.

The nostalgic statement. 'In the village I was a better man,' revealed to us more than once that even the educated man feels that he is a victim of the moral conflict between village standards and town ambitions. Nearly all value judgments we provoked in Nsensema's village were related to social behaviour. 'A good person is not quarrelsome, but peaceful; he does not use abusive words, he shares his food with others and is hospitable; he keeps secrets told to him, and tries to reconcile families who hate each other; if he sees a person developing bad habits, like stealing, he stops him and talks to him but not in front of others.'—'To be called a liar does not cause shame. But an adulterer will feel ashamed in the presence of his partner's husband, even if he is not found out.'—'Fornication between unmarried people is no cause for shame, unless the girl become pregnant; then the boy would be fined.'—'If you drink and then go home to sleep it off, it is all right; but if you become quarrelsome you are bad.' These statements of the Lunda people correspond with the ethics two Bemba girls were taught twenty-seven years ago, in a *chisungu* ceremony which A. Richards attended: 'Do not gossip. Do not talk when you are under the influence of drink. When your husband insults and scolds you, sit silent and merely raise your eyes. He will be ashamed and say, "Indeed, you have done well".' Though the future housewife is warned not to finish up her store of grain like a hawk pouncing on food, she is warned that in time of hunger she will be tempted to break hospitality rules—and to do that would be as abnormal as a tortoise climbing a tree. Respect for seniority and proper humility, the obligations to one's own clan and to one's in-laws, and loyalty to the tribe are taught together with the domestic duties and behaviour proper to a married woman. The social values inculcated with such emotional emphasis produce the bad conscience of the egotist town-dweller and the fear which sees the town as a dangerous place, full of violence, because nobody can be sure if the neighbours of different tribes which surround his house in the compound follow similar rules of behaviour.

Working conditions bring together men of often very differing tribes and Europeans of varying backgrounds, and the contacts certainly lead to social relations much wider than those which are made in the village and its tribal environment, or even through modern activities like fishing for sale, trading as a hawker in the country, or work in a Boma. It was perhaps inevitable that at the beginning the administration of the Mine and non-Mine urban settlements regarded the towns as a kind of extension of the rural communities, in which the same values and norms of social behaviour would function. Time has shown that this is quite impossible. The representation of the working man through Tribal Elders who were nominated by the chiefs lost public backing when the African Welfare Societies, whose members came mainly from the educated class, began to express the grievances and the requests of the people much more vigorously than the conservative, customary authorities. In labour relations, unity of interest cut across tribal divisions and the new urban leaders gained their following by competently dealing with 'any work calculated to improve the general welfare of Africans, to promote their contentment, and to make representations on their behalf' (Constitution of the Luanshya African Welfare and Recreational Society). The Welfare Societies became a training ground for the future political leaders; the present members of the Northern Rhodesian and the Federal Legislatures, African National Congress leaders and Trade Union leaders arose from this 'go ahead' body. This is not the place to discuss how the African National Congress grew out of the urban situation, cutting across all tribal organizations, and gained such universal backing. But it is important to note that in matters of labour and politics, the new principles have united people who in domestic and personal affairs are still divided and suffering under the conflict of customary behaviour, tribal loyalties and the new possibilities of personal freedom. A Nchanga African leader said, 'The so-called tension between Congress and the African Mineworkers' Trade Union is an artificial top level affair. The ordinary members of the Trade Union are all pro-Congress, for Congress expresses the working men's frustration.' It is not surprising that this idea of unity appeals especially to the young people. 'On the Copperbelt, there are numbers of young wives who have become very interested in politics, even though they have not had much education, and these try to persuade others.' One of the best educated women teachers said in a discussion on the participation of school-teachers in political activities, 'We cannot have this. If a teacher was known to be a Congress leader, all the children would follow his words blindly; he would be their hero and they might refuse to listen to anybody else.' She was referring to children in town, but one can have little doubt that the same applies to many in the upper classes of country schools. Political thinking is beginning to form a new social grouping which transcends the conflicting systems of tribe and labour, 'bush' and 'mine'. It brings the 'foreigners' together in standing up against the third, the real stranger—the white man.

This does not mean that xenophobia is expressed only in terms of races. The Nchanga miner is still very suspicious of all his neighbours who are not of his tribe or tongue. Long before the white man's rule, a number of small tribes had accepted the language of their Bemba conquerors. Sammy Ntara, a driver from Southern Rhodesia who was employed as instructor at Nchanga, was accused of having killed a fellow-driver, and when the police cleared him and found the real murderer, his neighbours still called him *munyama,* cannibal, and warned others not to go near his vanette lest he should catch them. 'And all this only because I am a foreigner; I come from Matabele, and can't speak Chitemba well.' Tribal marks like the filing of the front teeth are widely believed to be indications of sinister customs, and the magic powers and the 'medicine' of the foreigners are supposed to be stronger than the local tribal doctors. In the village we were told, 'People go from here to Itawa to send lions to an enemy. There they find people are going to Mweru to send lions to their enemies. And at Mweru the people may be going to Mbereshi to send lions. They are always to be found somewhere else.' The women of Nchanga crossed over the nearby Congo border to get protective charms and cures when the local remedies of 'wise women' or European clinics did not have the desired effect. They discussed frequently the reputation of the various 'doctors'—African and European *bashing'anga*—and got over their fear with the sophisticated 'Let us try, and see what happens'.

A welfare officer told us that one of his neighbours had twins born to him and he paid a lot of money to get protective medicine for these 'dangerous marvels'. Yet one of the twins died after a few weeks; he had had to give the women who had helped with the birth so many blankets (compensation) that there was no money left for buying things necessary for the babies'. After some time the welfare officer himself became the father of twins and he refused to use medicines. His relatives came and tried to persuade him, and he had many letters advising due precautions and blaming him for not wanting children. But he said, 'I want to make an experiment,' and sent his wife to the Mine baby clinic, and, he told us proudly, 'My own twins are still alive!' The experiment had turned out well, and this experience—not only the scientific education he had received in school—had convinced him and provided the courage to advise others to adopt a new attitude towards twins.

The willingness to experiment, and to take risks in ignoring the dictates of custom when deliberately accepting a new way of behaviour, is perhaps the result of an advanced formal education. As another African welfare officer pointed out: 'Most people change old customs or just drop them, without realising what they are doing.' Asked for an example, he told us about his own mother, the wife of a headman, who had spent her whole life in a northern village far away from any town. Her son married during his studies in Johannesburg and brought his foreign wife and first child home during his leave. He had discussed the custom of avoiding the in-laws (*tina mako*) with his wife, and she decided it would be wise to observe them, though she was an educated town girl. At the last stop before her husband's father's village, she got off the bus with her baby and waited till the customary gift was sent to her to 'make her look up'. The young man was met by his mother who immediately asked, 'Where is your wife?' 'She is waiting outside the village in order to keep our custom.' 'What nonsense,' the mother exclaimed, 'I want to see my grandchild,' and off she went without delay to welcome the stranger with whom she could not even talk. But, the young man said, 'If I had written to her and asked, "Do you want my wife to keep this custom?" I'm sure she would have replied, "Yes, she must learn our ways." '

Many of the social changes are made in this way without the consciousness of a choice, and that may be one of the reasons why they seem so inconsistent to a detached observer. It may also explain the ease with which people who return from the town to their village on holiday or on retirement fit themselves into the old pattern, which is, of course, never quite the old, since it too has changed. It is important to realize that the social development in the town is not a straightforward evolution of a 'civilized' or 'industrial' community out of a 'primitive' tribal organization. Who would dare to say that it is progress, with the implication of a change from an outmoded to a more perfect social order? Is the small family, which town conditions favour, not too heavily burdened when it has to take on all the functions which a much larger group of relatives carried in the village? The people who struggle with the problems of adjustment present a great variety of solutions, just as in the past the behaviour patterns were anything but uniform. The picture of social patterns is in many ways similar to that of the languages in Northern Rhodesia. The Bantu dialects can be seen as different stages of development from a common origin and the historical steps of phonetical and grammatical changes still persist in living use side by side in neighbouring villages and tribes, while over all of them is poured a wealth of new words and expressions from an entirely foreign source, which is nevertheless readily accepted because it meets new needs of communication. The purists resent the resulting mixture, which they call a corrupt language, and a few radical reformers would like to make everybody adopt English as the universal language. They forget that the Bantu languages are the best manifestation of creative thought in a culture poor in material art. We may feel compassion with the people who are forced into a life of difficult problems which demand quick decisions, but we should also recognize that this gives possibilities of growth, a challenge to be alive, to explore new lines of thought and action, and so gain a new social, as well as spiritual, security.

NOTES

1. Colonial Office, *Report on Northern Rhodesia for the year 1957*, p. 10.
2. Northern Rhodesian Chamber of Mines, *Year Book 1956*, Kitwe, Northern Rhodesia.
3. Hailey, *An African Survey*, OUP, 1945, pp. 675, 681. Also Merle Davies, *Modern Industries and the African*.
4. J. C. Mitchell, *African Urbanisation in Ndola and Luanshya* (Rhodes-Livingstone Communication 6), 1954.
5. One should bear in mind that the 'bridewealth' (Bemba: *mpango*) has not the same significance for all Northern Rhodesian tribes. The Bemba, Lunda and related people, who provide a large number of the mining towns population, used to have only a token exchange of gifts. 'The

important element in the marriage contract is the service undertaken by the husband for the parents-in-law over a period of years.' *Ethnographic Survey of Africa, Bemba and related peoples of Northern Rhodesia,* International African Institute, London, 1951, p. 5.

6. A. I. Richards, *Chisungu,* Faber & Faber, 1958.

7. A. L. Epstein, *Politics in an Urban African Community,* Manchester University Press, 1958, p. 17.

8. M. G. Marwick, in *African Studies,* 1954.

9. Richards, *op. cit.*

10. *Table of Beer Consumption*

Day	*Millet Beer*	*European Beer*
Christmas Day, 1957	1,575 galls.	221.6 doz quarts
Easter Sunday, 1958	2,665 galls.	119.1 „ quarts
		115.11 „ pints
May Day, 1957	2,721 galls.	100.0 „ pints
(Monday)		120.0 „ quarts
(Mine Holiday)		48.4 „ pints

11. Epstein, *op. cit.*, p. 60.

12. Epstein, *op. cit.*, p. 63.

13. Archives of the London Missionary Society; letter to the Rev. R. J. B. Moore, Mindolo, Kitwe.

14. Richards, *op. cit.*, p. 76.

15. Epstein, *op. cit.*, p. 143.

5

The Church in a Changing Society

AND where is the Church in this society? When we look at it as represented in buildings in the settlements seen from the air, we find it usually in several small or big meeting places on the fringes of villages and compounds, hardly ever in the centre. How far is that the symbol of a spiritual truth? Nchanga had fourteen church buildings and fenced-in sites, and only the three largest were really 'in' the compound among the houses. On the other hand, these church sites are fairly evenly distributed along the long outer border of the Township and not, as for instance, in Mufulira and other Mines, all in line next to each other on one road. It is only fair to say that this external position is not quite as detrimental to the life of the church as it would be in a climate where open-air meetings are not possible or are not often preferred to indoor sessions. But what of the multiplicity of churches? Is it wrong to say that in this urban setting, the church shows itself alive because so many small fractions of it exist side by side, yet at the same time to deplore that its witness is weakened by this lack of unity? In a strange contradiction the Church is both a unifying and a separating power in the urban community, and both tendencies seem to exist in all the big or small congregations of the many denominations.

Members of the town churches frequently answer the question about their church membership with a place name: 'We belong to Mbereshi—or Ndola—or Livingstonia.' The geographical distribution of mission stations and mission comity can be seen in the pattern of religious affiliation of the tribes. Only a few religious movements like Jehovah's Witnesses, who have no mission stations, schools or hospitals, are not restricted to people of certain areas in Northern Rhodesia. Immigrants when they arrive in the town look for 'their' church and they find there the people of their tribe, speaking their language, keeping their tradition of worship and church order. The process can also happen the other way round. Thus Sammy, who had been baptized while he was at a Primitive Methodist school in his home reserve in Matabeleland, Southern Rhodesia, felt that in Northern Rhodesia 'his spirit was dead', because he could neither understand the Northern Rhodesian church service nor take part in the church's activities as a lay preacher, since he could not speak Bemba. He met a fellow-tribesman at work who took him to the African Methodist Episcopal congregation, where the minister, who had been trained in South Africa, could speak and understand Sindebele. So he and his wife decided to join the AME church.

At Nsensema's the denominational affiliation was determined by the link of the headman with LMS when work was started from Mbereshi Mission Station in that district at the beginning of the century. Since the headship stayed in the family and many of the kinsfolk lived around Nsensema, the great majority of the villagers belonged to the same church, and they were the only congregation that had erected a church building in the village. Unfortunately we did not stay long enough to get a full survey of the inhabitants. It looked as if the few people who were Roman Catholic or AME or Watchtower lived further away, rather removed from the nucleus of the village formed by the houses of Nsensema's family, and they may have been newcomers. In two cases they were men who had married into the village. The only 'relation' of Nsensema's who belonged to the AME church was one of the wives of his maternal uncle, his predecessor. She spent her old age in the village among her daughters and, because she was infirm and could not walk far, attended the services in the village. 'She has not really got the right faith,' one of the elders told us.

Nsensema had been an active church member and trained as a lay preacher before he inherited the office of his uncle, and because he combined spiritual and customary authority, the constitution of the congregation was nearly identical with the village meeting. The same drum was beaten for the Thursday church class as for the public discussions, the same 'elders', in the literal sense of the word, gathered around the 'chair' of Nsensema, and the groups of men, women and young people sat divided in the customary way. The evangelist who lives in the chief's Township and carries the responsibility for teaching and the arrangements of preaching appointments could rely on the headman to stand in at the very shortest notice, and the church register, attendance list and collection money were in Nsensema's keeping.

The headman accepted the study of his village, if somewhat passively, after his 'brother', the Acting Chief Councillor of the Senior Chief

Kazembe, had explained to him that both the Chief and the Government, the Boma, had agreed to help us find a place for our research, and that we were linked with the Mbereshi Mission and did not want to bring another denomination into the village. He discussed the question of housing the research workers with two of the village-cum-church elders but, as far as we could see, made on his own the decision to let three Europeans live for six weeks in the village, without any consultation of public opinion. After we had settled in, he gave us an opportunity to explain the aim of the study at a village meeting specially called for the purpose. During question time a group of young men, including adolescent schoolboys, showed themselves as a distinct party aggresively challenging the elders and the church: 'Why are there so many different churches?' 'Why are Bibles not given away freely but sold?' 'Why do different denominations have contradictory rules, though they base them on the same Bible?' And the youngest son of Nsensema was put up by these older youths to ask: 'What happens to the church collections?' Nsensema was obviously annoyed about these questions. When the youngsters started on this attack, most of the women who had sat quietly in the background to listen to the proceedings rose and went away to cook the evening meal. It was probably a tediously repeated argument, a stereotyped clash between the generations in the congregation. Although the young people listened when we took their questions seriously and answered accordingly, an old man got up and as he walked away said, 'You always ask the same questions and when we answer them, you only ask them again.'

The nucleus of this young group were three blind boys, one of them being Saluki, the leader of the church choir (pp. 70f). He lived with his mother's brother, the elder Kayokolo, and had the self-assertive manner which, according to the local missionaries, is typical of blind people in that district. Saluki had been trained in Braille and handicrafts at a school for the blind, and was keen to organize claims for the advancement of the blind, in society as well as in the church. 'We'll boycott the schools for the blind if the Government does not provide work for us after we have been trained. Why should we not be given good jobs like the blind people in England? Both the Government and the Mission are only interested in advancing those who have sight. Why cannot the blind people become local preachers? In this country Christians are as much our enemies as others. They too laugh at us and treat us unkindly.' This last remark was quite contrary to the actual attitude of the congregation in a class meeting when Saluki asked more questions on the text of the lesson than anybody else; someone wanted to stop him but many others, especially the old women, said: 'No, let him ask. This is how we learn.' The elders threatened Saluki's leadership of the youth group when they appointed another choir leader, Lazalo, who had returned from the Copperbelt and was seeking office in the chief's administration. Lazalo had been a deacon and the choir leader of the town congregation and was keen to take the same responsibilities in the village church. After a few weeks he complained, 'I have still to find out what a deacon's job is here. On the Copperbelt the deacons were given responsibility for visiting in one particular section of the town, but as far as I know, this is not done here.' Lazalo tried to organize two regular choir practices a week, as he had done in town, but after only three weeks, he had to give up because of lack of co-operation, and Saluki was leading again. He made the choir sing choruses which he had learned at the Blind School, and which were not generally known, but they kept quiet during the general singing of hymns which were chosen by the elders.

The attendance at church services was very high. Out of the 105 permanent adult inhabitants of the village, an average of 60 came to the Sunday morning services during the dry, cold season, and the Thursday class meeting had about half this number. The women did not reach such a high average in their special Tuesday meeting, which was taken by an 'outsider', a woman who lived with her brother on a nearby peasant farm. It was definitely a grandmothers' group, not the women with young children, who attended the women's prayer meeting. The young mothers went the two miles to the chief's village where the woman missionary of Mbereshi regularly conducted women's classes together with clinics. The headman rebuked the women repeatedly about their slackness and said after the announcements at a Sunday service: 'Too few women come to prayers on Tuesday. Our hearts are hard. Why don't you come to hear God's word? And it is the same with the class on Thursday. We should always come to learn something new and to remember the old things.' The congregation had one woman deacon, but since she lived with her fisherman husband in the swamps during the dry season, the responsibilities assigned her and her work in the village congregation could not be observed. Her only appearance was at a funeral, an occasion which always gathers big kinship groups. Three women leaders from the neighbouring congregation expressed their dissatisfaction about the way the elders appointed women deacons. 'We women should choose our representatives ourselves, not the evangelist and the men deacons. The women deacons, not the men, go and visit the sick and bring them food.'

The traditional separation between men and women was very much in evidence in the village congregation at Nsensema's, as well as in the AME church which had a big congregation in the chief's village. They never sat together but always divided on either side of the church, and even when they went to more informal meetings, such as the traditional wakes (*malilo*), the women kept strictly separate. But that does not mean that women do not have a big influence on the way these meetings are conducted. The preoccupation with funerals and wakes is startling. People go away for a week or a fortnight when some relative dies. The church services and class meetings were attended by very small numbers when a woman related to many people in Nsensema's died in Mbereshi hospital and was buried in the chief's village. Everyone went to sit around her house to mourn. The heathen wailed, the Christians sang hymns.

The Christian women's group which was trained by a woman missionary of Mbereshi insisted that hymn-singing and prayers were the contributions which the Christian women's groups had to bring to these wakes (in addition, of course, to the traditional gifts of food for the meals of the mourners). They even took pains to send the pagans away to a house over the road, to do their wailing there. In Mbereshi hospital the nurses and other Christian women always tried to stop the non-Christians from wailing when a patient died. This is a much more courageous break with old customs than one realizes at first. One of the women leaders said, 'If you don't mourn, people say you have caused the death. If you stop wailing at the wake, they turn round and say "Witch" (*muloshi*).' This was probably in the mind of those who asked the District Church Council to put on its agenda: Should Christians wail first (i.e., before singing hymns)? The accusation of being responsible for somebody's death was felt to be one of the worst things that could happen to a Christian. The fear of witchcraft is still very much in the minds of people, even of Mbereshi Mission Station. When such fear is mentioned in a sermon, the congregation gets very attentive. Nsemsema himself was asked: 'What is the greatest temptation for a Christian?' Without hesitation he answered: 'To ask who has caused the death when perhaps a child dies.' The nurses in Mbereshi hospital have more than once shown that they are not free from this. One of the girls of the boarding school had a slight anaemia but was not recovering under hospital treatment. It was obvious that she was very scared about something. In the end her teacher found out that the nurses had told her: 'You are bewitched.' She did not get better until this had come into the open, and had been discussed with her and with the nurses.

A station clerk of Mbereshi had lived away from his wife for eighteen months, but when he heard that she was dangerously ill in hospital, he hastily came back and wailed loudly when she died. He had to show that he was really grieved and had not wished to kill her. Her people told him: 'In old times we would have killed you.'

When an Anglican African priest died, the missionaries had to take his wife into protective custody to save her from the wrath of her husband's relatives.

Christian women are still tempted to go through the ceremony of 'discarding death', *ukupose mfwa*, which relatives of the husband think necessary in order to free his spirit from the close bond with her. Otherwise he may become a revengeful, troublesome, *ciwa*. The custom includes cohabitation with a 'brother' of the dead man who formerly would have inherited the wife. In some cases this is disguised nowadays under a temporary marriage. If a widow is married soon after the funeral, sometimes to a much younger man, the church is suspicious that this is only a pretence for 'discarding death'. We were told that many of these marriages do not last longer than a fortnight and are easily dissolved by the chief's or Urban Courts. An Anglican missionary said that he had met three or four cases of pregnancy resulting from this custom, but he believed that only five to ten per cent of the Christian women do not refuse to observe this custom and that those who submit to it are nearly always older women. The congregations of the CCAR around Mbereshi want to Christianize the custom of wearing a bracelet of white beads, which indicates that the widow has come to an agreement with her in-laws not to go through the 'discarding death' ceremony. Women who wore such bracelets were very reluctant to explain the custom. Therefore it is not at all clear if the beads in the spirit colour (which is believed to be white) are a charm or a sign of refusal. A Christian woman in Lunda district refused very bravely to be inherited by her husband's family and stood firm though her old mother, then one of her grandchildren, and at last her own youngest child, all died within three weeks of her husband. The children and the old mother may have been neglected, left to sleep outside the hut during the wake, but the quick succession of deaths was of course terrifying to the non-Christians. It was a long struggle before they gave their Christian daughter-in-law the white beads, and with them the permission to marry again according to her own wishes.

Many Christians accept the fear of witchcraft, of evil spirits and of the use of 'magic' medicines as a matter of course. A small grandchild of Nsensema's had a bad cough and wore round her neck black thread into which sections of straw had been knotted. A group of old men who were asked about this seemed to count it as a genuine remedy, and only Nsensema himself was aware that Christians should not believe this, yet he did not yet understand the reason. They said that parents would not themselves go into the bush to fetch medicine (*muti*) even if it were a universally known kind, but would get it from 'people who know about it'. They did not mention that the native doctor (*shing'anga*) lived near by, but they assured us that his kind knew cures for snake-bite, as well as remedies against the effects of adultery on one's wife and children. Stories about warriors who used *muti* to change themselves into birds, and a European officer who possessed a charm which made him invulnerable, were all told without any distinction between one or the other. The 'magic' medicines did not seem to be regarded with more awe than the aspirins which Nsensema sold in his store. The daughter of a church elder did not show any anxiety when one of her small twin sons chewed his charm necklace and then lost it. On the day after the new moon, she wore three spots of whitewash, one on each temple and one in the middle of her forehead, and the twins had one each on their brows. She told us that people sang and danced on the crossroads that night and brought her gifts—always identical ones for the two babies. In spite of the evident sense of ill fortune, she said the parents of twins feel proud and honoured. The same mixture of pride and uneasiness was shown by an African minister's wife in Nchanga, who said that in their mine compound more twin births occurred than anywhere else, and the African welfare officer confirmed that some of the new moon ceremonies and the white marking of the twins and their mother was observed in the town as well. Some parents put their twin children on the compound rubbish heap and cover them with ashes. But I have never seen the marks on any of the twin children in a town congregation in church.

The attitude to medicines is in most churches, especially in the numerically small groups, one of the means of identification. The Pentecostal church members were taught to refuse all medicines, African or European. After a quarrel with the bishop over this matter, a member broke away and founded his own church with no ban on medicine or doctors. In the Lunda country both Jehovah's Witnesses and a small break-away group of them, the Bamulonda, refused the drugs of an African medical orderly, saying, 'We have faith'. An elder of the CCAR wished the church to discipline all members who went to seek help from African doctors or bought charms. But many of the Christians in town are as puzzled as Ba Nsensema about the difference between pharmacy and magic, and try both alternately or even together. Under conditions of tension, like a witch-finding hunt, quite harmless objects and herbs with proper medicinal properties may be regarded with fear and suspicion, and the difference between 'white' and 'black' magic is not easily drawn.[1] 'Man uses magic on those occasions when he is aware of his imperfect control over the course of events,' states Malinowski; and one can understand that in spite of the Christians' loyalty to a religion which 'casts out fear', economic and social changes increase the dread of witchcraft and the use of magic.

Kazembe's country was disturbed by the work of a witch-finder (*mucapi*) in 1957, and in the memory of the Christians at Nsensema's it was a time in which Christians had stood against such practices and suffered for it. When they refused to have their houses searched, or if they denied that any objects the *mucapi* found in them were used as magic, their fellow-villagers and the young rowdy followers of the witch-finder beat them up. The four Christian old men who brought a case against the witch-finder's accusations and then witnessed in the trial before the District Commissioner were remembered by him on account of their Christian faith. But at the same time the Christians of the district had not been united in the action, although some of the church leaders had said it would be good to get rid of witchcraft in their villages. The District Commissioner thought that the accusations were not particularly aimed against Christian men—no woman was accused in this case—but he confirmed that the trial was based on the stand of Christian witnesses, among them a young African minister. The case pointed at the tension under which the new Kazembe, the senior Lunda chief, took office. In many peoples' minds the chief himself was responsible for calling the witch-finder, who, as he went around, was accompanied by the chief's *kapasus,* officials of the Native Authority. His predecessor had died suddenly and quite unexpectedly, and his successor may have been afraid of retaliation, as many chiefs are. Since some Christians were openly critical of the new chief, he may have passed on his own antagonism towards them to the witch-finder. But the case was not at all a clear-cut question of Christian against pagan thought. The witch-finder himself was convinced that he had only been doing his job, and after the trial some people asked, 'Why has the District Commissioner imprisoned the one man who can help us?'

The Christians, however, seem to see themselves definitely as a group, a 'party', in the court and in public affairs, when a prominent member of a church is involved in a case. Several Christian leaders told us that the former Acting Chief Councillor of Kazembe's had been framed, and was innocent though serving a prison sentence. Some of Nsensema's church elders visited him regularly with presents—yet according to the case reports, he had pleaded guilty on a charge of embezzlement of public funds, and had asked for character to be taken into account. His wife, also a Christian leader, was working in order to pay back some of the embezzled money. These facts must have been known by the church, but they were overlaid by the knowledge of the jealousies and the tricks non-Christian court members had used against the Christian councillor.

The Christians in Kazembe's country showed the anxieties of a minority group, the sense of persecution, the aggressiveness against pagan customs, as well as the desire to conform, and to keep the precious harmony of social relations. Their influence had probably been much greater under the late Kazembe, who had been an active member of the local CCAR congregation. But the opposition to his Christian practice in matters connected with the chieftainship was clearly seen, for instance, in the tribal quarrel about his matrimonial affairs. He was an elderly man with children of school age when he was called to be Kazembe. His Christian wife took on the duties which the 'head wife' of a chief carried according to custom, and her husband sent all the wives of his predecessor away instead of inheriting them. But the old councillors and, we were told, especially the women of the tribe, were very upset that he did not take a new wife who might be the mother of a future Kazembe. Only a wife whom a Kazembe marries after his accession can bear a successor, and the Kashiba, a senior chief, has the traditional duty to find a girl of the 'right families' as soon as possible for the newly installed chief. The councillor who had selected a young and quite uneducated girl according to the tribal tradition had to wait for two years before the Kazembe agreed to marry her. In the meanwhile, people had argued and quarrelled with Kazembe's wife, making her life in the chief's village such a misery that in the end she had run away. She stayed with relatives in the Copperbelt till the Kazembe got permission from his congregation to divorce her.

The present Kazembe is said to be a Roman Catholic. Yet he is known to conform to some of the old ceremonial. He only eats what is specially cooked for him and what the hereditary food-taster has tried. When visiting the northern part of his district, he travelled a long way around because the direct road passes near the graves of his predecessors, which is forbidden ground for him. He is supposed to have called the witch-finder after his accession, to protect himself from the accusation of using witchcraft against his predecessor, as well as by way of a protection against the evil practices of his enemies. Since no witch-hunt could go on without the permission of the senior chief, the rumour is probably true. Like the headman Nsensema, the chief showed the uneasiness of an authority who is the centre of rival tensions. Though he had political powers under the Indirect Rule of the Northern Rhodesian Protectorate and used them, for instance, to arrest the leaders of a meeting of the African National Congress because they had failed to ask his permission, he did not seem to emulate the active part taken by his Christian predecessor in the daily affairs of the Native Authority, and in the Court which dealt with civil and minor criminal cases. His position is a very difficult one because he is, in the eyes of the young and politically ambitious, a paid official who has to enforce laws of the British administration, even if they are against his own wishes or those of his people. The conservative group is resentful, because he occasionally ignores customary restrictions to his personal freedom; for example, during an official visit to the Copperbelt, he slept in the ordinary resthouses though traditionally he must never sleep in a room where any other person has slept. This is not surprising. The old belief that the well-being of the whole country, the fertility of the soil, as well as the good or bad fortune of the people, is dependent on the blessing of the ancestral spirits is still strong, and the chief has always been the most prominent of the mortals whose ritual duties were jealously watched by the spirits. The Lunda of Kazembe seem to have retained this belief as much as the Bemba of Chitimukulu, though for nearly half a century both chieftainships have had a mission station within walking distance.[2]

Some of the educated Christian Lunda and Bemba see the dilemma of the chief and sympathize especially with difficulties which the older and little-schooled tribal officials have to face. D. Yamba, in *The Way of Marriage* (p. 79) answers the questions of a modern young man who is uncertain about the right behaviour in getting engaged and starting married life. He complains that he has grown up in a town where no elders could advise him, and he is already three times divorced. The author obviously identifies himself with the 'Elder' in the dialogue, and in a general discussion about modern ways says, 'The wise chiefs want to re-establish old customs and not just follow the European ways. Modern young men should help to guide the chief to return to good customs.

We hope that perhaps among you young people one may arise with God's help and lead the children of Israel out of slavery.' This last phrase has probably not the narrower, simply political meaning which it carries in the context of negro spirituals and prophecies. The 'slavery' might well be the feeling of helplessness among confusing problems. Neither the chief nor the European holds any longer the trust of those who find themselves in the bonds of relationships and circumstances for which they are not prepared with the wisdom of the tribe. New thinking under God's guidance, Mr Yamba teaches his troubled young man, a reformation in which the chief uses the best of his young people's knowledge, will deliver them from the oppression of old fears and new perplexities. But does the author think of the teaching in mission school and church when he refers to the 'new knowledge' of the young? He does not mention either of them. One may wonder if the setting of the dialogue is true to reality. Do the young men bring the problems of town life back to their village elders? Though we found no direct evidence of this at Nsensema's, it was quite obvious that the proceedings in the chief's court, as well as in the more impersonal and standardized Urban Courts, were based on and probably always preceded by the informal discussion of a 'case'. Such preliminary hearings, and even the Court proceedings themselves, are not so much a judicial enquiry as a discussion of the right and proper ways of behaviour. The friendly discussions of 'news from the town' on Marko's verandah and at Nsensema's store (p. 69) are the important basis of growth of new customs, since they are constantly reaffirming and at the same time adjusting the norms of behaviour; Christian teaching is made real in this, as far as it has sunk into that depth of mind from which notions arise as to how people ought to behave. And as Mr Yamba suggests, the new rules are the result of discussions in which the old tribal law and new unprecedented moral conflicts are considered. But the majority of the young men will not be able to wait till they are back in the village; they want to solve their problems in the vigorous, quick way of town life and are as impatient with the urban church discipline committees as with their village tribal elders.

The only minister of a Nchanga church who was young as well as educated and professionally trained belonged to an all-African denomination. His time was well occupied with the up-building of his church in every sense. His congregation was very scattered and they had only just started to erect their own church building. But he was well aware of the need to gather the educated young people and to help them to find the answers to their questions. He therefore registered under the societies' ordinance[3] a discussion group with the ambitious name, 'The Faculty of Christian Sociology, Nchanga Branch,' which meets fortnightly to read Christian magazines, discuss social questions and occasionally put on some display. It had only just started with eight English-speaking members and not made any inter-racial contacts. But after some initial suspicion, it had gained the approval of the European Manager in the compound and used the conference hall of the Welfare Centre for its meetings.

Preoccupation with money is perhaps less strong among the adult church members than one might expect. But members of mission churches are occasionally resentful about constantly increasing appeals, and some regard their church giving as a kind of tax—with the same universal dislike—and wonder if the funds are really used to their best advantage. A member of the CCAR congregation complained about the envelope system which had only recently been introduced with the consent of the session: 'How can one manage 6d. every week? The educated class specially object to this, for even they are badly paid.' Everybody agrees that the salaries of the African ministers and catechists are too low; some congregations are anxious to raise them locally, but at the expense of the sums which go to central funds. An African minister said: 'The town-dwellers are not enthusiastic about the assessment to the central fund which pays the ministers in the villages. They do not regard it as a missionary duty but think that it is a way of paying towards their home congregation, and say that they are not concerned about that now. They do not feel that the church as a whole has any claim on them.' The confusion of a free-will thank-offering with a tax is supported by the habit of checking the membership cards on which the payments of church dues are registered when people come to communion or want their children baptized.

The smaller congregations seem to manage their financial affairs better than the big churches. It was not easy to obtain information on this and not wise to probe deeply into it, because of the general suspicion that all Europeans, including the missionaries, are interested in African money for their own ends. The church showed their system of collection in a Sunday service which we attended at Nchanga. The congregation of a neighbouring Mine had come to visit and worship with the local congregation, and had their superintendent with them. He announced that both he and the minister had to go to a conference in South Africa. The uniformed women of the 'Ladies' Missionary

Society' then danced forward to the table on which two collection plates were placed, while the choir sang, clapped and stamped. When all the local women had danced round the table, put down their coins and returned to their places, two women counted the money. The minister gave out the sum and the women challenged their visitors to equal their collection. Then the men and the choir followed in the dance, and in the end the women again called on the rest of the people to reach a definite sum. Everyone enjoyed this.

School teachers on the other hand reported that in some church meetings the followers were enthused into paying blindly just because of the mass feeling, and went home without a penny left in their pockets. Sometimes it was sheer showing off, because people went up individually and put their offering in a plate.

The young minister of this congregation was meeting difficulties which were typical of the tensions that exist between the old and the new generations of church members. Some of the older people had specially joined his church because, although the young minister was trained in the south and spoke several southern dialects, they disliked his initiative in making decisions without referring them back to the Elders' Session, and they were concerned about the way in which he handled money. The local congregation was self-supporting and responsible for the salary of the minister, but they had been given financial help towards the church building from their American mother church, and the struggle for authority seemed to become centred around the control of these funds.

Accusations that church funds are mishandled are raised not only against the missionaries and ministers. The suspicion is so universal that often three or more people are appointed to check each other when counting collections, and more than once the attraction of the Watch-tower Society and the Lumpa Church to educated men was explained thus: 'They think they will be made treasurers and get some of the money!' The only church which showed no sign of preoccupation with finance, and whose attitude to giving seemed to have reached that form which many others taught as most desirable, though they had not achieved it themselves, was the small separatist group of the Roman Catholic Church, the '*Bana ba Mutima*', the children of the Sacred Heart (p. 167). At their Sunday Eucharist they have a 'Virgin Mary Silver Collection'. Gifts of cash or kind may be given. 'A small child,' we were told, 'is sent forward to put the plate on the table. This is to remind everyone that in their giving they must be as little children, small and not proud. If one is giving a large amount of money, it should be concealed in a piece of paper.' The local congregation has two officers who are concerned with these funds, a secretary and a treasurer. They are responsible for the money and the gifts. There is a room full of goods which have been given for distribution to the poor. They will seek out the very poor here and give them such gifts as hats, shoes, trousers, shirts, pots and plates, needles and cottons. But more often the gifts will be distributed to the very poor in the Northern Province, where some people have only a loin cloth. Those may be of any church, Watchtower, Protestant or pagan. 'If we say they are enemies, we have barred the Sacred Heart. The love of Jesus is for every tribe.' Their leader, Emilio Mulolani 'does not make himself rich. He goes barefoot and carries not even a penny.' He attempted to make a pilgrimage to Rome, when in a vision the Virgin ordered him to do this: 'She said: "Do not take money in your pocket; whatever money you are given, you must share with the poor. You must not pay money for your transport; you are my baby now, you are to be carried on my back." So he went, taking only shirt and trousers, writing materials and some books.' 'From the end of 1957, some of the *Bana* began to leave their houses, their work and their marriages and devoted themselves only to preaching. They are the friars (*fileli*). Other members pay the tax and other payments necessary to set the *fileli* free for this work. There are now twenty-two friars and seven sisters. In the Northern Province, the friars have built the Village of Mary, a few miles from Kasama (the Provincial Administrative Centre). That is their headquarters, from which they go out to give charity to others, and to it they gather the very poor and orphans and other sufferers, and support them there with the gifts from the Copperbelt.' The value they put on charity is so high that they insist: 'However small a piece of food you have in your hand at a love-feast (which has replaced the Mass), you have to share it, even a small nut, to avoid selfishness.' 'We learn that God is everywhere and in everything. If we eat food, God is in it; and if we refuse to give food to our neighbours, we refuse to give them God.'

How well this links up with the village ethics of sharing, especially that of sharing food. It is interesting to note that the *Bana ba Mutima* are an all-African group and that they are not free from the suspicion that the European missionaries use the church collections for their own purposes. 'They call the people to give money to help orphans in China, India and Australia, but here in Rhodesia are many orphans whom the Church does not help. The priests take the money but do not announce how much is collected. We know that about £70 was collected by

Christians in Nchanga for the new church, but still there is no building and the money is not accounted for, nor do they let us see if it has helped any orphan. Everything is done in private.'

The *Bana ba Mutima* are a very young group, the branch in Nchanga having been established only in 1957; but their concern for charity, and their attempts to show it in practical as well as symbolic actions, link them with the first apostolic church and many such groups through church history up to the 'Jesus Family' in mission-hostile China.[4] Will they be the salt of the Copperbelt, a light to show their fellow-Christians a way out of the conflict between the modern ambition to improve one's economic status and that Christian emphasis on unselfish care for others which may seem identical with the social responsibilities of the past and therefore outdated? Will the churches be able to overcome the suspicion that the missionary, like other Europeans, is part of the Western exploitation of Africa's wealth and labour? Do they see the possibilities for Christian social work in the existing mission institutions and find new ways of expressing Christ's love and care? Will some get over resentment against Western hypocrisy and maintain their slender link with the European congregations, so that the Church may grow into real unity?

The *Bana ba Mutima* seem to be the only Christian group in Nchanga which actually experiences that to give is more blessed than to receive. Their significance, therefore, for the life of both African and European Christians is much greater than their very small number might lead us to expect. Many African Christians, like the boys and girls who wrote the essays, look at the Church as a kind of insurance (p. 273), and many send money and clothing to their needy relatives in the villages, but only the *Bana* show a deep understanding of the way in which Christ's love solves the problems of social welfare and security. It is not surprising that this movement has grown out of the traditions of the Roman Catholic orders and their doctrine. The other denominations might find it worth while to discuss their economic problems, which are so intricately mixed with social ones, by rethinking the advice of the Bible and the practical solutions which the Church has demonstrated all down its history. The murmuring of the Greeks about the neglect of their widows by the Hebrew Christians in Jerusalem (Acts 6.1) may look like a very simple problem to us when compared with the complaints of the Copperbelt Christians, but it is essentially the same group of tensions in a young church which may lead to spiritual growth in unity of service.

Does the church help to stabilize social patterns? In a discussion about urbanized Africans, one of their ministers said to the missionaries, 'We have been converting people to Christianity, but have we been forming a new Christian society?' His two main concerns were the great number of marriage breakdowns and divorces in which both partners were members of the congregation, and the lack of responsibility of Christian parents for their children. It has not been possible to collect enough actual data about matrimonial and juvenile discipline cases in the churches to compare them with the secular case records. But the very large number of people who are disciplined and often suspended from their churches because of adultery and/or divorce shows that the African minister's question about the Christian society is not an idle one. How do the churches tackle the problems of stabilizing the family relationship of husband and wife, parents and children, in the new setting? Two African ministers of Nchanga Compound were discussing the problem with an elder. This is what they said: 'Long before Europeans came, Africans were living happily; the wives knew their place and the husband knew his place. Sometimes he had two, three or four wives; now, in these days, the women and men have one power in the house. We find it very difficult. There are few who live happily in their houses.' 'I don't agree with that,' a second speaker replied, 'I don't know how the problem of marriage is going to be solved. I can only think the Church may have failed to bring a right understanding about marriage. When we marry, we do not really think why we marry. European standards are quite different from ours.'

> 'No,' said a third, 'it has been the failure of the church not to put some more weight and emphasis on Christian marriage. The African minister is not licensed as an officer of marriage in proper standing, like the European. An African is not sure where he stands in marriage; he is split into three parts. First, there is the tradition, second, the urban and court authority marriage, and then there is the church; and all this involves one couple. The whole failure to make an African marriage a success is not only an economic or a domestic problem. An African does not know where he stands. Oh yes, in the old days the African woman was in charge of all food. If the man interfered, he was called a bad husband and could be divorced. In these days it is a matter of money. In a Christian family, the husband has taken the place of a woman, looking after the food. So there it is an economic problem. Long ago they paid cattle and hoes and the women worked hard, very hard, for family life. Urban marriage is in a different economic condition and there is divorce because there are a lot of children and they cannot keep up with the standard. There is a lower income and there is extravagance and that makes trouble. I would think educated people, especially here in the Copperbelt, have started

copying Western ways and would educate their children as well as we people who care for our children as Christians. It is Western culture, but Christianity has emphasized it. Christianity has done well; every real Christian is very careful to bring up his children, and all people are responsible for their own children. A friend of mine in the Eastern Province, even in 1937, paid for the feeding and education of his own children, instead of making the uncle take over this responsibility, because he himself was a Christian. But if he had not been a Christian, he would not have done that.'

This discussion shows that wide range of confusing ideas with which the Church has to battle. What is Christian, and what is simply Western in family and marriages customs? Does the law hinder the churches in their efforts to establish Christian marriages and family life? The desirability of allowing Africans to contract a marriage under English law or under an alternative African Marriage Ordinance has been in the minds of Christian peoples in Northern Rhodesia for a long time. In 1922 the discussions and investigations of the General Missionary Conference had already advanced enough to ask a commission to draw up suggestions for a Christian marriage ordinance. The difficulty of combining native customary law and Christian vows led to the proposal of a marriage licence which should be issued by the native commissioner, who had to be satisfied that the marriage was legal according to the customs of the tribe concerned. The licence would then be signed by the officiating minister after the Christian ceremony. The parties were supposed to relinquish by their own act the right to divorce for other reasons than those 'allowed by Christian law, the law of this territory for Europeans.'[5] This motion was defeated. The reasons are not reported. We may assume that, on the one hand, this compromise would not have seemed to help much towards the stability of an African marriage, and on the other, put an unreasonable burden on government officials. In 1947 the request was made by the African Christian Conference that Africans should be allowed to marry under the Marriage Ordinance and African ministers be registered to do this just like their European colleagues.[6] The Christian Council took the view that the Government should again be responsible for registration and that it should be the function of the minister to bless the marriage after registration. But the registration at a Native or Urban Court is definitely not the same as an English marriage at a registrar's office. It does not establish a legal marriage, but only confirms it when it is established by gifts and the consent of both parties according to native law and custom. Mr Moffat, the legal adviser of the Government to the African Court, said in 1957 that some Urban Courts nowadays recognize an African Christian marriage. 'If the Court is shown a certificate that a couple were married in church they will accept it as proof of marriage.'[7] That means that a new custom is in process of becoming a legal act, not by decree but by the strength of public opinion.

This has not yet been recognized by the churches in Nchanga compound nor, as far as we know, by any other churches in the Copperbelt. The attitude of the different denominations towards marriage customs is, of course, still very varied. The Anglican church does not recognise any marriage as proper for its members unless it has been celebrated in the church. That means that the so-called native customary marriage, which is the only legal one in Northern Rhodesia, is not valid in the eyes of that church. Roman Catholics in Nchanga told us that the priest insists that the couple show the registration certificate before he celebrates the nuptial mass in church. The Free Churches seem to have very few of their marriages celebrated in church. But the Presbytery of the CCAR recommended that if the minister celebrates a marriage in church, he should have evidence, preferably a registration, that this marriage is legal in the customary sense.[8] Watchtower insist on registration and have no special ceremony in their meetings. The most extraordinary exception is found in the case of the AME minister in Nchanga township. Inasmuch as he is the only African minister registered to celebrate marriage under the Marriage Ordinance, and as this Marriage Ordinance can be applied only to European and coloured persons, this means that the marriages between Africans which he celebrates in his Church have not the same legal status as marriages which he may be asked to celebrate for European or coloured couples.[9]

'One may well wonder how Africans manage at all in the legislative and dogmatic cat's cradle in which the colonial powers and the churches between them have contrived to wrap up their already sufficiently complex systems of kinship and marriage.'[10] A few congregations in Nchanga said that they had marriage councils to instruct the bride and bridegroom before a church marriage and to deal with the difficulties of their married church members, but that there seemed to be general agreement that these councils were not really doing much good. I think the reason is that, as the African minister said (p. 111), 'an African does not know where he stands in marriage in the compound.' Has the Church failed to bring a right understanding about marriage? They know that fundamentally the roles of men and women in homes and in married life have altered, but because the Church has not thought out the implications of their altered status under new social and economic conditions, people fail to realize what it should mean for them as Christians. 'Give us a new law,' they say; 'keep the family together by making divorces difficult,' instead of trying to upbuild the new family under urban conditions. Only a few have had the courage to alter the customary relationship of the sexes in a way which shows Christian freedom, and they are severely criticized and even slandered by outsiders who do not understand them. The most progressive in this respect are probably the Watchtower members. One of them said,

> 'There is very little real love in African marriages, so it is the concern of the church gradually to build up new relationships and leave people to live together as a family unit. The men are asked to do personal Bible study with their wives and family. We encourage them to sit together in church and to teach their children the elements of the faith. This obligation of the family cannot be abrogated, therefore the Society has no special Sunday schools or women's meetings. We try to give the parents help in teaching their children and have just produced a finely printed and illustrated book. If the instructions of the Bible were implemented, the problems would solve themselves. For instance, a naturally inhospitable person who forces himself to hospitality will eventually discover the joys of hospitality and become hospitable. We also encourage husbands to eat with their families. They will get to like it.'

This attitude of man and woman working together in their family units was very obvious in the homes of Watchtower members we visited. The women took their place in the meeting and in discussion without any embarrassment or the usual reluctance to speak. While it was rather difficult in most other congregations to find out who was married to whom, because husbands and wives neither came to the church together nor sat together during the service, the Watchtower families were easily recognized in their meetings as little clusters of father, mother and children. This new relationship is open to obvious misunderstanding. An educated Roman Catholic African told us that he remembered how the Watchtower Movement started in the country in his youth. He said that even then the rumour began that the movement was connected with promiscuity. This was because the members used to visit one another to greet each other early in the morning in their houses and to spend the day waiting for the Second Coming. They would go about in pairs telling people the Word of God, usually a man and a woman or a boy and a girl together. Young men and women visited each other at night for fellowship, calling each other brother or sister. Today on the Mine it is common to see a smart young Watchtower man going with a smart young girl. So the public suspects them. The elder of another church said about the Watchtower. 'They are called the society church; people go because they like a big crowd and because there are pretty girls. They go to see the pretty girls.'

Another church which stresses the basic family as a Christian unit are the *Bana ba Mutima*. One of the reasons they gave of their split from the Roman Catholic Church was their insistence that there should be no division in the seating of men and women in the church. They said that they objected to this because it was imposed on the Africans but not on the Europeans of their denomination. 'Do they think that we are not pure?' They remembered a Christian family crusade which was held in the Roman Catholic church before they separated from it and they quoted the slogan which had been used in that campaign, 'The family that prays together, stays together.' 'We cannot live without praying, so we meet to pray in our houses.' They remembered that the Holy Family had been set before them as an ideal. An American priest had said, so they told us, 'You Africans are lucky; Jesus, Joseph and Mary came together to Africa and they are still here now.' The practical implications of this belief are most interesting. 'Husbands help their wives in housework, washing plates and cleaning pots. This is done to defeat pride, because others will despise such a man. But if we are to love one another, pride must not prevent that love from going out to anyone and,' said our informant, 'this pleases the women.'

The difficulty as to how to work out this new relationship between the sexes, based on the freedom of the individual to make his choice, with or without the support of his or her family group, is the centre of the marriage problem. Most of the African young men, whether educated or not, regard love between the marriage partners as a prerequisite. The long and frequent discussions which are printed in the African newspapers show this quite clearly. The girls are not so outspoken about it, but from observation one can say that in a Mine town the girl tries hard to find her own marriage partner. For them as yet, however, the term 'love' has very little of its true Christian connotation; it is just as badly misused to mean only sexual attraction as it is in the usage of so many films and magazines from the West, which are, of course, available and influence African youth. 'We do not know what we want in marriage,' said a young Sunday school superintendent of a Free Church congregation. 'We must find out if the girl is the right one, and therefore we have to have the permission of the church to divorce the first wife and take second choice.' 'We are tired of each other; we do not love each other any more' is very often given as a reason for a divorce. The old conception that a marriage was not established until it had worked well for two or three years and children had been born, and the new idea that physical attraction and satisfaction are of primary importance, make many young men reluctant to vow solemnly in church that their first marriage is for life. 'Often a couple enter upon a trial marriage but the husband pays bridewealth after a period and only completes full payment when children have been born.'

A school-teacher told the story of one of his friends. Mulenga, a church member, fell in love with Kenefa, a woman welfare officer, but her father refused the bridewealth three times because the boy was of another tribe. The boy's parents then sent him home to look for a wife in the village but he could not find anyone whom he loved and so he returned to the Copperbelt and married his girl friend without the customary payment. After some time her parents approved and accepted the gifts which Mulenga sent and thus made the marriage legal.

This story shows the dilemma in which many young Christians find themselves. Their marriages cannot be solemnized by the church unless their families approve and make it legal through the giving and accepting of the bridewealth. 'There is growing opposition among African Christians in town to pay *mpango*. *Mpango* is nothing more than a price paid for a girl and it is simply done because our great-grandfathers used to do it. It would be much better if the money could be used by the married couple to start their new life. Sometimes a husband treats his wife badly because he thinks after they have been married for some time that he paid too much for her. It bring nothing but troubles.' Unfortunately this opinion is not shared by the parent generation. One woman, a deacon of her church, said proudly that her husband paid £20 for her. 'A big bridewealth is a good thing to make a marriage strong.' And the husband of another Christian woman said, 'I love my wife. I gave six cows and £12 for her.'

The question of bridewealth is not only important in connection with Christian marriage but also as related to the relationship between parents and children in a Christian family. 'Some tribes pay very little bridewealth and this is a weakness because the children remain the wife's property.' The school-teacher who made this statement belonged to a patrilineal tribe. Christian thinking has not wiped out the old idea. The bridewealth given by the young man and his family is in most patrilineal societies the price paid for the future children. This school-teacher had observed that in the many matrilineal tribes who had their matrimonial cases decided by Copperbelt Native Urban Courts, the mothers nearly always take their children when marriages break up, and this is hardly ever discussed or disputed in court. He regarded this as a great weakness, and attributed it to the small value of the gift, not realizing that the children were tied to their mother's family with a bond that was unconnected with the *mpango* gifts.

Only in a few cases church members showed that they had moved away from the old way of thinking, and that they no longer regarded the children as pawns to be shifted according to the rules of family group relationships, but as primarily a charge for which the individual parents were responsible to God. The daughter of an African minister was divorced by her husband because she refused to stay with him when he took a second wife. She claimed that she should retain both her children and that her father should keep the bridewealth to help her in bringing them up. The chief of her patrilineal tribe agreed that this was the sensible arrangement, though it was quite contrary to custom, and she won her case against her husband's strong opposition. 'We did not know what kind of a person he was when she married him,' the woman's father said; 'now we help her to educate her children.'

Some of the older educated Christian men showed very great concern about the insecurity of their daughters' marriages. Mr Mulima, a delegate to the Northern Rhodesian Christian Council, told me to what lengths of trouble and expense he had gone. 'I wanted to make her marriage really secure. She fell in love with a boy from another country. I did not object to that, because they are both graduates and must know their own minds. But can I see into the future? Do I know what kind of a person he is? Maybe he will get tired of her and perhaps I am then no longer alive. So I made him go to Southern Rhodesia for some time and then I took my daughter there and they were married under the European Marriage Ordinance in the Boma, and we all came back and they had their church wedding here at our Mission Station in Northern Rhodesia.'

This procedure was based on the same line of thought as the request which the African Christian Conference made in 1947 (p. 110). 'European laws are superior to ours. I want the best for my daughter, therefore I will have her protected by European law.' It is very understandable that people reason on those lines when members of one church are ruled by two sets of laws which divide them on racial grounds. Europeans marry under the Marriage Ordinance, Africans under customary law. Is the general acceptance of European laws the way out of the difficulties which arise from the breakdown of family relationships and the resulting insecurity on the part of individuals?

Mr Mulima, in insisting upon the European type of marriage for his daughter, had two main points in mind. He wanted to bind the son-in-law twice, with a secular ceremony enforcing the Christian vows, to ensure that he would stay married to her and to her only until death, and also that he would share his property with her and her children and in case of his predecease pass it on to her.

Unfortunately, African Christians in Northern Rhodesia have not yet seen that the present English marriage law is a compromise between the secular attitude to life and the Christian interpretation, and that instead of its strengthening the Christian principle against destructive forces, as they wish, new complications are introduced. In fact neither bigamy nor adultery nor the inheritance of property are considered by the law from the standpoint of Christian ethics.

Mr Moffat said that in territories where Africans are allowed to marry under the European Marriage Ordinance, for instance, in Southen Rhodesia and Nyasaland, the law of bigamy is simply ignored and a man can take another wife under Native Law and Custom without having a European type of divorce, which is expensive, costing at least £75. 'Several Nyasalanders married under the Ordinance without fully realizing what the consequences would be. Then they gave up hope of a divorce and are simply living with another woman.'[11] If the first wife is a Christian, she will either have to face permanent desertion, or stay in a polygynous household, or ask for a divorce herself. In either of the latter cases, she puts herself under church discipline. A similar dilemma occurs as regards adultery. This is a serious offence under Native Law, and the discussions of such cases in the disciplinary court of a Copperbelt CCAR congregation frequently showed such horror that one felt that the old fear of supernatural anger at the breaking of a strong taboo was still influencing the minds of the deacons. But under the Ordinance no punishment, i.e., compensation, can be claimed unless linked with a divorce. This puts Christian women who are married under the Ordinance into a dangerous position. Young men look for such women, as they know that they are fairly safe from a claim for damages for adultery with them.

It is a wrong conception that a marriage under the Ordinance includes the alteration of the native laws of property and inheritance. The *Survey of African Marriage and Family Life* tells us that in most territories a special provision has to be made regarding property and succession, and that such provisions have been the subject of judicial interpretation in numerous cases, especially in West Africa. It is fairly generally accepted that a statutory marriage entitles an African woman, in principle, to an enhanced legal status and relief from customary disabilities or obligations.[12] But if the court stops at a mere statement of the widow's independence, her new position is in reality very disadvantageous. She has no effective compensation for the loss of her claim to maintenance by the deceased husband's family, nor the control of his property.

Looking back at the marriage of Mr Mulima's daughter, it is distressing to see that her father's conscientious effort to make her future stable and secure put her into a most precarious position. Legally she stands in a no-man's land between inimical frontiers. Her real security lies in the facts that her marriage was celebrated in the church, that both she and her husband have thus accepted Christian foundations on which to build their family life, and that the fellowship of the church will support them when they need help and guidance. But Mr Mulima is not the only one in Northern Rhodesia who feels that the church has not really considered the problems of relationships between the sexes and the different generations in this new era, so as to be able to offer spiritual guidance and to create a new security.

Is there a way to true togetherness of two individuals who have been broken out of their family units by circumstances over which they have no control? How can a woman overcome the frustration of having lost her economic status as the producer of the family subsistence, and of now being dependent on her husband's generosity? To whom do the children belong (when they are a source of income, e.g., bridewealth), and who is responsible for them (when they are a liability, e.g., as costing school fees)? By whom should old people be looked after? By their sons or their daughters or their grandchildren? Or is it perhaps quite wrong to think about these questions in the old way, according to matrilineal or patrilineal orders of society? Should mutual responsibility and the care of the strong for the weaker supersede legal principles?

The churches will have to think over these and many other related questions again and again. There is no possibility of reviving the past, yet the mere acceptance of the patterns of Western society tends to add to the problems rather than to solve them. One of the most valuable services of the churches to society may be to interpret, to those who are brought into conflicts due to change, the meaning of what is happening to them. They may thus be encouraged to undertake spiritual adventures of new forms of togetherness in marriage and family life, so that these may become the firm foundations upon which a new equilibrium of Rhodesian society may rest.

NOTES

1. A. Richards, in *Africa*, October 1958, p. 453.
2. A. Richards, *Land, Labour and Diet,* International African Institute, 1939, p. 235.
3. *Northern Rhodesian Government Gazette,* 11.*vii*.58.
4. Wang Shih Peng and H. W. Spillett, 'A Christian Communist Settlement in China,' *IRM* XL, 1951, pp. 168-78.
5. *Report of the General Missionary Conference of Northern Rhodesia,* 1924.
6. The Christian Council of Northern Rhodesia, *Report* 1947.
7. Letter to the Social Welfare Officer, Kitwe, 13.v.57.
8. Church of Central Africa, Minutes of Presbytery, 1957.
9. *Northern Rhodesian Government Gazette,* 22.x.56.
10. Sir Philip Mitchell, in *Africa* XXIV, 1954, p. 154.
11. Letter to the Social Welfare Officer, Kitwe, 13.v.57.
12. *Survey of African Marriage and Family Life*, published for the International African Institute by OUP, 1953. p. 286.

III

THE CHURCH AND POLITICS

6

The Growth of African Self-Assertion

THIS is not a book about politics. Yet it is impossible to understand what is confronting the Church in Central Africa without paying considerable attention to the political scene. There are several reasons why this must be so.

In the first place, the Church, however much its members believe it to be *sui generis* in a theological sense, remains sociologically an association among other associations. Inasmuch as so many of these other associations have emerged, albeit ephemerally, to cater for the Africans' growing need for self-expression and a fuller participation within society as a whole, they are in the broadest sense political. The members of the different Christian congregations are inevitably affected by the relationship of their church with these other associations and by the extent to which their church loyalty appears to conflict with other group loyalties in the wider context of the political struggle.

Again, it is necessary to allow always for what might be called the 'this-worldliness' of the African Church—its reluctance to divide experience into separate realms of sacred and secular, spiritual and physical, and its insistance upon an ethic that is social and utilitarian rather than individualistic and pietistic. This is not the place to evaluate this point of view, but it must be taken into account if one is to understand why so many African Christians judge their church in terms of its effectiveness as a social institution. There are several exceptions to this generalization—notably the apocalyptic pietism of the Watchtower Movement—which must be examined in another place. Yet it remains broadly true that Africans will always find it hard to comprehend or to be satisfied with a church which appears to be either unconcerned or ineffectual with regard to their social and political aspirations.

Then, arising from the two previous considerations, there is the hard fact that, rightly or wrongly, a great many Africans today are deeply disillusioned with their orthodox 'Mission' churches on account of their failure, as they see it, to speak out on the major political issues of recent years and, particularly, on the matter of federation.

In order to understand the tensions within which African Christians are having to think out their position and to take their stand, it is necessary, therefore, to review the political movements in which they have been involved. Before attempting this, we need to reiterate two simple facts which are easily lost sight of, though their significance is obvious.

The first is that most Africans in Northern Rhodesia and Nyasaland have been in those countries far longer than most of the Europeans.[1] This means that while most Europeans, if they want to know the events of 1925 or even 1945, must consult the records, a great many Africans can remember them happening. Memory often distorts and, at best, over-simplifies, but people live with their memories more than they live with their reference books. In this sense the Africans are more aware of their political history than the Europeans.

The other fact to remember is that a high percentage of the Africans in the two northern territories have had first-hand experience of many different parts of Southern Africa. A few hours' casual gossip in any of the compounds reveals an astonishing range of experimental knowledge of affairs in the Union, in the Portuguese territories, in the Congo, in Southern Rhodesia and in Tanganyika.[2]

These two facts naturally predispose the African people to read the events of the past forty years in terms of political geography and history rather than of economics. The economic factor, in so far as it has entered at all into their consideration, has done so mainly at two points: their fear of dispossession from ancestral lands and their struggle for advancement in face of an industrial colour bar. To them, therefore, the dominant feature, even in the economic field, has been the conflict between African and European interests.

The growing self-awareness of the Africans as Africans, accelerated by the gathering of many tribes as a proletariat in the new industrial agglomerations, has been focused mainly upon three objectives, one negative and two positive: the resistance to political federation, the achievement of African self-expression, and the winning of the right to advancement in industry. All three are aspects of the same social struggle and have been so intertwined as to be historically inseparable. It is only for purposes of clarity that they are dealt with here one after the other.

African Resistance to Political Federation

It was the accidents of climate and the hazards of history that turned the River Zambezi into an ideological frontier. It is true that the white Southern Rhodesians chose to stand by themselves in 1922 rather than be incorporated into the Union of South Africa. Yet they had this in common with their southern neighbours: that they had made themselves a home on the soil of Africa in the determination that their way of life was to be preserved there for their descendants, uncompromised in any degree by the fact that they were living in the midst of Africans. Their allocation of the land of the territory and the status they accorded to Africans revealed a concept of the white man's place in Africa which belonged more closely to that obtaining in the Union than to the idea of trusteeship which was developing in the British Colonial Office. The northward thrust of the pioneers, however, had spent itself in Mashonaland; and although the extension of the British South Africa Company's administration north of the Zambezi was in accordance with Rhodes' original plan, it was in fact carried out by men who came not from the south but from the east, as agents of the Imperial Government empowered to enter into agreements on behalf of Her Majesty the Queen with the chiefs of Nyasaland and North-Eastern Rhodesia. From this beginning the two northern territories developed a distinctively different ethos from the countries south of the Zambezi. To the African of Nyasaland or Northern Rhodesia, as he travelled or heard travellers' tales, this distinction became more and more significant. In his eyes the important issues of the last thirty years—land apportionment, African advancement in industry, federation, the franchise, dominion status—are all only facets of the cardinal question: Is this ideological frontier to remain on the Zambezi or is it to be thrust further north?

That this was the real issue at stake can be seen from the fact that until 1930 most Europeans in the two northern territories had been staunchly opposed, for a variety of reasons, to any closer political union with Southern Rhodesia.[3] But in that year the United Kingdom Government, in a memorandum on Native Policy in East Africa which touched also upon Northern Rhodesia and Nyasaland,[4] had included certain references to the doctrine of the paramountcy of African interests. This provoked a protest from the elected members of the Legislative Council of Northern Rhodesia and a demand for amalgamation with Southern Rhodesia with the object of freeing their territory from Colonial Office control.

The Imperial Government turned down these representations in July

1931. In the same year the Joint Select Committee of Parliament on 'Closer Union in East Africa', which also referred to Rhodesia and Nyasaland, reiterated the principle that

> 'the interests of the overwhelming majority of the indigenous population should not be subordinated to those of a minority belonging to another race, however important in itself'.[5]

This conclusion had already been reached by the Hilton Young Commission in 1929 which said that

> 'any proposal for amalgamation would certainly meet with general disapproval in Nyasaland. . . . It might be welcome to the majority in the railway belt, but the interests and wishes of this area cannot be allowed to outweigh those of the remainder of Northern Rhodesia and the whole of Nyasaland.'[6]

Ten years later the Bledisloe Commission reported a similar conclusion from its investigations, namely, that the wide disparity between the native policies of the three territories constituted a fundamental objection to any scheme of union. The report went on:

> 'The striking unanimity, in the northern territories, of the native opposition to amalgamation, based mainly on dislike of some features of the native policy of Southern Rhodesia [is a factor] which cannot in our judgment be ignored. If so large a proportion of the population of the combined Territory were brought unwillingly under a unified Government it would prejudice the prospect of co-operation in ordered development under such a Government.'[7]

These arguments appeared to be conclusive; at any rate the question was not raised again during the war years.

In 1945 the Central African Council was set up, on the model of the successful East African Councils, as a means of achieving all the economic and administrative advantages of closer union without any form of political amalgamation. It consisted of the Governor of Southern Rhodesia, as Chairman, with four from each of the three Legislative Councils. It was strongly criticized in Southern Rhodesia as being only advisory, yet in 1949, when it was proposed to give it executive powers, it was Southern Rhodesia that turned the suggestion down. Nevertheless in its short span of life it had a number of valuable achievements to its credit. It had promoted a considerable measure of collaboration between the three Governments, sponsored a far-reaching agreement on the recruitment and protection of migrant labour, and investigated and reported on a scheme for hydro-electric development at Kariba on the Zambezi.

A new drive towards amalgamation was initiated in 1948 when Mr (now Sir) Roy Welensky, the leader of the elected European members of the Northern Rhodesia Legislative Council, raised the question of Responsible Government, the term used to describe Southern Rhodesia's status of independence from the Colonial Office. In February 1949 a private conference was called at Victoria Falls, attended by the Prime Minister and Finance Minister of Southern Rhodesia, unofficial Europeans from the Legislative Councils of the two northern territories and, significantly, one observer from the Kenya European Electors' Union. This conference decided that the desired union was more likely to be achieved in a federal than in a unitary constitution. As Welensky said immediately after the conference, 'Our best chance of breaking with the Colonial Office lies in federation.'[8] In the following December he moved in the Legislative Council 'that in the opinion of this House the time is opportune for His Majesty's Government to take the lead in creating a Central African Federal State.' During the course of the debate the Colonial Office was subjected to much adverse comment; the official members refrained from voting, though the Acting Chief Secretary had clearly stated, 'We on this side of the Council cannot vote in favour of the motion. We are not satisfied that the time is opportune.' All the representatives of African interests, both Africans and Europeans, voted against the motion, but it was carried by nine votes to five.

Almost a year passed before the Colonial Secretary, Mr James Griffiths, announced that he was calling a conference of officials 'to formulate proposals for a further advance to be made in the closer association of the three Central African territories.' This met in London in March 1951 and was followed by a delegation of unofficial members of the Northern Rhodesia Legislative Council which included the two African members. Their talks with the Colonial Secretary were postponed in order to consider the report of the Officials' conference, which was published in June, together with an 'Historical and Economic Survey' and a 'Comparative Survey of Native Policy'.[9] In September the Colonial Secretary arrived in Central Africa and after a two weeks' tour of the territories met with a general conference at the Victoria Falls which included African representatives from Northern Rhodesia and Nyasaland. A final communiqué stated that points of difference had been found to exist with regard to the *principle* of federation as well as to the proposals made in the report of the London Conference. For the first time the African voice had been heard at an official discussion of the issue. The position they adopted was that

'Africans would be willing to consider the question of federation, on the basis of the report of the London Conference, *after the policy of partnership in Northern Rhodesia had been defined and, as so defined, put into progressive operation.*'[10]

Mr Griffiths insisted therefore that further discussion was necessary and the conference was adjourned with the hope of reassembling in London about the middle of 1952.

A general election was impending in Great Britain and many of the champions of federation hoped that a change of party might secure a more single-minded commitment of the Imperial Government to their cause. The weekly journal *East Africa and Rhodesia*, for example, demanded that the new Government should lose no time in formally declaring its support for the principle of federation, because 'an entirely new set of circumstances would exist once it were made clear to Africans that federation was to proceed with or without their consent and co-operation.'[11] Such hopes were fully justified. The Anglican Bishop of Nyasaland later commented on the damaging effect of this change of approach upon the attitude of the African people.

> 'In 1951,' he said, 'when the first draft scheme for federation was published the then Secretary of State for the Colonies, Mr Griffiths, appeared to the Africans to be giving them a free choice for or against federation. They said "No", with, so far as my experience went in conversation as I travelled up and down the diocese, quite remarkable unanimity. . . . Then the Government in England changed and the new Secretary of State, Mr Lyttleton, lost no time in making an unequivocal statement that Her Majesty's Government were in favour of federation . . . and intended to proceed with it. This fatal mingling of two different techniques of government, consultation and direct order, seems to the African a breach of good faith, and the treatment his attempts to protest have received suggest to him that he no longer has the goodwill of Whitehall.'[12]

This change of approach was probably the real cause of the Africans' deepened sense of bewildered insecurity, which is often attributed to the non-committal neutrality of the District Commissioners during the earlier period.

For nearly two more years the negotiations continued. The case for federation was now based partly on the strategic needs of the Western world, but mainly on the economic argument. Immediate advantages were going to accrue to Southern Rhodesia through federation. According to the later survey of the Federal Apportionment Commission, the public debts of Northern Rhodesia and Nyasaland in 1952 were £21.4 million and £6.2 million respectively, while Southern Rhodesia had a debt of £134 million, a good part of which had been incurred through the programme of subsidies and services to European immigrants. It was also strongly argued that federation was bound to improve the financial position of the three territories as a whole, and this was generally granted without further question. But the economists C. H. Thompson and H. W. Woodruff wrote some time after federation had taken place:

> ' "The economic case is unanswerable," or some similar phrase, was the prelude to the fiercest of arguments on constitutional or moral issues. What was not always so clear was the process of reasoning by which this position, shared apparently by all, had been reached. Certainly some of the broad and often vague claims which were put forward under the heading of economic benefit require a measure of critical examination before being accepted.' They conclude with the warning, 'The question of race relations is an important one influencing both lenders to Government and private investors, as experience elsewhere on the African continent shows only too clearly.'[13]

At an informal meeting of officials of the four Governments in January 1952 it was decided that the Conference which had adjourned at Victoria Falls should be re-convened earlier. The Conference therefore met in London in April 1952, and prepared a draft federal scheme which was published as a White Paper the following June.[14] This time the four African members had declined to take part, though they had informal discussions with the Secretary of State before and after the Conference.

One feature of the draft scheme was an African Affairs Board, to consist of one European and one African from each territory, with a chairman appointed by the Governor-General, which was to cause to be referred to the Imperial Government any federal legislation which they deemed to differentiate to the disadvantage of Africans. This aroused strong opposition from many Europeans, particularly in Southern Rhodesia. At a further conference in London in January 1953 the constitution of the African Affairs Board was revised so as to bring it into the framework of the Federal Legislature, as a Standing Committee of the House drawn from those members who had been elected to represent African interests. There have been a few occasions when this watchdog committee's representatives have caused the Governor-General to reserve and refer to Her Majesty a Bill passed by the Federal Assembly. But so far the United Kingdom Government has in every case supported the Federal Government.

In April 1953 the revised federal scheme[15] came before the three territories for their decision. A referendum in Southern Rhodesia accepted it by twenty-five thousand to fourteen thousand, and it was passed in the Legislative Councils of the two northern territories. In both these assemblies all the representatives of African interests, European as well as African, voted against the scheme with the exception of two African members in Nyasaland, who had walked out in protest before the vote. The Act establishing the Federation was ratified on 3 September 1953 and on 23 October the new federal constitution came into operation.

The bewildering story becomes more complex when it is recognized that a large part of the European population was, and is, more inclined to be 'liberal' than their Government has ever dared to believe. So far from being white racialists, they were sincerely persuaded that a federation which would commit all three territories to the policy suggested by the word 'Partnership' offered the best chance of a 'third way' that was neither black nor white nationalism. It has been part of their tragedy that the goodwill of this white majority has been so little trusted by Africans. But the pattern of society—which this well-meaning majority too readily accepts—has not made it easy for a member of one race ever to discover what the members of another are really thinking.

The most significant feature in this story is the fact that for the first time in the northern territories it was felt to be wise and right to discount and override the consistent and almost unamimous opposition of the African people. Because of the far-reaching effect that this has had upon the life of the Church in Rhodesia, it is necessary to consider briefly the nature and the strength of the African resistance.

We have already seen that before the last war all the Commissions that explored the possibility of political union had reported on the unanimity of African opposition to any closer association with Southern Rhodesia, based on their experience of the native policy in that territory. After the war, when Mr Welensky's motion was being debated in the Northern Rhodesia Legislative Council, Sir Stewart Gore-Browne, speaking on behalf of the four representatives of African interests, of whom he was the leader, informed the Council on 11 December 1949 that 'the general verdict of the African public as disclosed at numberless meetings and gatherings in all parts of the country is overwhelmingly against Federation.'

Three arguments were advanced to support the contention that this opposition could with impunity be ignored. Sometimes it was asserted that the great mass of the Africans were unaware of the issues involved and largely indifferent to the outcome. This, however, was consistently denied by those who were in a position to know the facts. The Secretary for Native Affairs in Northern Rhodesia said in the debate on the White Paper on 4 June 1952 that he disagreed with people who claimed that the opposition was confined to a vociferous minority. Mr Nightingale, one of those representing African interests in the Northern Rhodesia Legislative Council, foretold that 'a most unhappy future would be in store if Federation was forced through while opposition remained as great as it was.' One missionary of long experience working in the Southern Province wrote in the same vein: 'Opposition is vocal and practically unanimous,'[16] and a well-known French Protestant missionary who had been visiting Barotseland reported: 'They are as one man against Federation.'[17] Sir Stewart Gore-Browne announced, 'I certainly told the Secretary of State at a private meeting that the vast majority of Africans (in Northern Rhodesia) were opposed to federation. That statement has now been proved correct.'[18]

At other times the spokesmen of the African cause were represented as irresponsible agitators. Yet the practically unanimous opposition to the scheme was being maintained, not merely by unofficial organizations, but by the two major bodies created by Government for the expression of African opinion—the Protectorate Council of Nyasaland and the African Representative Council of Northern Rhodesia. Lord Hailey in the debate in the House of Lords on 2 July 1952 described the members of these two councils as 'a body of responsible, respectable and intelligent opinion—by no means of the agitator type, but highly moderate in its forms of expression'. Many of the official statements of African spokesmen of this period compare favourably with those of their opponents in clarity and cogency.

Yet a third argument was that, though the mass of Africans objected to the scheme, they did so from ignorance and misapprehension. Yet the Blantyre Mission Council stated in the spring of 1952 that

> 'As missionaries we are surprised at the knowledge of the issues involved in Federation shown by ordinary Africans. Their opposition is not to details of the scheme but to the whole principle and it is for this reason that they refuse to discuss the details.'

Similarly an Anglican priest at Mapanza wrote about the world of the African villagers with whom he was in intimate contact, that

> 'as far as my observation goes, these are united in their opposition and they understand the issues as much as the average voter in, say, England understands what he votes about.'[16]

Mr (now Sir) John Moffat touched upon these three arguments when he spoke as senior member for African interests to the Northern

Rhodesian Legislative Council on 4 July 1952. A number of efforts, he said, had been made to get round the fact of African opposition by declaring, firstly, that opposition did not exist or was greatly exaggerated; secondly, that African opinion had been gravely misled, and thirdly, that it was completely misinformed. He continued,

> 'These devices carry no weight with me because on the evidence I have available the first contention is not true, the second is not material and the third could be remedied by instruction.'

Later in the debate he warned what would be the consequences of overriding this African opposition.

> 'We shall have given ammunition to that element in the African population which is already preaching the doctrine that racialism is the only salvation for Africans in Central Africa. These persons will never forget this matter, nor will they ever forgive you.'

The issue was this: granted in full measure all the substantial benefits which could be expected from federation, had the European minority the moral right to impose its will in a fundamental issue of this nature on the vast majority of African people who had indicated their opposition to it in terms which could not be misunderstood?

The ultimate significance of the events leading up to federation was the powerful way in which they emphasized the ineffectiveness of the Africans' voice. It is to this second aspect of the social struggle that we must now turn, and in order to do so we must look back again to the earlier period.

The Development of African Self-Expression

The gradual development of an African 'voice' has taken place simultaneously in the field of local administration and in that of industrial relations. In the early days of the copper industry the idea of a communal African voice seems neither to have been expected by the authorities nor desired by the Africans. The African copper miner was simply a tribesman in transit. On the Mines themselves discipline was maintained by compound 'police boys' armed with sticks, and any complaint or request had to be brought by the individual to the Compound Manager. Beyond the Mine precincts the government officers tried to apply to the growing urban population the same patterns of administration as prevailed in the rural districts, assuming that the tribe was still the only valid point of reference and the tribal chief still an adequate intermediary.[19] To a certain extent they had justification for continuing the old pattern. Even in these days tribalism is by no means a spent force.

Nevertheless the areas of social relationship in which the tribal authority was irrelevant were steadily widening. A man did not forget that he was Bemba or Nyanja by tribe, but the fact was not germane when he needed to express himself communally with other employees to the management, with other town dwellers to the local authorities, or with other Africans to the white rulers.

African self-assertion, both in politics and in industrial relations, was gradually achieved along two parallel channels. On the one hand, the powers-that-be experimented with various patterns of officially appointed spokesmen and intermediaries. To the African these were never wholly satisfactory since they were not their own freely chosen, freely replaceable representatives. So side by side with these official go-betweens there grew up the more genuinely popular organs of expression.

In 1931 one of the Mines first introduced a recognized Council of Tribal Elders, each elected by the members of his tribe working on the Mine. Shortly afterwards the same system was introduced in the neighbouring municipal location and it later spread to all the other towns of the Copperbelt. As a rule the men chosen were related in some way to the tribal chief and had also spent a long period on the Copperbelt. In addition to acting as intermediaries between the people and the authorities, they were frequently called in to arbitrate in disputes between Africans.

Side by side with the creation of this official mouthpiece there came into being a more popular and less conservative medium of self-expression in the form of African Welfare Societies. These gave visible form to the emancipated self-awareness of the 'new' Africans, among whom those from Nyasaland were giving the lead. As early as 1924 the Assistant Magistrate of the Fife Sub-District reported that Africans in the Mwenzo area had formed a Native Association which he welcomed as a helpful development. His comment was,

> 'They do not consider they are receiving from life what they believe they are entitled to. This impression is much more likely to increase than to diminish, and it seems to me that some method will have to be adopted to enable the natives to realize their reasonable ambitions socially, politically and materially.'[20]

The Assistant Magistrate of Fife is typical of a certain tradition in the Colonial Administration which recurs not infrequently in different individuals through the history of Northern Rhodesia. Another was the District Commissioner who spoke at a conference of Administrative Officers held in 1936, approving of the new Welfare Societies that were appearing on the Copperbelt as 'a representative body of educated native opinion' which reflected the point of view of 'thinking and politically-minded Africans'. Unfortunately there has always been the other kind of officialdom which perennially, as on this occasion, reacts against such associations as not representing the African population as a whole, being no better than 'debating Societies which give the educated native an opportunity to get up before his fellows and air his English'.[21]

Many of the most trusted and respectable African spokesmen of the present time had their first experience of responsible leadership in organizing those early Welfare Societies. In retrospect those associations appear moderate enough today, and it is a surprise to find how much suspicion attached to them in certain quarters at that time because of their concern with political questions. That the Welfare Societies were certainly concerned with politics at that early date can be seen from this resolution of the Ndola Native Welfare Association, passed in July 1933, in response to the first European demands for closer union with Southern Rhodesia.

> 'While this Association would welcome amalgamation with Nyasaland, where laws and conditions are similar to those of this country, it humbly asks that the Government will not agree to the amalgamation of Northern Rhodesia and Southern Rhodesia. Such a step would, in the opinion of this Association, be greatly to the detriment of the interests and legitimate aspirations of the Native population of this country.'

The Welfare Societies were certainly the only organs at that date which could have given expression to such opinions in the name of the African people.

The first hint that the system of Tribal Elders could not provide an adequate voice for Africans, if ever they wished to speak communally as Africans or as employees, came with the serious disturbances on the mines in 1935 caused by the sudden increase of African taxation. The Elders at Luanshya, completely discredited in the eyes of the African miners as being in league with the Europeans, had to take refuge in the Compound Office.

However, this incident did nothing to shake the confidence of the Government or of the Mine Companies in the possibilities of extending the old tribal controls in the urban setting. The number of Tribal Elders was increased at Luanshya and Mufulira and their responsibilities extended to cover almost all aspects of life in the Townships. Moreover by 1939 Urban Courts consisting of assessors appointed by Native Authorities in the tribal areas had been set up in every town of the Copperbelt to apply the tribal laws to the cases arising in the compounds. The astonishing thing is that the system appeared to work so satisfactorily, provided the Africans did not feel the need to speak or act communally as Africans or as employees.

In 1940, however, when fresh disturbances broke out at Kitwe and Mufulira, it again became clear that the intermediaries could not retain the confidence of the Africans whom they were supposed to represent. At Kitwe, where there were no Tribal Elders, the compound police were attacked. At Mufulira, according to the Commission of Enquiry, the Elders early in the negotiations were suspected by the miners of having come to terms with the management and by the sixth day had completely lost the confidence of their people. An attempt by the Bemba Elders to call a purely tribal meeting was angrily resisted by men of the other tribes.[22] The Africans needed to speak as employees, so a tribal representative was inadequate; they wanted a strong spokesman and could not be satisfied with a mere go-between. At Mufulira the District Commissioner, with great insight, invited them to select a committee of their own freely chosen representatives to act as strike leaders, and this action ultimately brought about a return to work without bloodshed.

When the Forster Commission enquired into these events some of the evidence strongly suggested that nothing short of an African Trades Union and an advisory wage board would now meet the need to make articulate the communal voice of the African workers. Contrary opinion, however, won the day and in order to avoid the 'premature' formation of African Workers' Associations, the Commission recommended an extension of the system of Tribal Representatives throughout the Copperbelt with facilities for training the chosen Elders in some of the rudiments of industrial negotiation.

As soon as these recommendations had been implemented, the District Commissioners took a further step in the development of this system of intermediaries by establishing in all the Copperbelt towns Urban Advisory Councils. This was an obvious convenience in drawing together for consultation with the District Commissioner representatives of the divergent communities of the Mine and the municipality. The members of each Advisory Council were elected from, and by, the Tribal Representatives and nominated by the District Commissioner himself, so that the Council had all the appearance of the traditional Council of Elders. It has continued to function efficiently and to be the basis of still further development. Nevertheless it shares the weakness inherent in the whole system of being devised and provided *from above* as a means whereby the administrators can communicate with the inarticulate African masses and gradually train African leaders to *co-operate* with them in the tasks of administration. It is the application to a colonial society of the 'prefect' system of an English public school.

In the meantime the African Welfare Societies, which in the late 1930s had fallen into a decline, took on a new lease of life. Not only were they able to make effective demands in the name of the African community for various improvements in their conditions, but they came gradually to supplant the Advisory Councils as the real mouthpiece of African political self-expression. In 1944, for example, the Luanshya African Welfare Society forwarded a list of topics for the African Regional Council, thereby usurping the proper function of the Advisory Council. In the following year Sir Stewart Gore-Browne, the nominated representative of African interests in the Legislative Council, proposed to the conference of Provincial Commissioners that the Welfare Societies should be merged with the Advisory Councils to form a more popularly elected body.

> 'In practice,' he said, 'the Welfare Societies are not infrequently more energetic and efficient bodies than the Urban Advisory Councils, the line between welfare and politics is difficult to draw, and in some townships at any rate a visitor desirous of sounding native opinion on any matter would be better advised to consult the Welfare Society than the Urban Advisory Council.'

The Administrators, however, found themselves unable to trust the Welfare Societies and Sir Stewart's proposal was rejected.[23]

The Welfare Societies, nevertheless, went from strength to strength and in 1946 they amalgamated to form a Federation of Welfare Societies with an annual Conference at Lusaka, the first unofficial organization of Africans on a territorial basis.

While this was taking place in the purely political field there was a similar development in the realm of industrial relations. By the end of 1942 Africans in the higher categories of employment had organized themselves in Boss Boys' Committees and Clerks' Associations in spite of the decisions of the Forster Commission. In 1946 a Works Committee was set up at each Mine made up of representatives from every Mine department. But this was only a step towards the creation of the African Mineworkers' Trade Union, which, following the successful campaign of a Colonial Office representative, was formally recognized in an agreement with the Mine Companies in March 1949.

During the next two years the conflict between the Trade Union and the intermediary Tribal Representatives became increasingly apparent and the more the Mine Companies tried to boost up the status of the Elders, the more they succeeded in undermining it. For example, during a fourteen days' unsuccessful strike at Nchanga Mine in March 1951, which had been called over the alleged wrongful dismissal from work of the treasurer of the Union, the Company tried to use the Tribal Representatives to induce the men to return to work. Again after the successful strike of the autumn of 1952, the mining companies called a meeting of all the Tribal Representatives in the Copperbelt. In return for closer collaboration with the Managements they were offered better housing and gowns of office. After this the Union pressed for the abolition of the Tribal Representatives. The Chamber of Mines agreed to a ballot of all African copper miners, and when this was held more than 82 per cent of the total labour force voted for abolition, only 2.6 per cent preferring their retention. So in March 1953 the system of Tribal Representatives came to an end.

Yet, though the system ended as far as the context of industrial relations is concerned, the 'Tribal Elders' have survived because they fulfil a function in the context of personal and family relations. Most matrimonial and many other civil cases are still brought before the Tribal Elders of a Township, and even school children born in the Copperbelt know, when questioned, who represent what they call 'our chief at home'. So gradually in an inarticulate way the departmentalizing of life is being recognized. This, as we shall see, constitutes one of the major problems for the Church in the Copperbelt.

While this adjustment was being worked out in the industrial field, the Administration was making a great effort to overhaul the intermediary system in the political field. Since 1946 the Urban Advisory Councils had grown almost moribund. But in 1949 they were reconstituted. Their membership became more representative of the new order that was arising in the towns. More of the young educated men obtained seats, several of them being also leaders of the Welfare Societies. It looked almost as if Sir Stewart Gore-Browne's hope of merging the two systems was going to be realized. At the same time the Advisory Councils were given a new function as electoral colleges in the new hierarchy of political representation for Africans. African Provincial Councils, which the Bledisloe Commission had recommended in 1939, had come into existence in 1943, and the territorial African Representative Council was first set up in 1946. But now all these Councils were constituted into one system. In its most recently developed form this system operated as follows. Each of the various wards of both Mine and township elected two or three representatives for nomination by the District Commissioner to sit on the Urban Advisory Council. The Advisory Council elected four of its members to the Provincial Council, which in turn elected four or five members to the African Representative Council. This had thirty-one African members under the presidency of the (European) Secretary for Native Affairs. It was able to discuss on a territorial basis subjects forwarded from the Provincial Councils; and it elected four of its members for nomination by the Governor to represent African interests on the Legislative Council, and two on the Federal Assembly.[24]

Even this rehabilitation of the intermediary system, however, could not remove from it the two fundamental weaknesses which all along have made it unsatisfactory as a vehicle of African self-expression. In the first place it was still too closely geared into the rural pattern of tribal authorities to meet the needs of the urban African population. This became evident as soon as the delegates from the Urban Advisory Councils found themselves overwhelmed by the greater preponderance of delegates from Native Authorities in the Provincial Councils. The Colonial Office reports might reiterate from year to year their gratification 'to note how well the rural and urban representatives mix and debate matters of general interest'.[25] Yet in 1950, when the delegates from all the Advisory Councils of the Copperbelt requested that the assessors on the Urban Courts should be chosen from residents in the towns rather than the rural districts, the delegates from the Native Authorities outnumbered and outvoted them by twenty-seven to nine. Then in the second place the whole system was still too much government-sponsored to be acceptable as a vehicle of African self-expression. If ever African opinion became consolidated in opposition to official policy, as when the question of federation was raised again in the late 1940's, this system of Councils was immediately felt to be not sufficiently independent of the Government to prosecute the African case forcefully and consistently.

So once again, side by side with the rehabilitation of the conciliar system, we see the further development of the more indigenous and uninhibited organs of African self-expression. Already, in 1944, the African Welfare Societies in Nyasaland had come together to form the Nyasaland African Congress. Now in 1948 the annual conference of the Federation of African Welfare Societies of Northern Rhodesia, meeting in Lusaka, reconstituted itself under the name of the Northern Rhodesia Congress, under the chairmanship of Godwin Lewanika. Three years later in response to the intensification of the political battle over the federation scheme, a further reorganization produced the Northern Rhodesia African National Congress under the presidency of Mr Harry Nkumbula. The inclusion of the words 'African National' epitomized the final crystallizing of African self-awareness *vis à vis* the white community, and the acceptance of a condition of racial conflict, which the drive towards federation had evoked. For, as one observer commented at the time, 'The issue of federation has changed the relationship between African and European from a relationship of employer and employed, of administration and administered, to one of black and white.'[26] In their National Congress Africans saw the achievement of their own vehicle of uninhibited and uncensored self-expression. Many of them might be critical of the Congress or its leaders; but, if a European criticized either, this was deeply resented as an attack on the Africans' right to an authentic voice of their own.

African self-awareness had found a voice, but it had not yet found a way of engaging in conversation. Herein lies the African dilemma. On the one hand, the Urban Advisory Councils and the African Representative Council do provide an opportunity for 'conversation'. Here African demands have to come to terms with immediate feasibilities and African aspirations have to reach a working compromise with other points of view. As one member of the African Representative Council said to us: 'The great weakness of Congress is that it provides no place for the meeting of African and non-African opinion. In the African Representative Council we learn to modify many of the resolutions which come to us, saying: "There is no sense in this as it stands; we must make it fit practical possibilities."' But on the other hand these Councils are felt to be inadequate as a vehicle for self-expression, partly because in them the African voice seems to be muffled by governmental control, partly because, even when the authentic African voice is heard in these councils, it is rendered insignificant through their lack of effective power. At the local level the power of the Urban Advisory Council can never be greater than the influence which the District Commissioner is able to exert upon other interests, which in many situations is extremely limited. And at the territorial level the African Representative Council, like the Councils which feed it, is only an advisory body and has more than once been reminded of the fact by white political leaders. Moreover, many Africans felt that the system of indirect voting through 'electoral colleges' was discredited by the fact that it was only responsible for such a small proportion of the Legislative Council; in this case it was the pyramid which laboured to bring forth a mouse! Hence, though many members of the various Councils have also belonged at the same time to the Congress, the Congress has had, as a body, no confidence in any of the government-sponsored organs of African self-expression and has often been openly opposed to them.

Dr Epstein cites a significant and complex example of the tension between a local Congress branch and an Urban Advisory Council in connection with the attempted boycott of butcheries at Luanshya early in 1954.[27] We ourselves met the same tension at work in the African Township of Kansuswa, five miles from Mufulira. Kansuswa is one of several satellite suburbs attached to the Copperbelt towns which are occupied only by Africans under nominated African Boards of Management with normal local government powers. I had been given special permission by the District Commissioner to reside in Kansuswa for two months in 1958 on condition that the African Management Board gave their consent. This, after long discussion, they agreed to do. The local Congress branch officers quickly seized upon this as an occasion for attempting a trial of strength with the Management Board.

At that time there was no member of the Management Board who was not paying his subscription to the National Congress or who did not fully support the general aims of the Congress of those days, namely universal adult suffrage and the dissolution of the federal ties. There was therefore no fundamental conflict of political ideas. The Board members, however, by accepting office had committed themselves to executive responsibility within the framework of local Administration. They were answerable to the District Commissioner for the good order and efficient development of their Township; they had to confer and co-operate with him and his junior officers, and their decisions were always subject to his veto. The Board Secretary was also a member of the Urban Advisory Council. The Management Board therefore was always liable to fall under the shadow of mistrust which is attached to all government-sponsored intermediaries. The opposition of the local Congress officers was partly a matter of personal jealousies; shortly before these events one of them had himself been a candidate for office in the Management Board, but had failed to secure enough votes. But it also arose from a growing tendency in the Congress as a whole to reach out after omnicompetence. Many Africans in the towns find it hard to accept happily a variety of associations each serving a different need; the idea seems to stimulate feelings of insecurity. So Dr Epstein reports that at Luanshya, when a by-election was held in 1954 to fill empty seats on the Urban Advisory Council, the miners could not be induced to take much interest, on the grounds that they had their Union and wanted no other organization. They quoted the Bemba proverb: *Uwaikete fibili afwile ku menshi*—'He who grasped two things was drowned in the water.'[28] In 1958 also we found in some of the officers of local Congress branches the same feeling that Congress must become omnicompetent lest its strength be undermined by other loyalties. Great satisfaction was evinced in the efficiency with which the Congress could still fulfil many of the functions of the old Welfare Societies. In Kansuswa, when a man died with no relatives on the Copperbelt, the local Congress branch made itself responsible for the funeral, which was attended by almost the whole population of the Township. One member boasted that day that 'we show more love for such people than the churches do'. These, then, were the motives underlying the opposition of the branch officials towards the Board of Management.

In this instance the challenge was first issued at a public meeting which the Board had called to explain their decision to allow a European to reside in the Township. The treasurer of the Congress branch had already had an interview with me at which he assured me that he believed in my good intentions and showed himself personally friendly. Yet at the public meeting he and other of the officials reminded the people that 'the more a white man appears friendly the more he is to be mistrusted', and attacked the Board for taking this step without consulting the public. This aroused an angry response and after a long discussion the decision was postponed for two weeks.

Immediately before the second public meeting, an event occurred which altered the situation. A body of some thirty Northern Rhodesia police raided the Township, searching through the rooms of many of the houses, even in the absence of the householder. Many of the women fled with their children into the surrounding bush where they remained until nightfall. No clear reason for the raid appeared to have been given. Some said it was a search for stolen bicycles, or for illicit brewing. But when it was known that Mr Harry Nkumbula was spending the night at Kansuswa, most people agreed that it was intended as a demonstration of the 'strong arm'. The action of the police was particularly resented as an affront to the authority of the Board of Management. The result was a unanimity of anger which swept aside for the time being all secondary factions. Surprisingly I was exempted on this occasion from the general upsurge of antagonism to authority, and instead benefited from the concord which was temporarily created between the Management Board and the Congress officers, who, at the second public meeting, withdrew all their objections to the action of the Board.

Three weeks later, however, the normal equilibrium was restored and the old conflict appeared again. The local Congress branch forwarded to the Board of Management a memorandum demanding, among other things, that building sites should be allocated and houses rented only to those who held a Congress membership card, and that the Congress subscription should be collected with the rent, just as the Mineworkers' Union dues were to be deducted from the members' monthly pay.[29] At the same time a second attempt was made to persuade the public to demand my withdrawal from the Township. The Secretary of the Management Board, however, urged me to remain because my departure at that point would be regarded as a defeat of the Board. A week later Mr Nkumbula, to whom the Board had forwarded a copy of the memorandum, administered a heavy reprimand to the local Congress treasurer, who shortly afterwards left Kansuswa.

This incident illustrates the tension which inevitably exists in these circumstances between those bodies of Africans which, being invested with responsibility, are suspected of compromise, and the more proletarian associations which, being uncommitted, can remain uninhibited. It also shows how the same tension arises within the popular associations themselves. Men such as Mr Harry Nkumbula, by virtue of their leadership, are bound to acquire a certain *savoir faire* and to use the methods of expediency and negotiation, but in doing so they become liable to be tarred with the same brush of calumny by the less responsible junior officials in the movement. As an African journalist at Chingola remarked: 'The heads of the Congress still think there can be a way through without violence, but the masses of supporters do not think this in these days. So they have started to disapprove of some of the Congress chiefs because their rule is weak. And everybody has it in mind that Harry is weak.'

Gideon Lisulo, then treasurer of the National Congress at Nchanga, who had suffered considerably from such attacks, described his difficulties to us in these words:

> 'These are very difficult times because everything is spoiled by suspicion. The great suspicion is of the white man. But that is not the only reason. Africans are afraid and suspicious of each other. I never know whether my neighbour is a straight man or not. If a man understands English and can speak with Europeans he is unpopular. If a man tries to give good reasons for a policy he is shouted down. Sometimes there is a good reason for throwing stones at a person, and I do

not oppose that. But it is foolish to think that you must throw stones at that person's brother also. So many of those who have local political power are illiterate. I'm not going to be made a fool of and take my orders from those people.'

This is one factor which tempts the precariously poised leaders of the popular movements to adopt a policy of non-participation in the normal political machinery, though they can never maintain this position for any length of time. So at Nchanga, as an African social worker commented: 'Congress boycotted the Urban Advisory Councils as being Government-sponsored, and so they lost their chance of getting Congress candidates in. But in a recent by-election all three elected were Congress candidates, for there has been a swing away from Independents to Congress men.' Later during the summer of 1958, however, the African Representative Council again voted against electing Africans to the federal parliament, and the Governor found it necessary to create a new electoral college by combining all the Provincial Councils together with Africans registered on the two electoral rolls.

The natural evolution of African self-expression, therefore, seems to have reached the point at which the official, intermediary machinery for sponsoring African interests should give way to the direct expression of the African voice through the Africans' chosen representatives on the executive bodies at all levels. Some recognition of this has been shown in the new constitution for Northern Rhodesia which replaces the nominated European representative of African interests by two Africans in the Council of Ministers, and has eliminated the electoral colleges in favour of direct voting by the enfranchised Africans.

If, as seems probable, the time has come when African self-expression should outgrow the need for intermediary machinery, then it is bound to struggle both for a much wider extension of the franchise, and for a greater number of African seats on the legislature. In 1958 African political concern was focused first on the franchise, during the discussions on the new constitution, and, later, on the question of African seats, when the African Representative Council asked for parity of African and non-official European membership in the Northern Rhodesia Legislative Council. To block both these avenues of development is to reduce the representation of genuine African interests to something less than it has been for a long time. Some leaders of the United Federal Party, however, would justify this on the principle of 'non-racial politics'!

At first sight the African Mineworkers' Trade Union would appear to be in a happier position, for there an organization that exists unequivocally to express the African voice is established in a direct, bargaining position in relation to the Mine Companies. Here at last one would expect to find a vehicle of self-expression that is at the same time authentically African and also responsible. To some extent this is in fact the case; and one may conclude that the same result will be achieved in the political sphere when the Northern Rhodesia African National Congress, or some equivalent body, is established as a political party in sufficient strength in the Legislative Council to fight its battle there in direct confrontation with other political parties. The example of the Mineworkers' Union, however, is not wholly straightforward in this respect, for there also tension has emerged between the ordinary members in the lower labour categories and the more highly qualified and responsible leaders. This subject, however, belongs more properly to the next section.

The Struggle for African Advancement

The gradual establishment of the Africans' right to advance into higher categories of industrial employment has been closely connected with the development of African self-expression described in the foregoing paragraphs. The issue, however, is a simpler one, and the story can be conveniently extracted from the main history and recounted quite briefly by itself.

When mining began in the Copperbelt, the local African labour supply was naturally completely inexperienced, and the Companies had to engage Nyasaland workers who had already had mining experience in South Africa and Southern Rhodesia. But the indigenous Africans of Northern Rhodesia proved themselves very quick to learn the rudiments of the work, and by the time of the disturbances of 1935 they had already proved themselves capable of advancing to certain jobs which in South Africa and Southern Rhodesia were the preserve of white mine-workers. At the same time the first hint that African labour might be allowed to organize itself for negotiation with the Companies had already appeared in evidence given by the District Commissioner for Ndola before the Commission of Enquiry, in which he recommended that Africans should be enabled to elect a representative body to state their demands in future.

It was this situation which brought up to the Copperbelt in 1936 the Secretary of the South African (White) Mineworkers' Union, Mr Charles Harris. According to contemporary press reports, he made it clear that his objectives were to help make Northern Rhodesia a white country, to assist white mineworkers to organize so as to prevent the Native from encroaching upon labour that was at present performed by themselves, and to ensure that 'Downing Street should not have its way' in the matter of Native Policy.[30] He started in the Copperbelt a branch of the South African Mineworkers' Union. But after a few months it was discovered that that Union had no power to operate beyond the Union of South Africa, so the Northern Rhodesia Mineworkers' Union was founded instead.

From the very beginning the white Union launched itself on a policy of entrenchment. Two years after its original agreement with the Companies it submitted a demand that 'non-European labour should be employed at all times under direct supervision other than that of the shift boys', which meant that no African should ever be allowed to rise to any supervisory post other than that of boss boy under the overriding authority of a white mineworker.[31] During the war years, the white Union used its strong bargaining position to secure an additional clause to their agreement, known as Clause 42, which in effect guaranteed that no job performed by a white miner in 1945 would ever thereafter be given to an African.

During the next three years, African workers became steadily more aware of the contrast between their standard of remuneration and that of the Europeans. Before the outbreak of the Second World War the average white mineworker's wage was something over £40 per month, though many were receiving up to £70 a month. The average African monthly wage was £2. 15. 4 for underground workers, and £2. 8. 9 for surface workers. (The estimated value of the rations issued is included in these figures.)[32] At the same time they began to challenge the contention that the Europeans' work was so indispensable or of so much higher quality as to justify this discrepancy. In the disturbances of 1940 'the African workers contended . . . that they were qualified to do the work normally done by Europeans. They issued a challenge that they should be so tested by one shift being worked by Europeans and one by Africans in order to show which shift achieved the greater production.'[33] From that time to the present day this theme has recurred in the African argument. Dr Epstein reports that African miners were complaining in 1954 that 'Europeans are very lazy fellows. After a short time they had to sit down and have a cup of tea.' 'They only stand and watch, but we sweat. In fact we should get more than they do.'[34]

In recent years the ratio of African to European earning power has risen steeply in the copper industry. Including bonus and food allowances, but excluding subsidized housing, both black and white, and the white pension and life assurance, the average wage of an African was 5.7 per cent of the average wage of a European in 1950, but almost 10 per cent in 1957. From July 1958 African mineworkers were allowed to participate in the bonus scheme on the same basis as white workers and this still further improved their average wage in proportion to that of the Europeans.[35]

But the concern of the African Union was not only the wage level but advancement in status and responsibility. The Forster Commission was the first of three commissions on the copper mining industry, each of which asserted that African advancement was a primary necessity. The Commissioners of 1940 said: 'We have formed the view that the African is so advancing in efficiency that the time cannot be far distant when the number of European supervisors could be reduced,' and went on to recommend that two or three Africans could replace one European supervisor with an adjustable wage standard scaled according to an efficiency ratio, such as had worked satisfactorily in the Katanga mines across the Belgian Congo frontier. These proposals, strongly resented by the white Union, were not implemented.[36]

It was at the request of the Rhodesia Selection Trust that the question of African Advancement was first formally discussed by the Chamber of Mines and the white Union in 1946. The following year, while the Colonial Office representative was campaigning for the establishment of African Trade Unions, representatives of the Government, the Companies and the white Union met again but reached no agreement. Later that year a new Commission under Mr Andrew Dalgleish arrived and was boycotted by the white Union. In their report this Commission said: 'In our view it is totally wrong in a country with such a large untrained labour force for Europeans . . . to be engaged in industry in the territory on semi-skilled jobs. . . . A start must be made for the advancement of the African.' They went on to pinpoint twenty-seven jobs which Africans could fill immediately and eleven others to be taken over in the near future. They re-emphasized a cardinal point, which Lewin had already made in his evidence before the Forster Commission, saying: 'We cannot urge too strongly that no European at present carrying out the work or operations involved should be discharged in order to make way for an African. The African should only be promoted when the European ceases to be employed or is himself promoted.'[37]

Early in 1953 the Arbitration Tribunal under the chairmanship of Mr C. G. Guillebaud recalled the Dalgleish recommendations which were still in abeyance, and asserted that 'the great cloud hanging over the industry remains the bar to African advancement'.

That was the year when the final decisions were to be made on the question of federation. In the United Kingdom most of those who were either enthusiastic or resigned about it were united at least in urging the necessity 'for imaginative action promoted by trust and understanding, to demonstrate to Africans that the intention behind the federal scheme is to provide the necessary political and economic framework within which all races can progress in effective co-operation'.[38] And one of the points most frequently proposed for such imaginative action was this matter of economic and industrial opportunity. The Mine Companies themselves appealed to the white Union to take some step to reassure Africans concerning the good faith of Europeans. The white Union however would make no genuine concessions in regard to Clause 42. It is true they had already had discussions with the African Union in which they granted the principle of African advancement only on the basis of equal pay for equal work. This in effect made their concession so unsubstantial that Clause 42 never required to be called in question. For, as the leader of the new Confederate Party was to reveal with disarming honesty a little later in the year: 'Equal pay for equal work was the Confederate formula for preserving the European position.'[39] Because of the obvious implication of the principle of 'partnership' in the field of economic opportunity, the subject of African advancement featured prominently in the campaign for the first federal elections in the autumn of 1953. At the end of September the African Mineworkers' Union announced its intention to press for the full implementation of the Dalgleish Report. Both the Federal and the Confederate candidates, however, were outspoken in their rejection of the Report's recommendations on African advancement. The Confederate party candidate for Kitwe and Chingola assured his audience that he regarded the Dalgleish policy as too dangerous to be implemented in the Mines. Mr G. W. R. L'Ange, a member of the Northern Rhodesia Legislative Council standing for the Federal Party, was able to announce: 'So far, I and my colleagues from the other Copperbelt constituencies have been successful in preventing its implementation in any aspect connected with jobs.'[40] And Sir Roy Welensky, the party leader, said: 'I feel that the Dalgleish Report is completely dead and it should be allowed to be buried peacefully.'[41] The two mining groups appeared to be divided on the issue. This had first become evident in the correspondence between the Companies and the white Union published earlier in the year, and it was underlined by an address given before the Royal Empire and the Royal African Societies in London by the Chairman of the Rhodesian Selection Trust, Mr (now Sir) Ronald Prain. Pointing out that comparatively few Africans were in fact ready for advancement, he claimed that it would be far better to accept the principle of advancement at this stage than to have masses of Africans advancing later. Three distinguished commissions, he said, had reached almost unanimous opinions on the colour bar. Yet nothing had been done—although the companies implemented every other finding. He ended by referring again to the principle on which the Federation claimed to be launched. 'Its future success depends upon the proper implementation of partnership and the question of partnership depends on the solution of the colour bar.'[42] Shortly afterwards the RST threatened to cancel its agreement with the white Union if it remained obdurate. In reply, however, Sir Ernest Oppenheimer, Chairman of the Anglo-American Corporation, made a public statement assuring the white Union that the Company had no intention of breaking their agreement, which included the famous Clause 42.

For another year, however, the discussions continued with no change and reached complete deadlock in July 1954. In September the Northern Rhodesia Government set up a board of enquiry under Sir John Forster which reported in October, offering, in place of the old 'equal pay' formula, a new proposal that while equal basic pay should be paid for work of equal value, work previously done by one European might be fragmented into several jobs. The RST intimated that it accepted the report and gave notice to terminate its agreement with the Union. At the end of January 1955, in spite of a last minute effort from the South African Union to boost its morale, the Northern Rhodesia European Mineworkers' Union decided by membership ballot to abandon its long entrenched position. On 27 September 1955 the Chamber of Mines and the white Union formally entered into a new agreement, on the lines proposed by the Forster Commission of the year before, whereby twenty-four new categories of work were opened to Africans and the principle of further African advancement through negotiation was accepted for the future.

Throughout this struggle for advancement, the African Mineworkers' Union seemed to be in such a strong moral position that they needed only to press consistently for the Dalgleish proposals to be implemented to be certain of winning their case in the end. But it was just this consistency which was lacking. With extraordinary miscalculation of their own best interests, the recently formed African Union had agreed in 1950 with the white Union's proposal to make equal pay for equal work a condition of African advancement. In the autumn of 1953, when the subject was so much to the fore, Mr Lawrence Katilungu again made it clear that the African Union was reluctant to abandon the principle of equal pay; and this was reiterated in March 1954 at a joint conference of the two Unions. There was, however, in the leadership of the Union a considerable faction who disagreed with the acceptance of the equal pay principle, partly because they realized it must nullify the promises of advancement, and partly through a fear that the few Africans who might qualify for a 'European' rate of pay would immediately lose all contact with the rest of the African labour force.

In this failure of the African Union to decide which policy was to its ultimate advantage we can see the same weaknesses at work as characterize the National Congress. Here again is the inherent mistrust of the responsible leader who stands at the point of contact with the 'white' world, enhanced by tribal rivalries. The large majority of mineworkers in the lower income groups imagine that 'advancement' means much higher wages for all Africans. The minority in the upper groups realize that it means the opening of doors to the most highly qualified only, so naturally the principle of equal pay for equal work appeals to them. Those Union officials who, not belonging to the highest groups, do not see any prospect of advancement for themselves, tend to suspect those of their colleagues who are in the highest groups of feathering their own nest, and can easily persuade the ordinary members of the Union that this highly placed minority are traitors to the cause.

This seed of discord was helped to fruition by the creation of the Mines African Staffs' Association. This exists for those mine employees who, working mainly as company officials or supervisors, are paid a regular monthly salary rather than on the basis of a 30-shift ticket. It appears to be widely believed by Africans on the Copperbelt that it was the Companies who created the Mines African Staffs' Association in order to weaken the Union by drawing off its potential leadership. In fact the idea of a Staff Association was first mooted by Africans as early as 1947, during the discussions with Mr W. Comrie on the formation of a Trade Union. The first African Staff Association was formed at Nkana in May 1953, and by September 1954 there were branches on every Mine. At first the Companies, from a general dislike of splinter groups, appeared not to favour this development. But in October 1955, when they began to implement the agreed proposals for African advancement, they drew up a fresh definition of the categories of work which should be paid on a monthly salary, and declared that in any matters concerning Africans in these categories they would only negotiate with the Mines African Staffs' Association. As soon as the members of the African Mineworkers' Union became aware of what was happening, they violently disagreed with the separate recognition of the Mines African Staffs' Association, and also challenged the basis on which the differentiation was made. Their Union leaders asserted that they had been compelled to agree to the recognition of the Mines African Staffs' Association by the Companies' threat to abrogate their contract with the Union unless its leaders signed their assent. In an attempt to force the Companies to withdraw their separate agreement with the Mines African Staffs' Association, the leaders of the African Union called a series of strikes with a boycott of clinics and welfare services, on the pretext of the underground workers' dislike of a new issue of leg-guards. The situation worsened throughout the summer until an emergency was declared and many of the Union leaders were rusticated by Government order to their tribal areas.

These events brought into high relief the inherent distrust of the ordinary miner towards the better qualified minority. In 1956 feeling between the Union and the Mines African Staffs' Association ran so high that, as was mentioned in the previous section, even the children of the two groups would not play together.[43] During that time the CCAR congregation at Nchanga was seriously divided by this clash, though by 1958 the tension had somewhat relaxed.

This general attitude of distrust towards the new middle-class group conceals, while at the same time it produces, a sharp differentiation among the middle-class Africans themselves. Some, like Gideon Lisulo, quoted on page 140, are the more deeply confirmed in their belief in moderation and common-sense, as they see it, and grow impatient towards what they regard as the unreasoning and exaggerated clamour of the less educated. Others, anxious to win back the lost confidence of the masses and frustrated by their failure, in spite of their advancement, to win acceptance into, or even a hearing by, the European world, turn into the most embittered and revolutionary group of all. These are the potential claimants to the throne of any African nationalist movement. It was from this group that Mr Nkumbula's position was most powerfully assailed, and from which comes the leadership of the rival Zambia Congress which split from the African National Congress in November 1958 and was outlawed in March 1959.[44]

From this outline of the Africans' twofold struggle for self-expression and for industrial advancement, it is possible to see the steady intensification of a conflict within the African urban community which is essentially the birthpangs of a class society. In the precarious position of Congress leaders, in the mistrust of such bodies as the African Board of Management at Kansuswa, and most of all in the clash between the African Union and the Mines African Staffs' Association, there is crystallized the inherent suspicion felt by the inarticulate majority of African workers towards the emergent middle class. But this simple and natural development is complicated by two other quite separate patterns of conflict which are superimposed upon it.

First is the pattern of tribal loyalty. By the exigencies of history it has happened that, broadly speaking, the men who came to the Copperbelt from Nyasaland and Barotseland cornered the market in clerical posts and in the more skilled jobs such as truck driving. The solid mass of workers in the middle groups tend to be Bemba or related tribes, while the Nyakyusa of Tanganyika have won a reputation for heavy, underground labour. It is one of the theses of Dr Epstein's brilliant study, to which the reader should refer, that what often appears to be inter-tribal conflict in Copperbelt relations is actually this same class struggle, but dressed up in the associations and emotions of tribalism. In particular, the developing conflict between the *evolués* and the African proletariat, between the Mines African Staffs' Association and the Union, between the Zambia Congress and the African National Congress, often appeared in the guise of a clash between Nyasalanders and Bemba. This is a most important theme which will recur later in connection with some of the problems of the Church.

But, secondly, upon this emergence of class conflict there is superimposed the pattern of race conflict. So to the ordinary working man's mistrust and jealousy of the new 'white-collar' class is added the deeper fear of being betrayed by the advanced men who by virtue of their position are compelled to enter into a responsible, mediatory relationship with the European. In such a situation every leader is liable to become a 'lost leader'. But while this suspicion operates to widen the gulf between one class of African and another, at other times the overriding racial conflict operates to close all ranks and present a united African front. In this emergent African society, racked by conflicts of its own differentiation, yet standing as a whole in the wider conflict of the two races, the congregations, ministers and missionaries of the various Churches are trying to discover what it means to be Christian. To their problems we must turn in the next chapter.

NOTES

1. The European population of Northern Rhodesia has trebled its numbers in the ten years 1947-1957. Besides this, it is a very fluctuating population. Census returns since 1946 indicate that for every three new white immigrants, one has left the territory. So the percentage of the present white population who have been in the country even ten years is quite small.
2. In 1946 the number of Africans from Northern Rhodesia who were employed in Southern Rhodesia alone was 45,413, which was more than twice the total white population of Northern Rhodesia. In 1951 the number had risen to more than 50,000, with an annual turnover, migrating and returning, of over 12,000. (Colonial Reports: *Northern Rhodesia 1952*, pp. 17, 101.)
3. See pp. 12-13.
4. Cmd 3573 (1930).
5. Cmd 184 (1931), para. 73.
6. Cmd 3234 (1929).
7. Cmd 5949 (1939).
8. *Rhodesia Herald*, 18 February 1949.
9. Cmd 8233-5 (1951).
10. Colonial Reports: *Northern Rhodesia 1951*, p. 2.
11. *East Africa and Rhodesia*, 11 October 1951: 'Matters of Moment'.
12. Letter to *The Times*, 6 May 1953.
13. C. H. Thompson and H. W. Woodruff: *Economic Development in Rhodesia and Nyasaland*, Dobson, 1954, pp. 182-193. See also the argument on both sides as set out in *Venture*, the journal of the Fabian Colonial Bureau, July 1959. Several developments, economic and otherwise have been credited to the federal constitution which in fact had already been initiated before federation came into being. For example, federation has been held responsible for the creation of rural development centres in Northern Rhodesia, though these were planned and provided for in 1947 under the Northern Rhodesia Ten Year Development Plan. It has been claimed that the Federal Government initiated the Kariba Hydro-Electric Scheme, yet as early as 1950 the Inter-Territorial Hydro-Electric Commission had made its first report on several possible schemes, and early in 1953 the Government of Northern Rhodesia appointed the Kafue Hydro-Electric Authority to carry out the scheme which had then been accepted. In a similar way the inter-racial basis of the new university was announced to the world so as to appear as the first-fruits of federation, yet that policy had already been agreed upon by the Inaugural Board before federation was established. See the letter from Dr Alexander Scott in *East Africa and Rhodesia*, 11 September 1958.
14. Cmd 8573 (1952).
15. Cmd 8754 (1953).
16. Letter to *Central Africa Post*, 18 September 1952.
17. Quoted by the Bishop of Chichester in the House of Lords, *Hansard*, 2 July 1952.

18. Letter to *East Africa and Rhodesia*, 4 October 1951.
19. A. L. Epstein: *Politics in an Urban African Community*, pp. 29-31.
20. *Report on the Native Affairs Department, Northern Rhodesia, 1924-5*.
21. Epstein, *op. cit.*, p. 47.
22. *Report of the Commission appointed to inquire into the Disturbances in the Copperbelt*, July 1940, pp. 19-21.
23. Epstein, *op. cit.*, pp. 69-70.
24. Since the constitutional changes came into force in the spring of 1959, direct voting by those Africans who have the franchise has superseded the electoral colleges as far as election to the Legislative Council is concerned.
25. Colonial Reports: *Northern Rhodesia 1950*, p. 92; *1951*, p. 87; *1952*, p. 90.
26. Dudley Hawkins, *Sunday Times*, 13 September 1953.
27. Epstein, *op. cit.*, pp. 163-197.
28. *Ibid.*, p. 190.
29. This arrangement with the African Mineworkers' Union, originally accepted by the Companies but abrogated by them after the strike in 1955, had just been restored on 12 March 1958.
30. Julius Lewin, *The Colour Bar in the Copperbelt*, South African Institute of Race Relations, 1941, p. 5.
31. *Report of the Commission* [on] *Disturbances in the Copperbelt*, para. 194.
32. *Ibid.*, Appendix III.
33. *Ibid.*, para. 121.
34. Epstein, *op. cit.*, pp. 109, 145.
35. Figures drawn from Colonial Office Annual Reports and Year Book of the Northern Rhodesian Chamber of Mines 1959.
36. *Report of the Commission* [on] *Disturbances in the Copperbelt*, paras. 195-197, 256, 270.
37. *Report of the Commission appointed to inquire into the Advancement of Africans in Industry* (1948).
38. Letter to *The Times* signed by leaders of the Churches, 4 March 1953.
39. *East Africa and Rhodesia*, 5 November 1953.
40. *Central African Post*, 2 October 1953.
41. *East Africa and Rhodesia*, 5 November 1953, p. 254.
42. R. L. Prain, *Selected Papers 1953-1957*, p. 19.
43. See the whole paragraph on pages 86-87.
44. In the last two years the United National Independent Party, successor to the Zambia Congress, has won the African, but its leader, Mr Kenneth Kaunda, faces fundamentally the same dilemma as Mr Nkumbula did in 1958.

7

The Reaction upon the Church

IT appears from the studies of social anthropologists in many parts of the continent that it is common for African people to judge the practice of religion by its results in terms of material good fortune and social status, and particularly by its efficacy in maintaining happy personal relations. To say this is no disparagement, and the inner significance of it will be discussed in the last section of this book. It is enough here to draw attention to this characteristic to show how vulnerable is the faith of many Christians and how damaging to the African congregations is the condition of conflict and mistrust which was described in the last chapter. This damage is greatly enhanced by the natural association of the Christian religion with the European race. It is not surprising therefore to find a growing disillusionment towards Christianity, especially in the younger generation. In a meeting of sixteen young school-teachers and welfare officers which the writer attended at Mindolo, near Kitwe, in 1957, one after another gave vent to a passionate attack upon the churches for their failure to practise brotherhood or to speak out about such things as the industrial colour bar. But finally one of them interposed the question: 'But are we supposed to be Christians because white people have been kind to us, or because we believe that Christ is true?' Only the minority, however, have been able to achieve such an objective and independent conviction and, though the survival of the Church may in the end depend on them, it is not possible to be indifferent to the steady fall-away of the 'weaker brethren'.

An African welfare officer with some training and experience in sociological observation summarized the causes of disillusionment as follows: 'The falling away is due to the general reaction against all organizations that seem to be inspired by Europeans, the disillusion over the colour bar and the Church's failure to make a stand about that or about federation; also the occasional conflict between ministers and the Trade Unions, as well as the occasional boycotting of the churches by Congress.' It will be well to deal with each of these heads separately. The general anti-white reaction and the question of colour discrimination in the churches will be held over to the next chapter. So we come to the effect upon the Church of the federation issue and the general condition of race rivalry in the political field.

We have seen that though Africans in the urbanized setting are becoming increasingly differentiated and thus liable to fall into a confused pattern of rival groups and associations, yet from time to time a crisis occurs which gathers them together in an overriding loyalty as Africans over against the white minority. Experiencing this themselves, they naturally expect to find that Europeans also, whatever their party or their religious profession, are subject to this ultimate solidarity of race. This expectation gives an edge of mistrust to every friendship with a European. 'The more a white man appears friendly, the more we do not trust him', was the reaction of the Management Board of Kansuswa township when they debated whether to allow the writer to live among them. 'We are reluctant at this time to have a white man here, for so many have been as wolves in sheep's clothing. If you are a missionary in a true sense we can trust you, but if you are hiding another motive then heaven must help us.' So in every offer of confidence there is always the fear that, when the test comes, the white man will 'revert to type.' Exactly the same reservation characterizes the friendships of most Europeans with Africans, where these exist. In these circumstances of suspicion, every failure of a European to go all the way in support of an African's contentions is likely to be interpreted as reversion to the white solidarity (and the same is generally true in reverse).

The fear that European friendship will prove to be a broken reed underlies the oft-repeated statement that Africans prefer what they regard as the honest racialism of the Afrikaans-speaking immigrants to the unreliable and equivocal liberalism of some of those from Europe. This is the fear which has created such intense distrust of the Capricorn Africa Society.

In the African congregations the federation issue seems to have been regarded by many as the ultimate test of the integrity of European church leaders. It provided a chance for them to prove whether they were prepared to make common cause with the disfranchised African majority in defence of their interests or whether they would take their stand with the rest of their own race. The fact that thousands of

Europeans, in Southern as well as Northern Rhodesia, voted against federation; the fact that many of the white Christians sincerely believed that federation was in the best interests of Africans as well as Europeans; or the fact that some church leaders did protest against the overriding of African opposition—these seem hardly to have affected their verdict. They remember only that their liberal friends, including the leaders of the churches, did not fight with them to the end over the federation issue.

So the Minutes of the Christian Council of Northern Rhodesia, meeting in June 1953, record that

> 'The Africans present were consistent in their opposition to the federal plan, and it was said that it had been conceived and carried forward hastily. . . . Further, it was felt that the missionary had also failed to speak soon enough on the great issues involved. As a result of this failure the African church leaders were themselves suspect amongst their own people.'

But not only is the local Church attacked because it appeared equivocal in this matter, but Christianity itself is beginning to be regarded as an agency for weakening African resistance. The leader of the Tertiaries in one Roman Catholic congregation on the Copperbelt said 'Today Christianity is losing ground because of the imposition of federation on this territory. Many have so lost confidence in the Europeans that now we are wondering whether they only brought the Word of God to try to blind us so as to take advantage of us and turn us into slaves.' In a meeting of elders and deacons of the CCAR at Nchanga the same fear was expressed: 'The Bible has made us slaves. Even our Christians are saying, "The Church will make us agree to federation." The Bible stops us from taking part in the affairs of the world. The preachers say "Do not trouble. Endure." But people want to fight bad things.'

The suspicion that Christianity is designed to soften up African opposition is not confined to the question of federation. The young son of a minister of the CCAR who was working in the Information Office of the Nchanga Mine, said to us: 'Young Africans find that the churches have come here as a blanket upon all African aspirations after independence.' A little later, when asked how he accounted for the fact that more of the African political leaders in South Africa were convinced Christians than in Northern Rhodesia, answered: 'Africans in Northern Rhodesia think they are the rightful rulers of this country. In South Africa Africans have resigned themselves to the present situation and abandoned the hope of self-rule.' His colleague, working in the same office, also remarked on another occasion: 'On the day that we give up hope you will see Africans flocking to the churches for comfort.'

During the strikes and boycotts of 1956, when mine-workers were disturbed by the creation of the separate Mines African Staffs' Association, feeling ran high against the Churches because, from time to time, it was alleged that preachers had spoken against the strikes. Often, as we have seen, there was tension within a congregation between the Union and the Staffs' Association, and if an African minister tried to mediate he laid himself open to such allegations by members of the Union. Any unguarded references either to the Trade Union or the Congress are liable to be misunderstood and are deeply resented, particularly if the preacher is a missionary. A common complaint against missionary preachers, both in the Roman Catholic and the Free Churches, is that 'they first read the Bible but when they preach they soon leave the Bible and start talking about money, Lenshina or the Congress.'

On such occasions, African critics appear as strict pietists, for, as usual, 'No politics in the pulpit' means 'No politics with which *we* disagree!' So, soon after one missionary had been disparaging the African National Congress, a schoolboy of fifteen wrote: 'The missionary should not take part in politics; politics for the politicians, the Church for the missionaries.' 'The Congress,' said an African minister in a staff meeting of the UCCAR, 'complains that African ministers and missionaries don't stick to church matters, but interfere in politics.'

One or two incidents in which the missionary appears to have sided with the Europeans against the Africans are sufficient to keep mistrust alive for a long time. In 1953 a missionary of great experience in the Luapula valley replied to a confidential Government circular saying that he thought it would be a good thing to introduce, as the circular suggested, a closed fishing season, although this was very unpopular among the African villagers. A copy of his reply was found by his African clerk and the ensuing resentment resulted in a considerable group breaking away from his church. Again, during the 1956 strikes, a missionary of the Dutch Reformed Church was alleged to have preached in their Mission at Nchanga urging all the mineworkers to return to work on the grounds that it was the God-given task of Africans to work for the white race. His congregation immediately left the church, and were persuaded to return only after some months. Their church is now named the African Reformed Church. Such stories, which may have originated from a misunderstanding, are passed from mouth to mouth and build up an inveterate idea that the Church only approves of Africans who are submissive. 'A reason for leaving the church is politics,' said a school-teacher at Nchanga who was also a consistent member of a 'Mission' church. 'Some churches give the impression that it is wrong for a Christian to be concerned in politics. But even when they do not say that, the church leaders are always on the side of the Government rather than on the side of the African'. 'Christians are unpopular because they refuse to become political and therefore they are called strike-breakers.'

This impression has become enshrined in a number of stereotypes which crop up in every discussion of the political scene and are quoted even by individuals whose earlier remarks are a contradiction of them. These were particularly noticeable in the essays of schoolchildren. 'Christianity was brought by white people to conquer Africans.' 'The churches enforce the law of the Boma' (Government Administration headquarters). 'Livingstone came to make Africans soft.' This last remark reveals a new myth which has developed around the name of the great missionary pioneer, in which he features as the archetype of European duplicity, arriving with the Gospel to disarm the African before the advance of the colonists, settlers and industrialists. When objections were being raised to the writer's presence in Kansuswa township, this myth was twice quoted: 'You see before you David Livingstone again. He came with the Bible in his right hand but, before he had finished, the Bible was in his left hand. We have had three successive Governments since David Livingstone came: Government by missionaries, a territorial Government, and now a Federal Government.' 'Livingstone came as a missionary at first, but afterwards he struck us.' It seems strange that Livingstone has been chosen as the villain when the history of these territories can provide several more suitable candidates. Probably the myth reflects a generation of mission-school teaching against which there has now been a reaction. The missionary is now too closely associated with the white race and the white rulers to be regarded any longer as the disinterested benefactor and counsellor of Africans. 'Priests,' said a Roman Catholic school-teacher at Nchanga, 'ought not to be weapons for the Government, telling people not to be politically active'.

That this is in fact not the teaching of many of the Missions is recognized by a small number of the more intelligent members of the various congregations. For example, a young welfare officer who, with his wife, is a keen member of the Roman Catholic Tertiaries told us that 'many priests encourage Christians to take an active part in politics, but they say you must speak in such a way as shows you are a Christian. During a strike at Kitwe in the Mine, Father X preached in church that Christians should co-operate fully with their fellows in all that pertained to justice, therefore they should co-operate in that strike; but at the same time they should pray to God that their struggle may remain in his hands: so can they fight a better battle.' A similar note was struck in the call issued by the Executive Committee of the Northern Rhodesia Christian Council in 1957:

> 'We urge both European and African members within the Church to meet together to consider their common Christian duty in relation to the crucial political issues facing the country at this hour.... We urge Christians to work for the widest possible distribution of political responsibility.'

Yet such statements appear to have made no impression on the Christians in the Nchanga African Township, if they ever came to their notice at all. The only 'evidence for the defence' which seemed to carry any weight in refuting these charges against the Church was the preaching of the Rev. Colin Morris, the minister of what was the European Free Church congregation in Chingola. In a series of sermons on race relations during the early summer of 1957[1] and subsequently in a number of addresses and lectures, he had made a stringent and well-reasoned attack on the attitudes of Europeans and the policies of the Government. This won him considerable notoriety in the press, in which he was violently attacked in the correspondence columns, so that the word 'Parson' alone in the headlines was sufficient to indicate who was the subject of the article. In May 1958 the church council of the CCAR at Bancroft invited him to preach a similar series of sermons on 'The African Christian's duty towards the Europeans.' This very emphatic stand had a marked effect upon African attitudes towards the Christian religion. So also to a lesser degree had the Joint Pastoral Letter of the Roman Catholic Bishops on 6 January 1958 in which they wrote:

> 'We realize that it is not an easy task to reconcile the rights of each group in a country like Northern Rhodesia, the population of which is composed of peoples who differ in many respects. But the differences are often wilfully exaggerated.... Sometimes it is said that it would be dangerous to grant every man the full and equal exercise of his rights, on the grounds that all men are not equally able to fulfil their duties to society.... By applying uncritically this argument to

one race, we may be guilty of an act of injustice to many members of the race who are fully able and willing to realize their responsibilities.'

In 1958 these were the only statements from Christian leaders which seemed to have caught the imagination of the African 'man in the street'. As one said, 'The out-spoken bishops and the sermons on politics by Colin Morris make people say: "Perhaps the churches will do good." ' We were told that the local branch of the National Congress at Luanshya was seriously discussing a boycott of all the churches in December 1957, when one of their officials said 'Let us leave the church of Colin Morris alone'; whereupon they agreed to drop the matter. My colleague experienced a similar reaction at Nchanga during the study in 1958. While she was sitting in the yard of a house in the compound talking to a group of women, two of the more radical Congress youths began to abuse the women, calling out, 'What does this white person want? Why do you talk to her?' Their shout quickly drew a crowd and the women became frightened by its hostile attitude. But at that point a third youth pressed through the crowd, crying 'Leave this European woman alone; do not stop her in her work. She is a friend of Colin Morris.' Immediately the atmosphere cleared, the youths stayed to listen to the discussion and the crowd showed no sign of hostility when the women accompanied my colleague back to her car.

Why is it that Mr Morris should have won this almost unique reputation? He himself would certainly be the first to agree that he is not the only white minister in Northern Rhodesia to have 'interfered in politics'. A certain amount of his reputation is undoubtedly due to the tendency of modern publicity to create a star in the firmament of popular imagination which, whether it is called Lucifer or the morning star, is none the less a luminary. But the full explanation probably lies in the fact that in this situation of acute disillusionment, the only guarantee for Africans that a European is to be trusted is that he is prepared to forfeit the trust of the majority of Europeans. Only as European Christians are seen to suffer at the hands of their own people will African Christians become assured that they are so committed to their principles that they will not 'revert to type' when the pressure comes. What very few African Christians have yet accepted is that the same applies in reverse to themselves.

This reverting to type under pressure has, in African eyes, been evident in the public statements of the churches in Northern Rhodesia on political issues, and is one of the reasons why such statements have not disarmed African criticism as much as they deserved to do. Until the Second World War, the General Missionary Conference, which was the precursor of the Christian Council, felt an obligation to speak on behalf of the unvoiced African people. This view of their function was formulated in the memorandum which the Executive Committee of the General Missionary Conference submitted as evidence to the Bledisloe Commission in 1938. 'Because of our continuous and intimate service,' they said, 'we seek the privilege of speaking for the African population of one-and-a-half millions—a population for the most part inarticulate—particularly, although not solely, the peoples of the great Reserves.' These words, of course, reflect the more paternalistic thought of those days; moreover, since all conferences and commissions were exclusively white, the Africans, being unrepresented, were more obviously in need of some body to speak for them. This responsibility the Missions had sought to discharge with boldness ever since the early days. The third General Missionary Conference in July 1922, for example, championed the Africans in no uncertain terms against the threat of further alienation of their land by the British South Africa Company.[2] Two years later they returned to the attack on the same issue. They also objected to the new poll tax as 'excessive and unjust', and pointed out the dehumanizing effect of so compelling African men to bargain their labour at a disadvantage in order to provide manpower where the Europeans needed it. 'This great annual exodus of tax-paying males,' they said, 'strikes at the whole fabric of tribal life . . . We venture earnestly to press for a general reduction of taxation.'[3] This also was the burden of one section in their memorandum submitted to the Bledisloe Commission in 1938.

> 'Today the African, faced with the demands of family life and the requirement of the Government for taxation, often has no alternative to migration to the industrial centres. Whereas the provision of suitable land for his crops and the general economic development of the rural areas would under the same circumstances provide him with an alternative . . . the absence of such power of choice dwarfs his personality and renders him less valuable as a unit of society.'

In a later section the Conference's representatives pleaded that generous scope should be given to the Africans'

> 'desire for expression and growing power in administrative and political affairs. . . . It is essential for the full-orbed development of the country that by a gradual progress they should be introduced to these affairs, and responsibility placed upon them always just a little in advance of their proved capacity. The tax collector and responsibility are great schoolmasters.'

That was written three years before the first Urban Advisory Council was established on the Copperbelt.

With regard to the main topic of the Bledisloe Commission, the question of Closer Association with Southern Rhodesia, this memorandum is quite unequivocal.

> 'The time may come when the real progress of the country may depend upon the initiative and enterprise of the African, and it would reflect undying honour upon the Immigrant if in that day he could safely leave the country to the African's care. We cannot with confidence regard this as the goal of many of those who seek Amalgamation. ... The danger that the prospects of the African are not receiving their rightful place in our present discussions is evidenced by the fact that Trades Unions are being formed in certain Industrial Centres which are avowedly seeking only to protect the interests of the Immigrant worker.... Our fears are intensified by the fact that the Government of Southern Rhodesia has introduced a colour bar into large fields of industry (*vide* the Conciliation Act of 1934 and its administration as indicated in Government Notice No. 107 of 18 February 1938). We definitely consider that a Government which could pass such legislation as is embodied in the foregoing would be inimical to the best interests of the Natives of this country.... We submit therefore that the case for complete Amalgamation of Northern and Southern Rhodesia and Nyasaland with the control of such a vast and important unit of the British Empire by its Immigrant population does not commend itself to our judgment.'

This quality of outspokenness had not been maintained without conflict with the powers that be. After the Copperbelt disturbances of 1935 Bishop May and the Rev. J. G. Soulsby, the Acting President of the General Missionary Conference, objected strongly to the composition of the Committee of Enquiry which the Governor had proposed to set up. Their Executive Committee passed a resolution urging 'the necessity of a strong, impartial Commission to investigate the causes of the trouble'. When the Governor himself altered his personal programme in order to attend the Conference and reprimand the missionaries for associating themselves 'with overt criticism of the actitivites of Government', the Acting President replied asserting the loyalty of the Conference but adding also:

> 'We claim the right to criticise when criticism is obviously deserved and our criticism is offered in kindness and with a desire to help both Europeans and Natives and also the Government. We think it does not quite deserve the castigation which it has received this morning.'

The same issue was joined in the industrial sphere in 1943 when the Mine Companies of the Rhodesia Selection Trust group, in sending their contribution to the support of the United Missions to the Copperbelt, felt obliged to complain that

> 'in one or two cases representatives of the Missions have shown an inclination to interest themselves in highly controversial matters affecting native affairs which do not appear within the scope of missionary activities as normally understood. For example, it is understood that one of the societies' representatives was taking an interest in the question of the formation of a Native Trades Union.'

Commenting on this to the Secretary of the United Missions, the head of one of the constituent Mission Boards wrote:

> 'We should always try to represent the needs, claims or rights of the African workers directly to the Mining Companies. But we must claim very definitely that the United Mission to the Copperbelt is interested in all matters concerning native welfare, even if they may be classed as "highly controversial". The scope of missionary activities cannot be limited in such a way as to exclude political questions. We must make it clear that money does not buy our silence in such matters.'[4]

Already, however, a more equivocal note was being sounded in the official statements of the Church. This seems to have been due, more than anything else, to the growing influence of the European congregations along the railway line. Missionaries living in a white milieu, while trying to serve both their European and their African congregations, were made aware, more than ever before, that there were two sides to every question. As one who served in that situation longer than any has said: 'As we developed the European church work we more and more cast our eye over our shoulder to see if our white congregations were behind us. This sensitiveness towards white opinion was specially marked in those ministers who had already had a home charge in Britain and then were pitchforked into a multi-racial charge on the Copperbelt.' Church leaders now felt that their calling was to be umpires rather than champions of one side. Yet this, from the Church's point of view, is a dangerous half-truth. For the Church is called not to champion this or that side, but indubitably to champion righteousness; and righteousness is not necessarily found at the middle point between two extremes.

Over the federation issue many of the Missions had been given a clear lead by their Home Boards. In November 1951 the Standing Committee of the Conference of Missionary Societies in Great Britain resolved that:

> 'Any attempt . . . to impose such a plan in the face of almost unanimous African opposition, even supposing it were ill-informed, would destroy the basis upon which its success would depend, and would set a precedent which would have far-reaching consequences, not confined to British Central Africa.'

In the same vein the General Assembly of the Church of Scotland in June 1952 moved that:

> 'The General Assembly, noting with interest the movement towards a Central African Federation, but viewing with concern the actual proposals now being made, urge upon Her Majesty's Government that full consideration be given to African opinion and that no scheme should be adopted without the consent and co-operation of the Africans.'

The London Missionary Society was given the same lead by its Africa Secretary who wrote to the *Manchester Guardian* in February 1953 that to ignore the Africans' opposition

> 'would be to abrogate all claim to responsible statesmanship. In these circumstances whatever risk is run by deferring the implementing of the Scheme of Federation is outweighed by the risk of irreparable harm to interracial co-operation attendant upon its being enforced now.'

To turn from such definite pronouncements to the Minutes of the Northern Rhodesian Christian Council is to realise what a divided mind existed among church leaders in the territory. In July 1951 the Council had resolved that

> 'the Christian Council welcomes the white paper on Closer Association as a statesmanlike attempt to raise this problem above party and racial issues. However, the Council calls attention to the fact that political developments in recent years have made the African suspicious of change and that the plan is unlikely to commend itself to African opinion unless there is a simultaneous clarification of the prospects of African political and economic development within this territory.'

But in January 1953, the Executive Committee moved that

> 'while recognizing that the Federation question is one over which sincere Christian people may, and in fact do, hold opposite opinions, it realizes that it is the function of the Christian Church to be vigilant in the interests of those who are not in a position to control their own political future. It desires to assure the African Christian community of its deep concern and of its determination (while maintaining a neutral attitude on merely political questions) to assert the necessity of applying Christian principles to public affairs.

The last meeting of the Christian Council before the Federation was established took place in June 1953. The African Christian Conference had forwarded a unanimous resolution calling for opposition to the Federation. The Minutes then record this:

> 'Great diversity of opinion was apparent. Whatever the course pursued, the Council was unanimous in its agreement that all should be done in love. A further note was struck when expression was given to the need for Christian bodies to bear themselves in hope and in creative Christian action.... From the European standpoint it was stated that Federation had this value at least, in that it had directed the attention of the world to Central Africa. Finally it was suggested that the Christian Councils of the three Territories concerned might issue a joint statement on their attitude towards Federation. In any event our first duty as Christians was to Jesus Christ.'

The Council, however, later adopted this resolution, the boldest note it ever struck on this issue:

> 'The Christian Council of Northern Rhodesia recognizes that it is primarily the right of every Christian to hold his own views on the issue of Federation in the light of his own conscience, but it wishes to express deep concern that the Government has found it necessary to proceed with Federation while African opinion remains so strongly opposed to it. The Council respectfully requests Government to issue such a declaration of rights for all men within the territory as shall remove all doubts as to their future well-being within the State. The Christian Council hopes that Africans will be given an increasing share in the educational, industrial and political life of the State.'

The resolution ended with a welcome to the multi-racial university and the negotiations on African advancement, and with a plea for non-violence.

The embarassment of the Council over its own divisions must have been acute. Nevertheless it is easy to understand why African Christians, remembering the championship of their interests by an earlier generation of missionaries, felt that once more the European friend had reverted to type. 'The churches let us down over Federation.'

It is not only the neutrality of the Christian Council and some of the Missions over Federation, however, that has given this impression of pietism in the churches. Many of the older African clergy, perhaps because they model their behaviour upon what they suppose to be the pattern of the missionaries, seem to support the idea that religion and politics may not mix. This does not mean that they have themselves abjured political aspirations and grievances; almost to a man they will, at times, express themselves as forcibly as any other Africans on these topics. Yet the majority of them would appear to agree that the Church and its leaders, as such, should keep clear of political opinion and action. This idea is based mainly on two grounds: the supposed other-worldliness of the Christian faith, and the assumption that political ambitions cannot be achieved apart from methods that are contrary to the teaching of Christ. Sometimes this leads church members to a total renunciation of political interests; but more often they divide their religious and social concerns into strictly separate compartments. At Nchanga a church member of twenty-three years' standing, uncle to one of the UCCAR ministers, told us that he is himself a member also of the National Congress, of the African Mineworkers' Union, and of his Native Authority Council in the rural area. 'I said to the Congress, "I must belong to Church, so that when I die I shall go to heaven; but I must also remember my country." '

Nor is it only the missionary churches which are criticized for their pietism. A minister of the UCCAR told us how, at one time, when he took prison duty, a cluster of hard-core prisoners who were Congress members boycotted his religious service and tried to make things difficult for him. But we learned that the minister of the African Methodist Episcopal Church, when it was his turn, fared no better. Indeed it is true to say that the religious groups which most dogmatically disallowed participation in politics were to be found among the all-African denominations. The New Apostolic Church, true to its precepts, everywhere forbids its members to belong to the National Congress, and this is strongly resented by other Africans. An equally rigid prohibition has been imposed upon their members by the Jehovah's Witnesses. This extended also to membership of any other association, including the Trade Union, and followers of this Movement were fiercely censured because they refused to join the strikes of 1956. So it was said of them then: 'Watchtower refuse politics and they join the Staffs' Association.' However, a social welfare worker told us they had recently begun to relax their rule in respect of the Union.

Some of the sects and break-away groups exhibit that strange combination of emphases, so characteristic of much South African Zionism, which is able at the same time to satisfy the anti-European sentiments and the other-wordly pietism of its adherants. This will be examined more closely in the next section of this book. In this context it is necessary only to draw attention to this phenomenon. The Jehovah's Witnesses, though they are supervised and guided by a small field staff of American missionaries, are nevertheless so organized as to have all the 'feel' of a purely African movement. The New Apostolic Church, while it comes under the authority of white 'Apostles', is an all-African church as far as Northern Rhodesia is concerned. Both organizations lay great stress on civil obedience, and the Watchtower adherents seem at present to have won a reputation for being almost a District Commissioner's dream of co-operative and reliable subjects! (see p. 230). At the same time it is clearly a source of satisfaction to the members of both groups that they are Africans running their own affairs with no missionary interference, and that their doctrine provides them with ground for teaching that the white missionaries of the other churches are the agents of Satan.

The so-called Lumpa Church of Alice Lenshina also exhibits an emphatic other-wordliness while undoubtedly channelling and, perhaps, sublimating the anti-European resentments of its members. 'They don't want the churches of the Europeans,' explained one headmaster at Nchanga, 'therefore the Lumpa Church is very strong.' Dr A. I. Richards has stated that not only do many preachers in this movement stress that it was not Africans but Europeans who crucified Christ, but she has twice heard them say, 'Let us go down on our knees and pray for the Europeans who committed this terrible sin; they need our prayers.' There is evidence that in the early stages African nationalist leaders attempted to adopt the movement, taking the platform at the open-air services as soon as the preachers had stepped down and calling on the crowds to support the 'Church of the African people.' Those adherents who are so inclined can read into the reference to 'the enemy' in some of the hymns and sermons a political significance; and, as in all the African sects, the white missionaries are presented as the principal deceivers and Roman Catholic priests are accused of witchcraft. 'In other churches the people, even the teachers, are weak; they are still possessing forbidden things.' 'The churches of this world call themselves of Christ but they do not obey . . . Take care, you murderers, you who disgraced the Son of the Lord.' But Lenshina herself appears to set her face against any political propaganda. The chief of one considerable district, himself a nominal member of the UCCAR, who has investigated her activities with some curiosity, told us that 'teachers and educated people join the Lumpa Church for nationalist reasons, but though they are politically minded Lenshina herself does not want politics.' All the evidence we could gather from officers of the Administration bears out the truth of this. Moreover, the essential emphasis of Lenshina's hymns and sermons is strongly pietist and other-worldly, though couched in the same evocative biblical metaphors of apocalyptic hope as appear in the sermons and spirituals of the American Negroes, and like them, always capable of temporal, as well as an eschatological interpretation.

> 'Gather all together for the Lord.
> We shall be spread far and wide in the beautiful country;
> We shall always roll in the dust, (*traditional greeting to a chief*)
> Hallelujah, always!'
>
> 'Look at the desert through which I send my children;
> They are shouting. Let all the enemies listen to it.'

Yet the most frequently repeated phrase is unequivocal: 'Do not look for the things of this world.'

Break-away as an expression of political feeling is more evident in some of the other groups. In Mufulira and in Chingola there have appeared in the last three years two small schisms from the Plymouth Brethren's Christian Missions in Many Lands; in both cases the reason offered was that the European missionary was too much an agent of the Government. We have already mentioned a similar incident in the Luapula valley. Again, there were many factors operative in the formation of a Tumbuka-speaking group who refused to remain in the CCAR. They wished to retain their separate identity as members of the Presbyterian Church of Nyasaland and have in recent times referred to the younger union of churches in Rhodesia as 'equal to Federation, the work of the missionaries'.

Another sect known as the Bamulonda, the People of the Watchman (see p. 238), was founded by Elliot Kenan Kamwana Chirwa, the Tonga evangelist mentioned in the first chapter, who learned the early Watchtower teaching from Joseph Booth and was deported from Nyasaland for causing disturbances in the Bandawe area of the Livingstonia Mission. The present Bamulonda reflect only a faint image of their founder's early Ethiopianism and have only a small following, mainly in a few rural areas. Yet their teaching contains a definitely political emphasis, albeit of a harmless nature. At an open-air meeting in Nsensema's the preacher said: 'King George had a flag and he set it here and wherever his flag was raised there was his kingdom. In the old times we were forced to approach the officers of King George humbly. We were not allowed to walk upright at Kawambwa. Today it is easier. But now, behold what kingdom has come! Look at the flag which is raised!' And he pointed to the flag of their sect which had been set up before the service began, bearing the words 'The Kingdom of God'.

'There is no European in our church at all. We don't tell you any lies.' 'The LMS teach the use of medicines, therefore all Europeans and Africans in their church are bad.' 'Elliot prophesied "Lusuba", a period of drought, for thirty years from 1955 to 1985, in which all the churches are being tried ... We think that this period started with Federation.'

The Children of the Sacred Heart are a break-away from the Roman Catholics (see pp. 106-8, 113). Though these people are beyond doubt primarily devotees of a more Franciscan ideal, their teaching contains, nevertheless, a strong element of protest against European domination. This is sometimes expressed in the claim that, in this present dispensation, Africans have a stronger propensity for the spiritual life than Europeans and so are the true successors to the covenants of God. 'When Jesus was persecuted by the European Herod, God sent him into Africa; by this we know that Africans have naturally a true spirit of Christianity.' This is an emphasis that recurs in the other break-away groups. The Bamulonda explained to us that 'the first people to have the blessing were the Jews; they lost it in 606 BC. Then the Europeans had the mission to preach for 2,520 years until 1914. The Africans are now blessed; they are like the Jews in the old times and they are wakening up from their sleep.' We were informed also that when Congress speakers addressed the congregations of the Lumpa Church in its early days, they used to say that 'only Africans had a true spirit of religion, for it was the Europeans who killed Christ.' In all this, however, we are to see not so much a calculated anti-European movement as an attempt to recover, in the hopes and promises of religion, a sense of destiny and significance and self-respect.

The preceding paragraphs may have given the impression that the National Congress is inherently antagonistic to Christianity. This, however, is far from the truth at present. We should not, perhaps, attach too much significance to Congress leaders' use of a 'Two-Day National Prayer' as a means of exhibiting, in April 1953, the solidarity of African rejection of the Federal Scheme, particularly as the Union members completely ignored the call. Nor is the common custom of opening Congress meeting with prayer necessarily a sign of the religious convictions of the leaders. Yet such practices would be inconceivable if the Congress policy was openly anti-religious. Congress leaders certainly share and, perhaps, underline the existing disillusionment regarding the Church, and naturally retaliate when preachers take upon themselves to disparage them. Many of the higher officials of the Congress were once active church members but have lapsed from church attendance. At Nchanga no Congress leader was an office bearer in any church in 1958. Like the officials of the Trade Union they tended to conduct their committee work and their public meetings on Sunday mornings but this was not from a deliberate policy of rivalry to the Church. Some Congress local leaders, particularly the younger men who were in charge of their Youth Organization, were avowedly opponents of Christianity and, from time to time, might suggest action against the churches. Here and there such individuals are trying the usual techniques of such propaganda; it was alleged at Nchanga that children were being taught to sing 'We praise thee, Nkumbula' in place of the usual canticle. But this was no part of official policy. On the contrary it has to be recognized that the majority in any African congregation on the Copperbelt (with the two exceptions mentioned above) are likely to be members of both Church and Congress with equal conviction and regularity. If a church member is definitely opposed to the Congress, it is more likely to be because he is a member of the Mines African Staffs' Association than because he is a Christian.

In the African freehold townships, such as Kansuswa, and also in the municipal African Townships, Congress is generally stronger than in the Mine African Townships because, as Dr Epstein has pointed out, there is not the same tension there with the Trade Union.[5] Congress also has a particular appeal among African merchants, especially those engaged in the fish trade between Lake Mweru and the Copperbelt, and those who are charcoal burners—in fact any independent, freelance traders. So it was not surprising to find that one informant who was in a position to make fairly reliable enquiries for the writer, said that at Kansuswa at that time 100 per cent of the adults of the Seventh Day Adventists' congregation, most of the CCAR and many of the African Methodist Episcopal Church were Congress members, but that the Roman Catholic congregation was more divided. Out of the presiding leaders of the nine congregations in that township, three were members of the local Congress committee and a fourth was brother to another committee member. Moreover these nine congregations included the Watchtower and the New Apostolic Church, whose members have no option in the matter.

In the Mine African Townships probably fewer of the church leaders are also exercising political leadership in these days. Dr Epstein has recorded that 30 per cent of the members of the Luanshya Urban Advisory Council in May 1954 were also office bearers in one or other of the local churches, and two of these were also officials of the African National Congress.[6] It seems likely that today fewer of the church leaders are so actively engaged in political concerns. Unfortunately in our own investigation, an attempt to find out what secular offices the elders of two African congregations also held was defeated by their reluctance to give such information to Europeans, but our impression at Nchanga was that the office bearers in both the Union and the Congress were not also church leaders. The general interaction between the churches and the African political leaders was described for us by one of the headmasters at Nchanga. 'It is not possible,' he said, 'to generalize about political leaders being against the Church. There are some who go to church and some may still be persuaded that the Church is a good thing when they hear that some of the European ministers, like Colin Morris, have the courage to oppose colour bar. But many fathers may be political agitators or have households in which political talk often goes on. Their children listen carefully and pick up all that is said. It is impossible to teach such children any religion. If one asks them if they go to any church they say, "What for?" and "Whose church is that?"'

One factor which should not be ignored is the part played by the Christian Church as a sphere in which Africans have been learning from experience the techniques of self-government. However true it may be that the Missions have generally been too slow in entrusting the affairs of the local congregations and districts to African leadership, it is equally true that the churches have almost always anticipated the Government in admitting Africans to executive power at all levels, and some missionary churches exhibit a degree of partnership in effective self-government which is a good deal nearer to the meaning of that much abused word than anything yet seen in the political sphere. We shall return to this subject in the next chapter.

So far we have considered only the effect of the condition of political tension upon the loyalty of the congregations. Its effect upon the status of the African ministry is far more serious. In the last chapter a constantly recurring theme was the suspicion with which most Africans regard any leader who appears to stand in an intermediary position between themselves and the European boss. We can analyse the difficulties surrounding such people under four heads:

1. African leaders who are selected on the assumption that tribal norms apply to town life are unacceptable to the proletarian population.

2. Any 'prefectorial' system created from above is opposed by the freely chosen representatives of African aspirations.
3. Advanced, 'white-collar' Africans are suspected by the ordinary workers of coming to terms with Europeans in order to improve their own status.
4. Tribal loyalties are often confused with these other conflicts, particularly in the association of Nyasas with the Mines African Staffs' Association and of the Bemba with the middle wage-groups.

It is not difficult to see how each of these tensions affects the status of the African minister in his congregation and in society at large.

(1) *African leaders who are selected on the assumption that tribal norms apply to town life are unacceptable to the proletarian population.* Therefore if a church authority in selecting an ordination candidate or evangelist is guided by the norms of the rural mission district, such a man, if he is afterwards posted to the Copperbelt, is likely to provoke a similar reaction to that aroused by the Tribal Representatives in the early 1950s. In chapter 5 we saw how the village congregation is guided by evangelists and elders who follow the customary order they have accepted from the missionary in the bush and modify it to coincide more or less with existing village patterns of authority. But the emerging middle classes of the Copperbelt who bring their knowledge of committee procedure and majority votes into the church sessions and parochial councils are not content to be ruled by elders or even clergy of that type. Yet the only candidate who actually left Nchanga during the period of our study to be trained for the ministry of one of the missionary churches was an ex-mission school-teacher employed as a clerk in the compound office, well over forty years old and very conservative in his attitude to Europeans. It is only fair to say that he personally expressed the hope that he would be allowed to spend the whole of his ministry in the rural areas. We could not but notice that almost always the African minister, evangelist or catechist who took charge of any congregation at Nchanga during our stay was one of the older and less formally educated men. A senior African welfare worker there commented: 'Our ministers are quite good at their theological so-and-so, but they lack general knowledge and experience. Most of them are old teachers or elderly men with a purely Mission (rural) background. Ministers in the Copperbelt ought to have some knowledge of sociology.' Another young, educated Christian complained, 'You can't keep your faith when you are disappointed all the time. Ministers who only generalize and can't give an answer to real facts make men lose faith.'

As in the secular sphere so in the congregations, an awkward tension exists between the nostalgic loyalty to tribal tradition and language and the new urban consciousness which rejects tribal divisions as a bar to the advancement of all-African interests. On the one hand, the traditionalists in the Church make much of language difficulties, and tribal rivalries appear to be much alive. On the other hand the impatience of the younger, more emancipated Christians was voiced by a Presiding Elder of the AME Church, who said: 'We do not allow any of our members to exercise tribal regime in the church. We are all Africans. We use any language in our church. If one wants to speak, we just give him an interpreter.' The very few clergy in the Copperbelt who belonged mentally and socially to the urban milieu were clearly exercising a more effective ministry than any others. This raises acute problems concerning the recruitment and training of clergy for the Copperbelt. Some aspects of the difficult question of vocation will be touched upon in the last section of this book. The time has long passed when it is possible to train an adequate ministry for the Copperbelt in some far-off rural retreat. But before men of the necessary qualifications can be expected to offer themselves in sufficient numbers, the terms of service, standards of salary, and the patterns of co-operation between African and European clergy will have to be fearlessly reappraised by a Church which has ceased once and for all to look at the towns from the standpoint of the villages.

(2) *Any 'prefectorial' system created from above is opposed by the freely chosen representatives of African aspirations.* It follows that far more needs to be done to correct the impression that the African clergy are the intermediary officers appointed by the missionary staff to act on their behalf toward the African Church. No Mission in Northern Rhodesia today intends that that should be the relationship. Yet in the context of social and political tension which we have attempted to describe, that will continue to be the opinion of African Christians until some really striking proof is afforded to the contrary. An African agricultural officer with experience in many parts of Northern Rhodesia remarked that 'when a man of some education becomes a minister he goes down in almost every respect. Not only in salary, housing, etc., but also in status, because it is known that he will always be subservient to the missionaries and he is regarded as a Yes-man.' And he went on to enumerate the African ministers of the various Missions who, instead of being sent out into a charge of their own, are stationed at the Mission centre as colleagues of the ordained missionary. The words which Dr

Goodall and the Rev. Erik Nielsen wrote in 1954 are still fundamentally true:

> 'When such a man (the younger African minister) absorbs himself in the organizational life of the Church, he is faced with the whole organization and tradition of the Western mission. Here, too, he is (very often subconsciously) afraid; at any rate, he is not sure of himself. He feels that things are decided *for* him, that he is part of a machine, the whole pattern of which he does not know. He has all the ambitions of the young educated African, but has no real possibilities of 'advance', humanly speaking. He has a low salary and he has (whether we like it or not) a feeling of white supremacy within the Church. . . . The African Christian community seldom sees the office of the ministry as an integral part of the life of the Church itself. It is regarded as belonging to the pattern of Western missionary activity, and not really to the African church. The minister is therefore thought of in terms of a continuation of the missionary's function. From this angle we were told that some of the young nationally and politically self-conscious Africans disparage the ministry as belonging more or less to the realm of "white missionary domination".'[7]

It seems unkind to repeat such words when all Missions that we have met have been making valiant efforts to eliminate the traces of 'white missionary domination'. What such efforts ultimately involve must be considered in the next chapter on the supra-racial Church. Yet more remains to be achieved, and that quickly; for we found that in the missionary churches on Nchanga Mine, with the possible exception of the Roman Catholic Church, the African congregations and their elders did not seem able to see a missionary in relation to their church in any other way than that of the white 'boss' to his gang underground. It is not surprising that African clergy are still called 'slave', 'Mission stooge', or 'the white men's dog'. Something startling is required to shift this pattern which is stamped so firmly on people's minds. That might be done if the Church proceeded to make its African clergy the exact equivalents of their European counterparts in respect of the scope and the autonomy of their ministry. It would also be a considerable advance if the Christian Council of Northern Rhodesia were to consist of at least as many African as European delegates.

(3) *Advanced, 'white-collar' Africans are suspected by the ordinary workers of coming to terms with Europeans in order to improve their own status*. It is not surprising, therefore, that an almost irresolvable tension exists for the African minister in respect of his status within the emerging class differences of African society. We have seen that often there is conflict in the various congregations between the Union

members and those on a monthly salary. An interesting example of this appears in the organization of the Roman Catholic Church. There are two lay adult groups, the Catholic Action, known as the Actio's, and the Franciscan Third Order, or Tertiaries. The former are to be found in the country districts as well as in the towns. Until recently the Actio's were selected and appointed by the priest-in-charge, while the Tertiaries are volunteers. The Actio's in any congregation are made responsible for the discipline of the local congregation, rather as elders in the Free Church; the Tertiaries, on the other hand, are concerned more with their own spiritual life and with acts of charity—visiting the sick, helping elderly folk and entertaining travellers. While it is not possible to make a hard and fast distinction between the two bodies, these features coincide sufficiently with some of the main differences between the secular associations, for many people to look on the Actio's in much the same way as they once regarded the Tribal Representatives or the Urban Advisory Council, as intermediaries of the priests, while the Tertiaries appeal as a more free and authentic, and at the same time more sophisticated, expression of African insight in the Church. So one man in Kansuswa, who during his working life as a hotel waiter had been an Actio and had been made chairman of the local group, as soon as he retired in 1949 and started his own private business, left them and joined the Tertiaries. He explained his preference, saying: 'The Actio is a military kind of organization; its members are selected by officials who send them as their delegates to do their job . . . But the Third Order is voluntary; it teaches people to be humble, not to fight for authority and position. It makes people simplify their lives and forget worldly things.' A similar differentiation, this time on a more obvious class distinction, was seen in two Roman Catholic youth groups at Ndola; the 'Jocists' was for working men with education up to Standard V, and the 'Seniors' for white-collar men with education from Standard VI upwards. It was explained that 'This division enabled each group to feel at home in its meetings.'

Where such differentiation exists in a congregation, with whom does the minister appear to stand? Hitherto, because of their educational level and standard of living, the clergy have tended to belong more to the 'ticket' men than to those on a monthly salary. So at Nchanga, during the tension in 1956 between the Union and Mines African Staffs' Association, the minister of the CCAR, though he thought he was being neutral, appeared to stand more on the Union side. But a variety of factors are now bringing the clergy much more definitely into the orbit of the salaried staff. As their education qualifications improve, this will be even more marked. The new Franchise Bill which has accorded them the vote may arouse some jealousy against them. And the more they are taken into real partnership with the missionaries the more they will become suspect, like the Mines African Staffs' Association, of compromising with the Europeans. Already they are quite frequently called informers by their people.

If it is true that the price of solving the previous problem must be paid largely by the missionaries, then it is equally true that this third problem must prove very costly to the African clergy. Unless we are to cut the knot and opt for separate racial churches, the African minister is bound increasingly to be exposed to this loneliness and calumny, and there is no way out. Yet, when we have said that, we are still left with a problem, for no one who is concerned for the Church in Central Africa wishes to see it failing, as the Church in the Western world has failed, through becoming so linked with the bourgoisie that it loses the real working class. It is just conceivable that at this juncture it is a certain kind of European missionary who may yet, by his self-abandoned presence in their midst, bring the Gospel to the new African proletariat.

(4) *Tribal loyalties are often confused with these other conflicts, particularly in the association of Nyasas with the Mines African Staffs' Association and of the Bemba with the middle wage-groups.* This confused picture of pseudo-tribal loyalties, and loyalties which are genuinely tribal, combines with other factors to affect the position of the African minister. The high proportion of Nyasalanders in four congregations of the CCAR was shown on page 61. In 1958, the CCAR minister at Nchanga was a man from Nyasaland, and at a church session which we attended all the seven elders who were present were also of that country. When we attended service in the Dutch Reformed Mission it was not surprising that there also the great majority of the women in the church were Nyanja-speaking. But what in fact is the significance of a minister from Nyasaland, or of the Bemba or Nyasa minority in any congregation? As we have seen in the previous chapter, the answer to those questions will depend upon the context in which they are asked.

For example, there was, in 1956, imminent danger of a break-away from the Roman Catholic congregation at Ndola. 'The Ngoni', a young member of the Tertiaries told the writer, 'were disappointed when announcements were always given in Bemba. One day one Ngoni elder demanded that the Ngoni Catholics should be given an equal chance of getting positions in the Church. They held a meeting and complained that church offices were always given to Bemba and only Bemba hymns were sung. The different groups met to discuss the issue. They agreed to have hymns in different languages on alternate Sundays but pointed out that the other demand was a silly idea as leadership is not based on tribe but on ability and intelligence.' What was the significance of that dispute? Without written evidence and at a distance of several years, one can only guess. But, considering the year in which it took place, it seems most probable that it was in fact a reflection of the rivalry between the white-collar workers and the Trade Union, though it took on the outward trappings of a tribal quarrel. In that context the voice of the Church had truly to say, 'Leadership is not based on tribe.' Or, as the Presiding Elder of the AME Church put it: 'We do not allow any of our members to exercise tribal regime in the Church. We are all Africans.'

But in another context the minister has to know that he is dealing with a matter of genuine tribal concern. The same young Tertiary told the writer of a case with which he was dealing as a social worker. A church member who was a Mambwe had married a wife who was a Senga. He was of a patrilineal tribe, she of a matrilineal. He wanted to return for a time from the Copperbelt to his home but planned to leave her behind because of her quarrelsome nature. She feared that if that happened their children would go with him and would remain there with his parents. Here, in the context of personal relations and family custom, tribalism was valid and the Church, in the person of the Tertiary, had to take it seriously.

In these two incidents the distinction is plain. But it is not always so easy for the minister to decide, when dealing with angry or troubled people, whether the question of tribe is relevant or not. But the problem is not only a pastoral one. It is a problem of apologetics, of 'public relations'. The African mineworker still lives in two worlds, the world of his personal and family relationships in which tribal values are still operative, and the world of labour and politics in which he is simply an African and a worker, transcending all tribes. As we have seen, the two worlds appear often to be in conflict. To which of them does the function of the Christian minister seem to belong? In which of them does the Church appear to be relevant? The answer should clearly be: Both. But no association in the Copperbelt has so far succeeded in meeting the demands of both those worlds, though both the Union and the Congress have tried to be omnicompetent and to deal with the personal as well as the communal needs of their members. Obviously, as a pastor, the minister will often be called to meet his people at the point of personal perplexity. He will come to them then as part of their personal world of family relationships and old rural disciplines, in which the village church was the way to God. But if that is how they think of their minister, then at those other times when they belong to the world of labour and of African aspirations and advance, he will be identified with the outworn sanctions, the irrelevant values and the weakening divisions of tribalism. This was the experience, for example, of the preacher who complained in his sermon, 'Don't give an evasive answer, saying, "We are now citizens of the mine towns, we have left agriculture behind, we don't keep Sunday."' If on the other hand he stands in their eyes as one of the new men, with no 'tribal regime' permitted in his church but with a message relevant to the realm of their industrial solidarity, then, when the personal and private blow falls, it will not be to him that they turn. He will then be one of those preachers of whom they complain, 'He talks about politics instead of the Word of God.' This is perhaps the most pressing dilemma for the African clergy on the Copperbelt. It may be that, for a period at least, it will only be resolved by the provision of two types of clergy, the parish pastor to meet men on the personal and tribal level, and the industrial chaplain to speak the Word of the Lord in the new context of modern society. So gradually may the fullness of Christ be understood.

NOTES

1. Published as a pamphlet, *Anything but This*, USCL, 1958.
2. Report by C. T. Loram in *The Livingstone Mail*, Christmas 1922.
3. *Proceedings of the General Missionary Conference of Northern Rhodesia* (Lovedale Press) 1924, p. 24.
4. Memorandum sent to Rev. Cullen Young from the Management, Roan Antelope and Mufulira Mines, 17 June 1943, and Letter from the Rev. J. W. C. Dougall to Miss Gibson, 1 July 1943. From Archives of the Church of Scotland.
5. Epstein, *op. cit.*, p. 191.
6. *Ibid.*, p. 242.
7. *Survey of the Training of the Ministry in Africa*, Part III, IMC, 1954, pp. 32, 34.

8

The Church and Race Relations

> 'There is too much failure among all Europeans. . . . The three combined bodies—Missionaries, Government and Companies, or gainers of money—do form the same rule to look upon the native with mockery eyes. It sometimes startles us to see that the three combined bodies are from Europe, and along with them there is a title, CHRISTENDOM. And to compare or make a comparison between the MASTER of the title and its servants, it pushes any African away from believing the Master of the title.'[1]

These words were written by a convert of the Livingstonia Mission in Nyasaland in the first decade of this century. They serve to remind us of two facts: that the African complaint against colour prejudice—what Mr Van der Post has called 'the wrong look in the eye'—is not a new thing; and that it has continuously fostered disillusionment towards Christianity.

It is impossible to understand the problems confronting the Church in Northern Rhodesia unless one bears continuously in mind the convention of prejudice which is the atmosphere in which it lives. The operative word here is 'convention', for inherent in every convention is its own private standard of judgment. Customs and attitudes, which to the outsider seem ludicrous or reprehensible, are not only acceptable to those who conform but any breach of them appears as wrong-doing. Godfrey and Monica Wilson emphasized this point in their observations in Central Africa fifteen years ago.

> 'If, for example, an African believes that his child has died of witchcraft he is compelled to take steps against the supposed witch; yet if he does so he may be prosecuted. Similarly, a European pastor with African and European parishioners cannot, even if he wishes to do so, have easy social relations with both groups. If he invites Africans to his house the Europeans will feel that he is "letting down the prestige of the white man"; if he fails to entertain Africans some of them

at least will think him a hypocrite. He is forced into behaviour which half his congregation finds immoral.'[2]

We shall return later to the problem of the European pastor. At the moment the quotation is offered simply to illustrate the different standards of judgment which are applied inside, and outside, a particular convention. However objectively one attempts to describe the race relations in Northern Rhodesia, the facts will still evoke a different reaction, and will therefore carry a different significance, in Europe from that which they will among the white population of Central Africa. Nevertheless the attempt must be made if any picture of the Church in that area is to be drawn.

Within any convention there are greater or lesser degrees of individual conformity, and this is true of colour prejudice in Northern Rhodesia. For this reason, as a recent sociological survey of the colour problem has pointed out,

> 'there is a danger of making sweeping generalizations which are not substantiated by the facts. As always, there are Europeans in British Colonial Africa who are quite free from prejudice against Africans and many, particular teachers and doctors, whose lives are devoted to the improvement of their material welfare and social status. At the opposite end of the scale are Europeans who hold Africans in the utmost contempt and rarely miss an opportunity of expressing hostility towards them. Between these two extremes fall the large majority of Europeans who tend to share a stereotyped view of the African, which suggests that there is some inherent difference between the races. It is often sincerely believed that, while the Africans may eventually achieve a higher standard of living and acquire, at any rate, the outward signs and symbols of Western civilization, they will never really rise to the same cultural level as Europeans. Although, as we have seen, science disputes that view it is still widely held.'[3]

The basic relationship between Europeans and Africans in Northern Rhodesia has always been that of employers and employees, though understood in nineteenth-century terms of 'master and man', with a wide gulf between the two.[4] But this basic relationship has been enveloped in a complex of fears, rivalries and conflicting ideals, expressing itself in an insistence upon social segregation and in an attitude of superiority which ranges from benevolent patronage to contemptuous dislike. The Commission of Inquiry of 1940 reported that

> 'many witnesses, European and African alike, drew our attention to the bitter resentment caused among the African workers by the terms of address and the sneering attitude which, it was stated, were not infrequently used towards them by the European mineworkers'.[5]

Eleven years later the *Comparative Survey of Native Policy* reported that in Northern Rhodesia

> 'restrictions are imposed on Africans regarding the possession of liquor, and discriminatory practices include the habit of certain shops serving African customers through hatches, the barring of Africans from European cinemas, hotels and restaurants and the provision of separate accommodation for Africans on the railways and in buses.'[6]

It would be possible to fill a chapter of this book with incidents of racial prejudice and social segregation which came to our notice during the course of the study. Yet the most important factor in the situation is the change which is evidently taking place in the attitudes of the white population. It is not a uniform change working wholly in the liberal direction, but a much wider differentiation appearing between European points of view. This produces a confused picture so that one 'old settler' bemoans the hardening of antagonism on both sides, while another white resident asserts confidently that 'there is no doubt that the rank and file of Europeans in the whole of Northern Rhodesia are becoming very, very much more liberal in their outlook'. The fact is that both these assessments are true, just as they were ten years ago when the United Missions in the Copperbelt reported that they were 'concerned at a deterioration in racial attitudes; at the same time we are conscious of the prevalence of a greater amount of goodwill on the part of the Europeans towards the African than ever before.'[7] And this should not surprise us, for the history of Europe seems to suggest that the moment of revolution and the point of extremest bitterness occurs, not when oppression grinds most heavily, but when for one reason or another it begins to relax.

Pressure from African leaders, pressure from European liberals in the territory and the pressure of world opinion, resented but still effective, have all played their part in creating this change of attitude. The preamble to the Federal Constitution laid down the principle of partnership. It is true, as Sir John Moffat said, that

> 'this woolly term has been interpreted in an astonishing number of different ways and every individual has been free to say that the word meant what he wished it to mean. [8]

Nevertheless the word has clearly been a weapon in the hands of the liberals. In the summer of 1953 the African National Congress launched a campaign of demonstrations against discrimination. In August of that year the Government of Northern Rhodesia announced that those Post Offices which still had separate entrances and counter services for

Africans would be redesigned to provide the same facilities for all races. Early in 1954 a new series of demonstrations was staged. After ten days' picketing by Africans, the custom in 'European' shops of serving Africans through special hatches in the wall came to an end at Ndola and other Copperbelt towns, and the Chamber of Commerce signed an agreement with the African Advisory Council that in future all should be served at one counter.[9] Later that year African representatives in the Federal Legislature made the first of several attempts to introduce legislation against discrimination in all public places. This, however, has been consistently rejected. On that occasion the Federal Prime Minister said significantly:

> 'Let us for the sake of the Federation, which was for economic advantage, not for the preamble, which was forced upon us, have patience.'[10]

Slowly, but steadily, here and there, bars have been lowered. European commerce with hard-headed economic sense has often been a liberalizing influence. White salesmen in the 'second-class trading area' seem often to maintain exceptionally friendly relations with their African customers and speak highly of them; in the Nchanga Mine Compound one of the two most trusted Europeans is the owner of a chain of stores; and early in 1958 a business organization in Southern Rhodesia offered to finance the Rhodesian team entering for the 1962 Empire Games on condition that the team should be multi-racial. Local Race Relations Committees have also played some part in reducing discriminatory practices. The multi-racial discussion groups which exist in every town are generally disappointing and ineffectual, partly because they consist too largely of 'officials', both European and African, who attend because it is expected of them, and partly because timidity leads them to eliminate all but the safe subjects which are also the dull ones. They seem very rarely to lead on to spontaneous personal contacts between European and African members. There are in fact alarmingly few real friendships between individuals of the two races. The new university is bound to create these, but not for a long time to such an extent as to make any appreciable difference to Copperbelt society. What is probably of more significance is the evidence of a greater *camaraderie* between African and European mineworkers on the job, particularly among the underground workers. No one would claim that there is much of this as yet, but there are stories of African miners paying a visit to their European boss at Christmas time.[11] Though there has been no systematic study of the racial attitudes in the European community of the Copperbelt, it seems likely that the same would be true there as has been proved by surveys in Britain, namely that most people imagine that others are more prejudiced than themselves. This not only inhibits many individuals from making a stand which they are inwardly convinced they should, but it probably misleads the white politicians into adopting a party line less liberal than it need be. It may be that the Federal Government is so dilatory in effecting the removal of discrimination not only because of the predilection of some of its leaders but also because the others misjudge the temper of European opinion, just as some clergy have frightened themselves into believing that a bolder liberalism on their part would cause trouble in their white congregations.

Such fears, however, among the leaders of both Church and State are not without excuse, for, as has already been said, white opinion is not moving uniformly in a liberal direction, but rather is being more widely diversified. As a greater number of the white population is shifting tentatively towards the 'left', so others are reacting with more outrageous declarations of racialism than before. Unfortunately this attitude more frequently finds expression in the press than the other, and even at times in the Legislative Assembly, so Africans are persuaded that it represents the opinion of the majority of the whites. One quotation from a letter which appeared during 1958 from a fairly frequent correspondent who uses a *nom de plume* will suffice to show the note of impatience which characterizes this hardening opinion:

> 'Northern Rhodesians have been about surfeited with partnership, racial relations, multi-racial society and all the other absurdities which mean nothing. . . . At best this so-called "partnership" or "racial relationship" is but an uneasy peace. Most of us are just too busy to bother about it. The breaking down of barriers at post offices and banks and public offices has not really been achieved. We stand in queues with Africans, we white men and women, but we do not fraternise.'[12]

The most serious aspect of such a statement is that it is almost identical with what a growing number of Africans are also saying. At a meeting of teachers and welfare workers at Mindolo in 1957 one young African gave vent to this *cri de coeur*, which was taken down verbatim:

> 'We have waited too long for the privilege of being accepted. First we were not educated—so we went away and struggled until some of us were able to come back with our School Certificate. But then we were still separated by the barrier of culture—so some of us went off to Britain or America and learned to be on equal terms there and to

> think and behave like the other students. But still we are just as far away as ever from being accepted by you. For you are a thousand years of civilization ahead of us, and however far forward we progress you have moved on also, so you say. So now we say: "You can keep it. Keep your thousand years' advantage over us; keep your friendship and your society to yourselves; keep your wonderful way of life." We shall fight for the things we must have in our own way—justice and equality and opportunity. We can win them by fighting, not by friendship. And when we have got them we shall not be much interested in the friendship of people like you.'

Very few are as articulate as that, and only the more educated are so completely disillusioned. As a member of the Staff Association at Nchanga said to us:

> 'The white man is always aloof and mentions the thousand years that it has taken him to become civilized, and he says: "You cannot become civilized quickly." We educated people get angry when we hear that. But less educated people say: "Europeans know the Bible better than we do, therefore they must be right." '

Yet the less educated also are wounded by the so-called 'pin-pricks' of European insult and discrimination, and accept more readily the stereotypes of anti-white prejudice. This emerged particularly clearly from the essays of the children of the different schools in Chingola, in which the recurrence of certain phrases indicated that they were stereotypes of this kind. 'Europeans despise us'—'They call us dirt of Kaffirs'—'White people do not want to eat with us'—'They chase us from their churches'. The crude European misconception of Africans as sub-human types is particularly resented. A schoolboy wrote: 'God made all human beings created in the image of God, not as animals'. One church elder in Kansuswa said: 'We received the first Europeans, giving them everything they needed free of charge. We carried them on our backs, as I myself have done. Yet now they tell us we are only monkeys, not made by God to be human beings.' And another, touching on a familiar point of tension and rivalry, complained: 'They say that Africans smell. But we notice that they can only smell during the day; for at night they come after our African women, and then it is: "Hallo, darling".'

Such quotations—and they could be multiplied *ad nauseam*—should not mislead the reader into imagining that the Copperbelt is dark with sullen looks and seething resentment. Nothing could be further from the truth. When a European drives his car through a Mine African Township children wave and shout greetings, and adults of the two races conduct whatever business they have together with smiles and often with a joke. The conscious thoughts of Africans do not, as far as we could tell, dwell continuously on their grievances. Yet we would wholly endorse the warning given by Philip Mason in his book *The Birth of a Dilemma,* where he says:

> 'There is a level of consciousness at which men go about their work, eat their meals; laugh, dance and drink; tell the boss they have no complaints—and mean it. There may in the same man be another level, of which they are most of the time unaware, at which there is a deep, perpetual, and bitter resentment. But at an emotional summons of a particular kind this may leap into view.'[13]

That is the situation in which the Church in Northern Rhodesia stands at the present time. There is not much disagreement, even in the Dutch Reformed Church, as to the principles which it is bound to proclaim; its problem arises from the difficulty of practising what it preaches. Yet it is on this issue of race relations that 'Christendom' is on trial in Central Africa to-day, as it was fifty years ago. 'And to compare or make a comparison between the MASTER of the title and its servants, it pushes any African away from believing the Master of the title.' The question at stake is whether European and African Christians maintain an inward attitude towards one another essentially different from that found in society as a whole; but, as usual, the test is focused upon a few points of external conduct of which the most important is joint worship. The Africans' most regular charge against the Church is that it countenances racial segregation within its own ranks. 'Europeans came to bring us the Gospel, but when they built churches they made separate buildings for white and black men. We ask ourselves if we have two different Gods.' 'The Europeans who advocate the precepts of Christianity don't hold to those principles. I know the churches have a genuine way of teaching the Africans, but if the churches cannot convince us that Africans can also be regarded by the Europeans as one family of God, then I don't find any reason why Africans should be going to the churches.'

Is there in fact a policy of segregation in the congregations? And is there any genuine demand from African Christians to be allowed to attend English-speaking churches?

In the Dutch Reformed Church the principle of segregation is accepted as it is in the Union of South Africa. The Jehovah's Witnesses also never combine their African and European meetings; their American leaders in the territory have a sense of uneasiness about this but maintain segregation on the grounds that the Witnesses are not called to change any of the *status quo* in this present world. Apart from these two, and the all-African Churches, every other denomination subscribes officially to the principle of the 'open door'. Yet undoubtedly there are quite a number of Europeans in all the English-speaking churches who do not like to see Africans actually coming through the door, and succeed in conveying that fact if any do venture in. Two young communicants in the Anglican congregation in Chingola European township ceased coming to Holy Communion early in 1958 after finding on one occasion an African nurse kneeling beside them at the Communion rail; and their mother was astonished that the Rector would give her no assurance that this would never happen again. The writer overheard one member of a Free Church women's fellowship ask another as they left a meeting at which the subject had been 'Africans and social change': 'Do you think they are really human like ourselves?' Similar instances could be quoted from nearly every white congregation in the Copperbelt.

As in society at large, so also in the Church, a wider differentiation of attitude is appearing in the European community. The move towards liberalism is somewhat bolder and more deliberate within the churches, but there also it is accompanied by reaction. In another of the Free Churches a few Africans and one coloured woman had been attending the English services spasmodically for several years without comment. From the middle of 1957, however, a small number of the younger European church members together with a few enthusiastic missionaries began to press for some bolder demonstration of inter-racial fellowship in their congregation. The committee of the church bazaar invited the African women's fellowship to run one stall, but a reiterated request that members of the African girls' club should serve the teas proved too much for several white women who left the church; and shortly after, when twenty Africans attended the evening service, one European family walked out. At the beginning of 1958 the liberal element in the congregation renewed its pressure, inviting Africans to accompany them to the evening service. The reaction came to a head when the secular inter-racial club asked for the use of the Free Church Hall. Although a majority on the church committee actually voted in favour of granting them this permission, a minority of the 'pillars of the church' voiced such strongly racialist views that the chairman of the club, who was also the minister of the church, decided to seek other quarters for their meetings. Later in the year the same minister was able to report that 'in our European congregation we are still in the middle of this fight but there is no doubt that steadily the tide in our congregation is changing'.

From within the convention of prejudice this change of the tide is eventful and full of promise; but to the African Christian the pace of the change seems too calculated and slow to suggest anything like repentance and a change of heart. A few of the most firmly rooted of the African Christians are able to recognize a substantial improvement. For example, the minister of the UCCAR at Nchanga said; 'I can see that this matter of integration is moving up a bit, though we cannot expect things to be carried forward all at once. But I can see in Chingola it is now a fact that educated Africans can come to the European church and feel there is no fear. But the Europeans, they haven't started yet to attend African services; it might be because the language is difficult for them. In the future this integration will become a real thing.' But in general the pace of improvement in the attitude of European Christians has not come up to the pace of disillusionment and secession among African Christians.

In 1954, in conformity with their campaign of demonstrations against discrimination, the Congress was initiating test cases to challenge the colour bar in the Church. Groups of young Africans, prepared for a scene, presented themselves at English-speaking churches at service time. But the church leaders had been forewarned and the Africans were surprised to find themselves admitted without trouble in every congregation except that of the Dutch Reformed Church. This incident has led some Europeans to suppose that every African who comes to the English services does so only in order to assert his rights. There are, however, a considerable number of educated Africans in every Copperbelt town who find the worship at the vernacular services intellectually and aesthetically unsatisfying; there are others, also, such as police or hospital staff, whose place of residence or whose times of duty make it almost impossible to attend the churches in the African residential areas.

But it is not the mere right of admission that African Christians are seeking in the European congregations, but the evidence that the fellowship of believers is a reality, and that within the Church different norms apply from those which are accepted in society at large. As an elder of the Anglican church at Luanshya said to us: 'If I sit beside a white man in church on Sunday and he cuts me in the street on Monday it would have been better if I had never gone to his church.' So it is often the manner of their reception by the European congregations which brings disillusionment. 'When I was a proper Christian I was a member of a church choir. When invited to take part in a festival with Europeans we were given reserved seats at the back.' Among Roman Catholics and Anglicans, Africans have got hold of the idea that if they attend Mass in a European congregation they should communicate last, out of consideration for Europeans' fear of infection. They respect this convention but not without some soreness.

African criticism of the white Christians' failure in fellowship is focused most bitterly upon the unfortunate missionaries, for it is felt that they, at least, should be blameless in this respect. 'This matter of attending the European church', said one African headmaster, 'is a minor point; what is more serious is that so many missionaries don't really show love.' And an advanced underground worker remarked: 'We are the Samaritans, the missionaries are the Jews.' As we shall see later, a great deal of this is the result of the invidious position of the Copperbelt missionaries who are responsible to both black and white congregations. Much also is due to pure misinterpretation by over-sensitive people of other people's actions. 'Father X when giving the ashes on Ash Wednesday did not touch any African's head with his thumb, but sprinkled the ash from above.' 'At Chipili I saw a certain missionary always had separate Masses. He celebrated first with the white people and took his Communion then, but when he came to celebrate for Africans he did not even partake at all himself.' Although neither of these actions could in fact have taken place as reported, the relationship between the races in society as a whole predisposes Africans to put the worst interpretation on something which has been inaccurately perceived. Sometimes it is a matter of language that is misconstrued. 'They tell us Africans when crossing ourselves to say "*Kwi shina lija Kwa Tata*" ("through the name of the Father") but they say "*In* the name". So they show that they think that we Africans are not in the Cross but only near it.'

There has obviously been a long build-up of resentment against the authoritarian position of some missionaries, particularly on the rural mission stations, and on the Copperbelt this becomes associated with the general antagonism to white dominance. An African minister of the UCCAR told how easily his congregation at Mporokoso had been split by a local preacher of the AME Church who was accusing them of being under the rule of the missionaries. Very often what a missionary regards as legitimate admonition and guidance appears to the African congregations as autocratic, simply because the words are addressed to them from above, or from the outside. It is of course immensely difficult in the present state of relationships for the missionary conscientiously to fulfil his responsibility to the African church with the right tone of voice, the right look in the eye. But if an African Christian attempts to point this out, the European all too often seems unable to hear what he is trying to say. This can be illustrated from a scrap of conversation between a missionary and an African headmaster, an elder of his church. It is taken from a verbatim transcript of a discussion group:

'Headmaster: Sometimes where a missionary reads the Gospel, and when it comes to preaching, he tends to despise or to speak something against Africans which leads them to be disappointed. He is preaching on what he read from the Bible, yet he brings in a different topic altogether.

Missionary: Because the preaching is not fundamental Bible teaching therefore it is unsatisfying?

Headmaster: Most of them preach contrary to what they have read.

Missionary: Would you say that orthodox churches are failing because they are not supplying enough in the vernacular for their preachers?

Headmaster: The big point is the attitude of the ministers. They preach very well. But when it comes to behaviour it is different. Some of such ministers do not show any attitude of being friendly with their people.

Missionary: Does that apply to European and African ministers?

Headmaster: That applies mostly to European ministers.'

The way in which resentment can be built up in an individual church member is well illustrated in this account of one man now working at Kansuswa. It should not be read as an objective statement of fact but rather as a demonstration of how a subjective frame of mind can be moulded through a combination of missionary authoritarianism, African inadequacy and misunderstanding:

'My father was a cook at Chipili. When he had been there a long time others became jealous and brought false accusations and he was dismissed. Missionaries listen too readily to false reports and this brings hatred. I also began to hate the rule of the missionaries. A lady missionary once gave my sister a pair of shoes. One day I put them on to go to school. But I was beaten and sent away from school for a time. We are realizing that the early missionaries never came for the sake of the Gospel but only to make their living. The Mission wanted to be a kind of government to show their own power. We came to fear the Mission like an enemy or like a great empire walking all over the mission-district. No one was allowed to go about after 9.0 p.m. If any was found outside his home after that hour he was called, charged and punished.

'I tried to become a good Christian and the Mission praised me in my reports. In the Anglican Mission we were taught how the Saints had lived. I was trying to follow the same method of becoming a Saint. I had been baptized Benedict and I tried to be like him, even fasting many times. . . . In 1942, being tired of living only in one place, I took a long leave and came to Lusaka. I worked there for two years as a mechanic, then the Mission called me back to be a teacher at Broken Hill. I was afraid to go back to Chipili because I had left that place with hatred owing to the way my father was treated.

'At first the missionary in charge liked me because he knew I had some knowledge of the old history of my people. How he came to hate me I can't tell. Perhaps it was because I was found reading the Seventh Day Adventist papers and books. Perhaps they disliked me because I would not confess what they expected; the priest said I had omitted to confess adultery, yet I had never done it. I have never understood the reason, but, whatever it was, in 1949 I was expelled from Broken Hill. No explanation was given. Only a great curse from the Bishop when I claimed three pounds for my travelling.

'Even in the Seventh Day Adventists, the missionaries all show the same colour bar in their thought about Africans. Recently a Seventh Day Adventist missionary said to us: "You have got a very dirty church where no angel will ever come to join with you in prayer." This offended us because he despised us. We kept writing letters to those in authority. Last week he came to discuss the matter, but he showed that no African can be allowed to oppose a European. Always the Europeans want to show that they are holy people or righteous in the eyes of the people for whom they work.

'I cannot speak about Government; that side of things I can't tell. I stick only to talking about the Gospel; and there I see that missionaries don't have fellowship with Africans in this country. God himself will release us from the white people. Or it may be that God will send the Holy Spirit in the last days to unite us in true Christianity with the white people. But in these days there always comes misunderstanding from the way the missionaries behave. Yet, after all, we talk to ourselves as Jesus talked about the Rabbis: "If they tell you to do something, do it, but never follow what they do themselves." '

This reference to Matt. 23.3 sounds perhaps a little self-righteous. But it is typical of the way in which white behaviour is judged by the Bible's precepts. In the school children's essays we frequently found references such as: 'Jesus taught, Love your neighbour and your enemies, so the colour bar is against Jesus' teaching of love'. A young man who was a regular churchgoer from childhood until his sixteenth year told how 'in my last year at school I began to learn that the practice of the Europeans does not agree with what they taught from the Bible.' The application of the Bible to the relationship between the races was well illustrated in the sermon that was preached by the African President of the Synod of the United Church of Central Africa at the service which inaugurated the integration of the European Free Churches with the African CCAR under one constitution. His text was: 'Till we all come in the unity of the faith'.

> 'The Israelites were loved and chosen by God to be members of his household. They were so fond of their nation that they looked down on other nations. They were ignorant of God's purpose that people of all nations were the same in the eyes of God, though they may be different in appearance and traditions and customs. God was gradually teaching them to do away with selfishness and pride so that they might stop despising other people. . . . Jesus taught the Jews, his own people, that unless they repented of their sins, particularly the sin of spiritual pride, they had no hope of salvation. . . . Let us turn to St Paul again. This man was a true Jew in race, in tradition and in following the Law. When God showed him the spirit of love in Christians, he first of all protested against it and persecuted the Christians; and then he began to doubt the Jewish way; then Jesus showed him the power of love. Now Paul could see why the Jewish way failed. It helped to make people good, but it made them proud at the same time. Pride spoils good people; only the love of God can conquer pride and bring men together.'

One aspect of the disillusionment of so many towards the Church is the widespread belief that Christianity is essentially a white man's religion. The use of religious pictures in schools, religious films and film strips in the compounds has had a far greater influence in confirming this false impression than most missionaries seem prepared to allow. We became convinced during our study that the visual aids commonly used by the churches need to be most critically reviewed with this in mind. Some missionaries, for example, who commended the beautiful Bible pictures of Miss E. A. Wood 'because the characters are obviously not Europeans' seemed unable to realize that to African eyes this would be far from obvious. After a film of the *Pilgrim's Progress* had been shown in a school at Nchanga during 1958, children asked their teachers: 'Why are there no black people in Heaven? All the angels were white.' One child wrote in his essay: 'I have never seen a picture of Christ helping a black man'. But another had been deeply impressed by a picture of Saint Martin handing half his cloak to what the child supposed to be an African. Yet a mere Africanization of pictures will no longer suffice to redress the balance. The Roman Catholic Mission in Bancroft bought from the Congo a series of Stations of the Cross portraying Christ as an African; but these were rejected by the people, who said: 'This is not true. You are trying to deceive us.'

Some Africans are confirmed in this error by the remarks of a certain type of white mineworker who, irritated perhaps by the facility with which his gang of African miners will turn their conversation to a religious subject, will begin to challenge them. Several informants at different times mentioned incidents such as these: 'There is one shift boss who asked an underground worker in Cikabanga (the Copperbelt pidgin vernacular)—"Do you go to church? Our God is not your God. Jesus Christ was a white person."' 'Europeans sometimes ask Africans who are at work with them: "Why do you go to church? Jesus is not the brother of an African. You are wasting your time; your father is the devil, for he is black."'

The ministers of the different denominations do what they can to combat this falsehood. One of the Tertiaries at Kansuswa reported: 'Father has tried to convince every Christian that the church is not a European church.' And the bishop of a small break-away sect, the African Holy Spiritual Church, said: 'Most Africans think Jesus Christ was a white man. I don't, because I know he was the Son of God who came down to save all men's souls. There is no difference between souls—mine is not a black soul and yours is not white. We all had the same grandfather and grandmother, but they had three children, and we are the children of Ham. That I know. So we are black, but our grandparents were white.'

It is among the younger generation that this concept of the 'white man's religion' is most establishd. The idea occurred fairly consistently in the essays of children of every denomination. 'All churches in the world help white people only.' 'Jesus was born by a white woman; we cannot follow him.' 'I do not want to believe in a white God.' As the headmaster of one school said, naively: 'Most of the children know that Jesus was a white man.' Sometimes, no doubt, the children who say such things are only repeating slogans, but often a note of genuine spiritual search is audible in their remarks. 'I have found my own way of praying; for it is bad for one to pray to God blindly. My own way of praying is only praying in my house and singing songs of God in my house. If I consider it deeply I cannot even talk about Jesus in my prayers, but only God. Because Jesus was not an African, but he was a European; so it is no use to say, Jesus died for us. I should advise every African man and woman not to pray under any church but by himself or herself in the house, without mentioning Jesus. Jesus came to the Europeans and found that they were very cruel. So they killed him at that time. But after that they came to Africa and started preaching the death of Jesus Christ. But, if they don't believe in Jesus, how should we, who did not see him?' Even among the educated Africans, the white-collar workers, there is a strong feeling of the foreignness of Christianity. One who holds a position of great responsibility, a mediocre Roman Catholic, was speaking of the deterioration of his own character during his years on the Copperbelt. 'If I could go to my village', he said, 'and pray to the older gods, I would be a better man. We had no Jesus because that never happened to us. But Christianity now has destroyed all those things.'

Apart from the difficulties that we have already discussed—the white convention of race segregation, the alleged authoritarianism of missionaries and the fallacy of the 'white religion'—the Church in the Copperbelt faces certain special problems that arise from the close juxtaposition of European and African congregations.

First, there is the embarrassing contrast in standards of various kinds. The most obvious of these are the economic differences. Again the children's essays provide succinct statements: 'We have poor buildings and furniture, but the church for the white people is beautiful'. 'Only the white priests have cars, yet they say they are poor.' 'The missionaries teach, Love thy neighbour as thyself, but European ministers get higher salaries than Africans.' Many adults also referred to this difference in salary. In the Anglican Church, for example, a married European priest is paid an average of £60 per month; his African colleague gets £18 if he lives in the towns and the Church pays for the education of his children. In the United Church of Central Africa the discrepancy is still wider.[14]

Then there are the different standards of discipline applied to Christians of the two races. Even in small matters, these cause irritation in the African congregations. The disagreement which occasioned the break-away of Emilio Mulolani and his followers from the Roman Catholic Church was over the rule, common in African congregations of almost all denominations, that men and women should sit on opposite sides of the church. Emilio objected that this was imposed not on Europeans but only on Africans, thereby imputing to them a lower standard of purity. The problem can assume much more serious dimensions than this, however. When discussions were taking place on the integration of black and white congregations into the United Church of Central Africa, one of the questions raised by African leaders was whether the discipline for European and African members would be the same in the new church. In that church a rule of teetotalism was imposed on African members but not on the Europeans. Africans in the Anglican Church undergo a very strict procedure of discipline with a system of public penance and restoration to which European penitents are never expected to submit. These anomalies raise serious problems for a would-be non-racial Church, to which we must return later.

An even more perplexing question posed by the proximity of black and white congregations in the Copperbelt towns is how the available clergy of both races, and the other missionaries, should apportion the pastoral responsibility for both sides of the work. In all but the Dutch Reformed Church and Mission, the white clergy regard themselves as having a responsibility to both Europeans and Africans, and this in practice provides a fruitful ground for misunderstanding. We saw in the last chapter how far the missionaries in the Copperbelt live in a white *milieu*. Their friendships and recreations, their homes and gardens, their children's schools, their participation in civic responsibilities, as well as all the unconscious affinities of race and language, involve them closely in the European community. A good part of their work for the African congregations is administrative, and therefore does not bring them into pastoral contact with Africans. Whether their responsibilities to the African community are supposed to be full-time or part-time, missionaries are in fact spending a far smaller proportion of their working hours among Africans than most of them realize; and, of course, their off-duty time is spent almost always with Europeans. Most of the missionaries on the Copperbelt seem to be painfully aware of this tension, but that does not mitigate the misunderstanding which this situation creates in the minds of Africans. 'We cannot know,' said a schoolboy, 'if the missionaries really love us. They do not live with us.' 'The missionary made the people build the church but he does not help them or visit them.' 'Missionaries do not give themselves to Africans; they will not learn our language.' In one discussion group, however, the African treasurer of one Anglican church in a Mine compound defended their missionary because the responsibility for African and European congregations in two towns was far too great for one man. Their numerical superiority is certainly one of the reasons why the Roman Catholic priests have won such a reputation for pastoral work in the African community. One headmaster at Nchanga told us that the most popular church among the children of the school was the Roman Catholic, 'because of the efforts of the priest. No missionary or African minister visits the school except the Roman Catholic priest, who comes in three or four days a week. His religious instruction class is very popular and he has sweets for the children.' The welfare worker in Kansuswa commented:

> 'Father X used to visit African homes. Father Y is the best example, very free with Christians, playing with the children, carrying them on his back. Father Z came and had meals with me sometimes when I was in Kitwe. Many of the priests do that. But the modern Fathers are a bit proud and don't want to mix with Africans. We are very keen to note that and comment on it.'

What makes it so hard for African Christians in the Copperbelt to understand the position of the European clergy is that they cling to the picture of the missionary as they remember him in the rural districts.

> 'At home,' said one young man, 'the missionary seemed to spend his time trying to help us Africans. He looked after the schools and visited sick people and helped in the church. If we were in trouble or needed some money for a journey we could go to him. But when I came here I found the missionary is not like that. He is very busy with the European church. Only he sometimes comes to preach in our church. But he does not know us or visit us, and if we go to him for help we feel that is not his job. It would be better to tell us that there are no missionaries in the Copperbelt, but only sometimes a minister from the European church helps us by taking a service. Then we would understand and would not be disappointed. But because they still call themselves missionaries, we are confused and we say we have been deceived and Christianity is not true.'

This view is linked also with the idealization of the rural past which naturally takes place in the Copperbelt. 'The missionaries in the village are good;' wrote a schoolboy who may have lived all his days on the Copperbelt, 'they know their people; but not so here.' Adults look back to the 'Golden Age' of good relationships. 'When I was a schoolboy,' said a headmaster, 'we would very often see the missionary round the villages with medicine and gramophone to entertain the people. People had great faith in the missionary, but as time went on things changed.' And a minister who had worked as a pioneer missionary's colleague at a rural station added: 'He was well known. Most of the time he was out, and when he came in he had to deal with all the problems that were waiting for him. They were more popular with the people then, if I compare with the present time.' Continually judged by that unfair comparison, it is not surprising that sometimes a missionary finds the tension too great. The same church treasurer who had defended his overworked missionary told, on another occasion, how in a meeting of the African church council 'the missionary had so many questions put to him that he said finally. "I am not really your priest; I am paid by the Europeans."' 'Such things', he commented, 'bring about bad feelings among Africans, because they expect the missionary to show by example that he really is there for them.'

Such bad feeling is exacerbated, in this multi-racial society, by the dilemma which so often confronts the white pastor when, as already quoted from Godfrey and Monica Wilson's book, he 'is forced into behaviour which half his congregation finds immoral'. So again we heard missionaries bitterly censured for failing to override the convention of segregation in their own homes. 'Sometimes missionaries show themselves to be loving at church, but if one invites you to his house and at the same time has European guests, he puts a chair for you outside until the Europeans have gone.' 'When he has called the African minister to discuss their work, he keeps him standing on the verandah.' As we have seen, such complaints may reflect innocent behaviour misconstrued, but, as most missionaries would be the first to allow, not always.

Despair at the intractability of these various problems and frustration over the failure of the multi-racial church to demonstrate a real fellowship of all believers is leading some African Christians towards deciding that they would fare better on their own as an all-African church. The existence of the AME Church and of various African sects raises the question continuously, and the members of these bodies are proud of their status. 'Our Church belongs to the Africans;' wrote one child, 'we do not pray with Europeans.' So in the missionary churches the idea is growing that African Christians must work out their own salvation, though it is at present little more than an emotional reaction. 'We do not mind the failure of the missionary; it is not he that can save us.' In their moments of impatience African ministers voice the same sentiments: 'The members of the Church of Central Africa want an all-African church.' 'It would be better if all missionaries left the Church of Central Africa in Rhodesia and we could have the funds that are spent on them instead.'

This tendency, however, should not be too lightly dismissed. Educated African Christians are seriously debating the pros and cons of separate development in the Church, and the need for reducing the Western externals of the faith. A pointer is that in more than one group we found the use of European baptismal names being questioned. One church register showed a definite drop in attendance on the days when a missionary was due to preach and we were assured that this occurred in other denominations also. The only exception to this was the Dutch Reformed Church. 'Catholics prefer to get confession from African rather than European priests.' 'Many Africans want to keep the spirit of being a Christian, but they don't want to go to church to listen to a white man.' One factor in this preference is that the white missionary is on some occasions an embarrassment when he visits African Christians who live in a strongly anti-European *milieu*. 'People want to know what the European has come about. You are suspected of being an informer.' The missionary churches are therefore open to an imputation which the all-African churches do not have to bear. This probably lies behind the complaint of a school child about his local church: 'It is bad that a missionary is the head of the church, he makes people look foolish.'

Is it possible, in view of all these things, that the other missionary churches would be wiser to accept the principle of separate development on which the Dutch Reformed Church bases its mission? This is not a question which can be given a quick answer. Here are facts, for example, which have first to be faced.

Experience on the Copperbelt suggests that missionaries may never become as completely committed to the African community as they should be until a clear distinction is made between those who are missionaries to the African townships and those who are chaplains to the white community.

Worship in the African congregations will never be more than a poor imitation of Western modes of expression until African Christians feel free to introduce music, ritual and forms of prayer in their own idiom, as some of the break-away sects are doing; but it can be argued that they will be inhibited from doing this as long as they have to 'keep their end up' in a multi-racial church.

Fifteen bishops of African race sat in the last Lambeth Conference, yet not one of them came from South or Central Africa; does this mean that the so-called multi-racial church always frustrates and delays the emergence of African leadership?

Economically, we are bound to doubt whether it is right for the sake of a unitary constitution to saddle the African Christian community with forms of ministry, machinery of government and other ready-made institutions which Europeans feel to be necessary but which the African congregations can neither manage nor afford. In such cases either the African side of the Church becomes permanently dependent upon its

European benefactors or, in the name of self-support, the Church as a whole is involved in a denial of charity.

Christians in China, and in some of the other 'younger churches', have testified in the last few years to the spiritual maturity which has come to them only through being compelled to stand alone. Confronted with outside decisions and no longer having Western guidance as a substitute for their conscience, they have been thrown back upon the Bible and upon the Holy Spirit in the Church and, for the first time, made their own discoveries of God. Can we expect any comparable maturing among African Christians in Northern Rhodesia as long as they are constitutionally yoked together with the more traditional, more wealthy and more dominant European congregations?

Sociologically, it is certain that until the Christian Church has taken hold at the cardinal points in the cultural pattern of an African people, it is bound to remain a foreign and unrooted institution, an easy prey awaiting the advent of Islam. So we are driven to ask whether a Church, as an ecclesiastical entity, can 'belong' to an African society while it is so evidently a part of the Western way of life.

Psychologically and pastorally, it is necessary to recognize that the religious life, prayer and worship of a people are the vehicle through which they lift up to God their communal aspiration and suffering. As the cry of the Negro people against their slavery was breathed into their spirituals, so the protest of the Bantu in South Africa finds both expression and comfort in their vernacular hymns. Creative religious experience must tap the subliminal level of consciousness, where lie those fears and grievances, those memories and desires, the sharing of which makes a people one. If the integration of two races in one church means that those deep emotions, which ought to be voiced and offered and purged in prayer, have to be left in the church porch, while worshippers allow themselves only the lowest common denominator of passion in the polite deference of a multi-racial club, that church will die, either from the boredom of mediocrity or because all its most vital members, black and white, have drifted into the sects.

These are solid arguments; so weighty that for several months during the study the writer was inclined to conclude that the separate-development policy of the Dutch Reformed Church and Mission was justified, though personally persuaded that in practising it they were guilty of T. S. Eliot's

> 'greatest treason:
> 'To do the right deed for the wrong reason.'

In the end, however, we came jointly to the conviction that the Church in Northern Rhodesia must embrace all its members, whatever their race, in one Body under one constitution. But in asserting this we must emphasize that the drawbacks and difficulties are so great that they can only be overcome by a much more radical and far-reaching unity and fellowship between African and European Christians than has been demonstrated hitherto. It is difficult to say these things without their sounding like a sermon. We would set it down as a conclusion reached objectively from our study of the situation that unless the Church can set about realizing immediately this far more radical fellowship, it would be more honest and prudent to establish quite separate African and European church structures, each autonomous and independent, with missionaries put at the disposal of the African Church, as they are elsewhere in the continent. The present state of cautious semi-commitment can only accelerate the disillusionment and falling away of African adherents from the Church. The words of a distinguished Roman Catholic are pertinent for all the denominations:

> 'Amid all the complex questions which face us in Africa today, nothing short of undiluted Christianity will save the day. If we water it down with selfish or expedient heresies or half-truths, we shall lose Africa—for God and for democracy.'

If the Church in Northern Rhodesia as a whole is to commit itself to being an actual and visible fellowship of black and white Christians, it will need to be securely convinced of its reasons for doing so. The fundamental grounds for choosing the way of integration rather than of separate development are twofold. The first is theological, and rests simply on the belief that the Church is *de facto* not a man-made institution but a new humanity in Christ Jesus, in whom the old dispensation is superseded and old distinctions 'cannot be'.[15] This, however, is not the place to argue the fundamental tenets of Christianity.

The second reason is both theological and sociological, and involves a refutation of the argument advanced on page 196, and a rethinking of much that has been said in missionary circles about 'the indigenous church'. We should on no account abandon that insight which the modern ecumenical movement has given into the particularity of the Church's relatedness to each local society in which it stands. But a situation such as the Copperbelt reveals that it is inadequate and misleading to describe that particularity in terms of *volksturm*, or of rootedness in a cultural soil, Such a metaphor, in the first place, conceals the fact that the culture of most societies at the present time is fluid, indeterminate and increasingly cosmopolitan. Moreover, the Church also, for all its given-ness, is always in a state of becoming; it lives by obedience not to a definitive norm but to the existential call of God. Therefore the relatedness of the Church to any society does not consist essentially of *roots* going down into the particular soil, but of obedient *response* to the particular situation.

The situation in the Copperbelt does not in fact present two separate traditional cultures existing in parallel but one emergent cosmopolitan society in which members of two races are inextricably inter-related in a variety of ways. If a whole Church is to respond to this total situation, it can do so only as a single fellowship embracing both races.

But as soon as the Church wholeheartedly attempts to realize this single fellowship in practice, it quickly runs into some very considerable difficulties. The most important of these seem to fall under five distinct heads: how can such a Church embody a genuine oneness in its organization, in its worship, in its discipline, in its finances, and in its ministry?

The Problem of Organization. This is in some ways the most obvious problem and the easiest to solve, and the various denominations have gone further towards racial integration in this sphere than in any other. There have been some considerable achievements, the importance of which lie not so much in the value of ecclesiastical constitutions, as such, as in the fact that these commit a Church to further action at a more local and personal level.

The Roman Catholic Church naturally claims to be one and the same Church for all, irrespective of race. Her Mass is celebrated without variation of ritual or language in every church. Her finances are entirely centralized so that in theory the buildings, the priests' stipends and other expenses are met, as need arises, from a common fund. Through her universal use of the Confessional all are submitted to virtually the same discipline. Because of her very prolonged seminarial training and her celibate priesthood, her African priests enjoy a status and a standard of living far closer to their white colleagues than can be found in any other denomination. In all this, she has an immense advantage over other churches. Yet because of the strictly hierarchical character of her government this enviable state of affairs cannot be said to be due to the personal choice of her adherents. In the few areas where such choice might be exercised there does not seem to be any greater fellowship between black and white Christians than in other denominations.

The Anglican Church also enjoys the fruits of a polity that is not based mainly on the democratic principle. But since the establishment of her synod in 1948-9 the clergy and laity, both African and European, have had a more responsible share in making decisions. The area of moral choice in the matter of race relations is therefore much wider for the rank and file of the Anglican Church and the problem of organization more real. At the congregational level the pastoral work among Africans on the Copperbelt is organized in what are still called 'mission-districts' (a term borrowed from the rural set-up), whereas the unit of European church life is called a parish. The use of these terms suggests that the Rector of the European parish is also Missionary-in-Charge of the mission-district, even when there is an African priest there; in fact, however, these mission-districts on the Copperbelt which have an African priest are practically parishes in their own right. Both the parish and the mission-district have their elected church council, and each sends its lay delegates to the diocesan synod. This means that, above the congregational level, the governmental system of the Anglican Church is racially integrated, and even at the congregational level there is nothing constitutionally to prevent, for example, an African being elected to the parochial church council of a European parish. At Luanshya the African priest regularly attends the meetings of the European church council as an *ex officio* member. From time to time there have been valuable joint meetings of the two church councils in one or two places, and recently at Chingola the Anglicans have made a successful experiment with a small joint executive committee drawn from the two councils. This seems a particularly promising development in view of the fact that, presumably, as soon as there are one or two more African priests available, the mission districts on the Copperbelt will be turned into fully fledged parishes. Such a step seems to be necessary in order to give the African priests the same standing and responsibility as their European colleagues; but it could easily be a step in the wrong direction, closing for good the opportunities for co-operation and for making a witness on this issue, unless there were a deliberate effort to provide a more substantial link between the African and the English-speaking parishes than normally exists between neighbouring parishes in one town.

It is well known that the Dutch Reformed Church maintains constitutional separation between itself as a white Church and its Mission. The latter is in process of being developed into an independent Bantu Reformed Church, with its own organization from top to bottom, as has happened in the Union of South Africa. There are, however, two important bridges between the two bodies, though they only carry one-way traffic. A number of delegates of the white Church—not missionaries but ordinary lay members—sit in the presbytery of the Mission Church as assessors and advisers, while at the congregational level the same is done in the African church session. A greater number of ordinary white church members of the Dutch Reformed Church show a responsible participation in the church life of their African fellow-Christians than can be found in any other denomination.

The Church of Central Africa in Rhodesia and the European Free Church Council were constitutionally separate bodies until 1958. In order to understand the difficulties of their growth towards integration it is necessary only to remember the nature of the presbytery in the polity of the Church of Scotland. Hitherto congregations of Scottish nationals overseas have been organized under an Overseas Presbytery, thereby giving them representation in the General Assembly. This has meant that European congregations have not been linked with the presbytery of the Church of Central Africa in Rhodesia which governed the African congregations. The first step towards integration was taken in 1951, when it was proposed that a Liaison Committee should be formed on the Copperbelt to provide a link between the Copperbelt District Church Council of the Church of Central Africa in Rhodesia, the Central Free Church Council of the European congregations, and the Methodist Synod. After further negotiation they finally created, by the act of union in 1958, the United Church of Central Africa in Rhodesia, with provision eventually for four inter-racial presbyteries under one Central Synod. Below presbytery level there are still separate African and European District Church Councils in the Copperbelt, and at the congregational level separate church sessions, corresponding to the separate church councils of the Anglicans.

There were at least as many misgivings on the African as on the European side in the negotiation that preceded this act of union, and the reasons for these are revealing. First there were fears that reflected the political tensions. The African National Congress was suspicious because of its distrust of any inter-racial co-operation. We were told of one candidate for the ministry, who was also closely connected with the Congress in Chingola, who almost gave up his vocation when he heard of the proposed integration. Others said they disliked it because it seemed like 'partnership' in the Church. The best African church leaders saw that they must disregard these grounds for objection but it is important to remember that this was in the background of their discussions.

Some African ministers expressed the fear that integration would inhibit African leadership in the Church. 'In a single Church Council Africans will feel that they cannot make a good contribution among Europeans who are doctors and lawyers.' They also foresaw difficulties in requiring a multi-racial Consistory and District Church Council to handle with sufficient understanding many of the pastoral problems that would be referred from the separate African and European congregations. On these grounds the members of the African District Church Council had firmly resisted being merged in a multi-racial District Council; yet after the act of union Africans frequently complained that integration had stopped short of the District Church Councils and Consistories! Such are the complexities of the search for unity.

Others objected that the act of union would be interpreted by African church members as initiating greater changes than the Europeans intended that it should, and so would lead to greater disillusionment. 'Africans will assume that the act of union means they can go freely to the European churches, but this will destroy fellowship instead of promoting it, because the Europeans will feel uncomfortable and some will walk out.' An African minister told us that immediately after the act of union one of his lay preachers had said to him, 'Now can I go to the European church and preach through an interpreter?' This minister also expressed the criticism that there had not been enough preliminary consultation between the lay members of the African and European congregations. 'It was talked out by the ministers and then they came together saying that their people agreed, but that was not really the case; so the act of union was dangerous.'

The strongest objection, therefore, was that the act of union was too much a piece of top level organization that would induce complacency without bringing about much change in practice at the congregational level. Africans appear to have less faith than Europeans in the value of writing a principle into a constitution either in the political or the ecclesiastical field; they are more concerned with the realities of everyday practice. 'Now the act of union is a fact everything depends on how much difference it makes in practice. Europeans despise us; will they now think of us as people?' One African minister said, 'I cannot see the point of an act of union in a church which is already one; it is like making a fuss about the marriage of two people who have lived together for years. The need is not for an act of union, but for making the oneness which already exists into a reality.' The concern of a growing number of European church members to make the union real in practice gives good grounds for hoping that these African misgivings may be dissipated. But there is no doubt that, in all the Churches, the need to realize a truer fellowship between races at the congregational level is the most urgent of all tasks. As one school-teacher said, 'I am sure that often a black and a white member of the same church meet on the job but each has no idea whether the other is a Christian or not.'

The Problem of Joint Worship. The last remark shows how any Church which commits itself to the principles that have been accepted by the Roman Catholic and the Anglican Churches and by the UCCAR must inescapably come to terms with the need to express a common fellowship in Christ through acts of worship in which Christians of both races share together. We found several of the African church leaders were sympathetically aware of how hard it is for white Christians, living in the midst of racialist attitudes, to overcome the prejudices of their society; yet they all agreed that the Church cannot compromise over this issue and remain true to its Gospel. A headmaster said, 'The European minister must teach them the truth. It is better for them to go away from the Church knowing that they cannot accept the truth than to remain in it imagining that they have accepted the Gospel when actually they have not.'

It is generally recognized on both sides that for reasons of language and custom there are bound to be separate English-speaking and vernacular-speaking services. The conduct of worship, the content and presentation of the preaching should be adapted to the capabilities and background of the congregation. One Anglican headmaster with an excellent command of English was honest enough to say, 'I do not think I would enjoy having my services always in English. Besides, our African women come to church with their babies, but if they were mixed up in one congregation with Europeans who don't have babies there would be a lot of interference.' He did not specify who would interfere with whom! Yet, while separate services may be accepted as the norm, there remain two aspects of the problem which have to be taken into account: the needs of the educated African Christian, and the call of the situation for a distinctive witness on the part of the whole Church.

There are already many, and there will be increasingly more, Africans who by virtue of their education and experience are intellectually and aesthetically more at home in what has been, but is no longer, an exclusively white world than they are among the simpler people of their own race. If such men are prevented from finding their spiritual home in the English-speaking congregation and its fellowship, then the pretension of being a multi-racial church falls to the ground. It is argued that such men are needed as leaders in the African Church. To this one would reply, first, that constitutionally there is no 'African Church', there are only vernacular-speaking congregations; secondly, that if the African who is at home in the English-speaking world ought to help and guide the vernacular congregations, so also should the European Christian. Both of them have, as it were, a missionary and fraternal responsibility towards these fellow-Christians. Though the educated African by virtue of his race has greater obligations to his own people, nevertheless when he goes to worship with them and to lead their church life, he is in fact going forth and going down, just as the white Christian would be doing, and he therefore needs the support and sympathy of the English-speaking congregation. To insist that such men should be relegated to some specially arranged English-speaking services in the 'African' churches is an unjustifiable evasion of the issue.

There remains the call to the Church to offer the kind of witness to society which inter-racial worship epitomizes. Precisely because this is so often the stumbling block to white Christians, the Church must make its stand at this point without compromise. The paramountcy of such witness in this particular society has often to be allowed to override other considerations, as will be seen in connection with church discipline. Several groups of African Christian leaders independently offered a suggestion which appealed to us as eminently practical—namely, that a vernacular-speaking congregation should invite the English-speaking congregation to send a dozen chosen representatives to attend their service one Sunday morning, and then to meet their minister and elders in order to get to know them and learn how their church activities were organized and what problems confronted them. On the following Sunday the European delegation should be given an opportunity of reporting to their own congregation on what they had seen. After a short time the African congregation should be invited to send a similar group on a return visit. Such interchanges might eventually lead to a regular combined service, monthly or at less frequent intervals, to be held alternately in the 'African' and the 'European' church, as a deliberate act of witness and fellowship.

Even in the worship of the separate congregations European and African Christians ought to be made aware constantly that they are part of a wider whole. Reference has already been made to the need of every people to bring into their worship their deepest fears and longings and the difficulty that this creates in a Church which embraces two groups whose aspirations are different or even opposed. The problem can only be overcome through a mutual sympathy which expresses itself in intercession. The leading of intercessions is an educative as well as a devotional act, and prayer for some aspect of the need of the other race should be a regular feature in the services of a multi-racial Church. Those denominations in particular which follow traditional liturgical forms need to examine them critically with this in mind. The African child's complaint that 'the missionaries pray for the Queen but not for Chief Chitimukulu' raises questions which cannot be brushed aside.

The Problem of Discipline. At the time of our study the only Christian body which was applying exactly the same forms of church discipline to its members irrespective of race was the Salvation Army. One of the questions posed by African ministers in the negotiations that preceded the integration of the Free Church Council and the Church of Central Africa in Rhodesia was, 'Will European and African church members be included under the same discipline?' In the event the answer has been, 'Not exactly'. There are separate African and European consistories, and hitherto African congregations have accepted a rule of total abstinence, for example, which obviously could not be imposed on European Free Churchmen. The Anglican Church has been operating in its African congregations an exacting form of public penance which could not easily be applied to Europeans, and its baptismal regulations were a good deal more stringent in the case of Africans.

These apparent inequalities arise from the difference which *de facto* exists between a convert Church and a Church many generations old, and the combination of these two in a multi-racial society is bound to produce such tensions. In essence the problem derives from the fact that non-Roman missions tend to regard the convert Churches as 'the gathered community', the *corpus Christi*, drawn out of the surrounding pagan society, while still treating the whole European community as a *corpus Christianum*, a Christianized society, just as is done in Great Britain. There is, of course, a certain practical justification for these attitudes, though they are hardly defensible theologically.

As the Church develops a closer integration of its European and African congregations, so it moves towards a uniform discipline. For example, the Anglican Bishop of Northern Rhodesia has informed us that since his arrival in 1952 he has been trying to bring the position of the two races closer together in ecclesiastical discipline, as in other ways. The baptismal regulations have been made stricter for Europeans and lighter for Africans, so that now they are very similar, and for the past two years the same form of application for Infant Baptism has been used for both races. Marriage discipline with regard to admission to Holy Communion is identical for both races. In most country districts the catechumens are still dismissed at the traditional point in the Eucharist in African congregations, but this is no longer done in the towns. The use of public penance is much more rare and in these days is reserved for cases of gross scandal among African churchmen. Throughout the Province of Central Africa the lay and the clerical disciplinary courts are the same for Europeans and Africans. The Bishop, however, states that many of these changes have been forced upon them by the urgent necessity of making a witness in the racial situation and were not made because they were really considered best for the African Christians. He points out that in most new Christian communities anywhere in the world, the Church in its wisdom has imposed a stricter discipline than is needed after several generations, and in the Anglican Church in Rhodesia every suggestion for relaxing the disciplines has met with strenuous opposition from the African priests and certain laymen.

Sooner or later, as the Church develops a homogenous discipline, the thorny question of the Marriage Ordinance is bound to be raised. At present the Administration in Northern Rhodesia recognizes only marriage by tribal law and custom in the case of Africans; the Marriage Ordinance which applies the English civil laws of marriage and divorce is reserved for non-Africans only. Ecclesiastical marriage has no legal validity on its own account but must be supported by civil marriage under the Ordinance in the case of Europeans or, in the case of Africans, by tribal customary marriage. The latter institution, however, has been seriously undermined by the mingling of tribes and the breakdown of old sanctions on the Copperbelt, and naturally the multi-racial Church would like to enable those African members who are married by its rites to enter into a more stable contract than the present practice of the law offers them. This raises such complex issues that it requires a volume to itself, and it would be superficial to attempt to deal with the problem here. The writer feels competent only to offer for consideration one or two principles based on his own and others' experience elsewhere.

First, the matrimonial affairs of an African, as of a European, should be governed legally by the civil law to which he is subject, without reference to his religious beliefs or whether his marriage is blessed by a Church service or not. To seek to bring automatically all Christian Africans by virtue of their religion under a different code of *law* from that applied to other Africans is to court disaster. Secondly, however, in a plural society, it should be made possible for an African couple to make voluntary and responsible choice to opt out of their subordination to tribal marriage law and to enter into liability under the Marriage Ordinance. This, being a very serious undertaking, with consequences for others beside themselves, should not be permissible without certain safeguards. If they wish to marry in the first instance under the Ordinance, it would probably be wise to insist that the guardians of both the man and the girl, as well as they themselves, should formally assent to the step being taken. If a couple, already married by tribal customary law, wish to transfer into a contract under the Marriage Ordinance, they should probably be required to have lived happily together for at least five years before they are allowed to commit themselves in this way. Thirdly, the Church would be free under these conditions to rule, if it so decided, that only those who chose to contract under the Ordinance should have their marriage blessed by its rites; but experience in other parts of Africa suggests that it would be ill-advised, as well as theologically questionable, to do so.[16]

The Economic Problem. As the Church becomes increasingly one Church of the black and the white, the glaring discrepancies between the quality of the African and European church buildings and furnishings, and the standard of living of their ministers, will grow more conspicuous. The Church's dilemma consists in the choice between mutual charity and fellowship on the one hand and, on the other, the need to foster real responsibility and self-respect in the African congregations. In the circumstances of the Copperbelt at the present time, there is probably very little to be lost and a great deal to be gained by putting the emphasis on fellowship and mutuality between black and white. One step in this direction is to unify a Church's funds, including the contribution of the Missionary Society, or Societies, under a single board of finance which can disburse all salaries and all maintenance grants according to an agreed scheme. But over and above such centralization there remains a great scope at the congregational level for European Christians to express their concern for the African side of their Church. In all such ventures the giving of funds is of far less value than the personal contact and interest provided when a party of white Christians goes round to consult with Africans on the needs of their congregation and to work with them on some project. The question of ministerial salaries raises a massive problem not peculiar to the Copperbelt nor to the mission-field. One of the great advantages of the Religious Orders, either Roman Catholic or Anglican, is that they do provide at least an enclave within which a few Africans and Europeans can live and work as a team on a common standard. Where this is not possible, a sensitive and fraternal collaboration of the European minister with his African partner can alleviate many of the discrepancies; and some occasional gift, like an 'Easter offering', from the European congregation to their African minister would carry the special benison of a personal concern.

The Problem of Relationship between African and European Clergy. We have already seen the grave disadvantages of placing one missionary in charge of both European and African work in a town. In theory the arrangement should be a witness to the oneness of the Church but in practice such a man is so hard-pressed and belongs so much more to the white *milieu*, that it results only in deeper misunderstanding. It appears that the norm in a multi-racial Church should be an African and a European minister, responsible respectively for the African and the European congregations but co-operating in a deep and evident collaboration, with as much interchange as is feasible. The need to make this co-operation more real calls for advance along two particular lines: the training of African clergy better qualified to exercise their ministry in an urban and multi-racial setting, and the training of missionaries in the use of a vernacular. These are matters concerning which pious hopes are constantly being expressed, but which have proved extremely difficult to attain. Nevertheless, both are of such absolute urgency that only a deliberate plan resolutely put into operation will suffice.

But even when the Church is provided with an African and a European minister in every town in the Copperbelt, there will still be an important place for the additional missionary giving full-time service to African work. In the first place, such a man is a token and witness as a European totally given to the service of Africans. And secondly, there is still great pastoral scope for the European missionary in the African townships provided he is able to give his whole time to it. The Roman Catholic Church is demonstrating how the life of the African congregation can be strengthened through the regular visitations of a European priest, particularly in the schools. Conversations with African Christians revealed that, while for most of their spiritual needs they prefer the ministrations of a fellow-African, there are certain problems, especially those arising from their contacts with Europeans or European ways, which they would take to a white minister if it were possible. Many admit that the visit of a European may be an embarrassment to African Christians who are thereupon suspected of being informers or 'Capricornists'. But on further enquiry it was generally admitted that this state of affairs is due to the spasmodic, hit-and-run appearances of the part-time missionaries who cannot appear frequently enough to be known in the neighbourhood; the full-time workers, such as the Roman priests or the women workers of the non-Roman missions, quickly become familiar figures and cause little or no embarrassment by their visits.

The battle, therefore, at the moment must be for the unity in Christ Jesus to be made patently real in a Church in which there shall be neither Jew nor Greek, Scythian or barbarian, bondman or free. But after that battle has been thoroughly won the true problem of the multiracial Church will emerge more clearly, namely, how to maintain the diversity of the gifts, including the mysterious gifts of culture and temperament, under the one Spirit. It is a problem which the Church in Africa will evade at its peril; yet a Church which has not yet won the prior battle against discrimination is radically unfitted to tackle it. But those who are in the van of the fight for the oneness of all believers are thereby often less qualified to grasp the dimensions of the later problem. For the African and the European whose ground of meeting is the world-wide cosmopolitan culture of modern 'Western' education are prone to forget that only the *élite* of both their peoples will ever be at home in that *milieu;* but everywhere faith's Amen must be spoken in the vernacular. Moreover such Africans are too often aware of being representatives rather than leaders, so that they act towards others rather than towards God and his call to them. In the context of the present tensions, if one asserts that African people are different it is assumed that by difference one means inferiority. Yet in spite of that, it must be said; and the Church should champion as something most precious to its life both the strangeness and the validity of the African contribution. This will not be achieved by what are usually understood as joint activities, for unfortunately, in present circumstances, in any gathering in which Europeans number more than one third they exercise a majority influence and determine the methods of procedure. Somehow, within the unbroken mutuality of the one Church, means must be found to enable both European and African Christians to be obedient to their own insights and to make their own discoveries of God out of their own spiritual travail, in order to be able to offer to one another for the service of the one Lord the diversity of gifts with which the Holy Spirit has been enriching them.

NOTES

1. Shepperson and Price; *Independent African,* pp. 163f.
2. G. and M. Wilson, *The Analysis of Social Change,* CUP, 1945, p. 152.
3. Anthony H. Richmond, *The Colour Problem,* Penguin Books, 1955, p. 150.
4. Major H. K. McKee, Address to Royal African and Royal Empire Societies, 29 May, 1952. Cf. L. H. Gann, *The Birth of a Plural Society,* p. 180.
5. *Report of the Commission* [on] *Disturbances in the Copperbelt,* para. 193.
6. Cmd 8235 (1951), p. 21.
7. United Missions in the Copperbelt, 9th Annual Report, 1948-9.
8. Sir John Moffat in Northern Rhodesia Legislative Council, 29 July 1954.
9. *The Times,* 10 February 1954.
10. Circular from the Department of Native Affairs, Northern Rhodesia, 3 September 1954.
11. Dr C. L. van Doorn's Report. MS. held by the World Council of Churches Department on Church and Society (1958).
12. *Northern News,* 24 September 1958.
13. Philip Mason, *The Birth of a Dilemma,* OUP, 1958, p. 328.
14. An African Anglican priest receives £13 per month in the rural districts. Anglican salaries are higher for both European and African priests in Northern Rhodesia than in Southern Rhodesia or Nyasaland. In the UCCAR an African minister receives £11 10. 0 in towns, only £9 5. 0 in rural districts, and his education allowance is less (1958 figures).
15. Col. 3.11 (RV); Gal. 3.27-29; Rom. 2.11 and other references.
16. Letter from the Bishop of Masasi in *Tanganyika Standard,* 1.xi.1930; 'Christian Marriage in Nigeria' by S. H. Childs, *Africa* XVI, 1946, pp. 238-46; 'Marriage Ordinances for Africans' by Martin Parr, *Africa* XVII, 1947, pp. 1-7.

IV

SOME INDEPENDENT CHURCHES

Some Independent Churches

Mention has already been made of the difficulty of discovering the various Christian groups which live and work in an African Township like Nchanga (pp. 57ff). Members from the most diverse religious streams are caught in this big reservoir which may destroy their identity or on the other hand make them more conscious of their need to be alive in their faith and to propagate it if they want to keep it. For all of them, the Copperbelt is at the same time a threat and a challenge. The response to this may be either an anxious avoidance of all publicity, a tendency to introspection which is found even in the big, well-established mission churches, or an outgoing, fighting spirit which may give to a group a recognition by the public, and an influence out of proportion to its numbers. The investigators did not find it an easy task to discover all the groups in Nchanga, and even at Nsensema's village the investigation into the religious affiliation of every villager had to be left incomplete. An assessment of their numbers or even their comparative weight of influence is not possible on the available data. We have to restrict ourselves to a description of those with whom we came into contact, and the limitations of this study should not be forgotten when conclusions are made about the significance of these churches and their life in the Mine Township.

It is an onerous task to divide the Nchanga churches into groups and to choose those which are to represent their type in a more detailed description. Since the study was undertaken with the help of the Christian Council of Northern Rhodesia, it is perhaps advisable to distinguish between those which are members of that body and those which are not, or not as yet, connected with it, although the line cannot be sharply drawn and observed in every case. The term 'independent' in this section is meant to denote various 'outside' groups; it gives no indication as to their dogma, polity or importance—if one is inclined to pass such judgments at all.

The registration of all religious groups under the Societies' Ordinance, which became applicable to 'every association of ten or more persons whatever its nature or objects', provided up to 25 April 1959 the following list:

1. Spiritual Assembly of Bahais, Chingola.
2. Blackman's Presbyterian Church of Africa.
3. Roman Catholic Church.
4. African Methodist Episcopal Church.
5. Mohammedan Church.
6. African Reformed Church (DRC Mission), Chingola and Bancroft Branch.
7. South Africa General Mission, Chingola.
8. African Covenant Church, Chingola Branch.
9. Jehovah's Witnesses, Chingola Central Branch.
10. Jehovah's Witnesses, Chingola East Branch.
11. Jehovah's Witnesses, Chingola North Branch.
12. Christian Missions in Many Lands.
13. Anglican Church.
14. Seventh Day Adventists.
15. Last Church of God and His Christ.
16. The New Apostolic Church, Chingola.
17. The Assembly of God, Chingola.
18. The Christian Brethren, Chingola.
19. The United Church of Central Africa in Rhodesia.

The Free Church, Anglicans, Roman Catholics, African Methodist Episcopal, and African Reformed Church (DRC) and Mohammedans have 'churches'. Each of the others has a place where its adherents congregate, but these frequently change.

When comparing this list with that of the members of the Spiritual Round Table, we find two omissions in the registration: neither the Lumpa Church, the followers of the Prophetess Lenshina Mulenga, nor the small group of break-aways from the Roman Catholic Church, the *Bana ba Mutima* (Children of the Sacred Heart) had up to that date asked for official recognition.

The churches listed as numbers 4, 6, 7, 13 and 19 above are members of the Christian Council; No. 12 is closely affiliated, and, for example, on the African Education Advisory Board, represented through members of the Christian Council. For our purposes, these churches, together with the Roman Catholic Church, come under the heading of 'orthodox' churches. At the time of investigation, however, No. 4 was not yet a member of the Council, and thus stood on the dividing line.

During the study we made some kind of contact with nearly all of the independent or 'non-orthodox' groups, met their leaders at the sessions of the Spiritual Round Table or some of their members in a discussion group, attended their service or visited a family of their denomination. Some of these encounters were too brief to lead to any real knowledge of that church. We chose three for a detailed investigation; the opportunity they offered was good, they were representative of definite types of church life, and as such they were easily recognisable bright threads in the multi-patterned tapestry of religious life in the Mine African Township. These were (1) the African Methodist Episcopal Church (AME); (2) Jehovah's Witnesses, which are more frequently called the 'Watchtower' people (*Ba Citawala*), after the name of their church magazine; and (3) the Lumpa Church. The first is an all-African Church, the second a sect of non-African origin, and the third an African separatist movement.

9

The African Methodist Episcopal Church

AMONG all the churches with an entirely African membership which we met in Nchanga Mine African Township, the African Methodist Episcopal (AME) Church was the nearest to orthodoxy in our narrowly defined sense. It has already become a member of the Christian Council since our study was undertaken. In 1952 an application for membership was rejected because the training of its ministry did not meet the standard required by the churches who formed the Council.[1] With the approval of their American bishop, with whom they discussed this matter during his visit in 1957, they decided to apply again, since their old untrained ministers have nearly all retired and have been followed by younger ministers of higher educational standards and professional training. The youngest of their three ministers, whom we learned to know, was only twenty-seven years of age and had been educated at the Wilberforce Theological College in South Africa, after a full secondary education. The initiative and ecumenical thinking which he showed right at the start of his work in Nchanga (p. 104) promises that this first all-African church to enter the Christian Council of Northern Rhodesia may quickly prove itself to be a very valuable member indeed. During the village study the AME congregation at Chief Kazembe's township gave us a very friendly welcome, and understanding help in our investigations. Two of their ministers and the president of their 'Laymen's League' attended the final study conference. Both in the urban and the rural district there seemed to be an eagerness not only to be on friendly terms with the members of the 'orthodox' mission churches, but also really to co-operate with them and with their missionaries. This was remarkable at a time in which an all-African congregation might be tempted to exploit the widespread anti-white feeling. African church leaders of the UCCAR in the Lunda country said that in the past there had been friction, members of the

AME saying of the missionaries, 'They rule your church'; but they agreed with the impression of their district missionary that these were things of the past and that the relationship was now a harmonious one. The principal of the Kashinda Bible School for the training of African ministers and evangelists in the UCCAR must also have had a good relationship with AME congregations in the Bemba country when he wrote in a letter about a visit to an AME church: 'We met the Presiding Elder (i.e., the senior minister) of the Native Church (a term widely used for the AME in Northern Rhodesia) and he gave us the best sermon I have heard from an African.'[2]

This is not the place to go into the history of the African Methodist Episcopal Church. Its origin in the opposition to the colour bar practised in the Methodist church in America in 1787 made it attractive to South African independent church leaders, who decided in 1896 to seek affiliation with this American Negro Church.[3] Its membership spread rapidly in South Africa, and soon attracted Christians from Nyasaland and the Rhodesias working in the South, and others who looked there for help in their spiritual growing pains.[4] In the early days the General Superintendent of the South African branch of the AME, James M. Dwane, had an ambitious programme of mission work to spread into the north over the Zambezi and through the Rhodesias, with the aim of linking up with the ancient Christian Church in Ethiopia,[5] for which he formally asked Cecil Rhodes' permission. But the internal difficulties of the work in South Africa hindered this expansion, in spite of the interest and help given by the American mother church. The Northern Rhodesian ministers of the AME church date the beginning of their local church history from 1930, a time when the mutual exchange of mine-workers brought the peoples of Northern Rhodesia and South Africa into rapidly increasing contact. In 1933 the oldest of the three Northern Rhodesian ministers we met was ordained in Wilberforce[6] and went back to start work in the Abercorn district.

In the Lunda country around Kazembe's Township, the Presiding Elder of the AME Church was looking after 525 full members, ten of them living in Nsensema's village. With him worked two other ordained men and seven 'brothers'—evangelists with little training, whose work was largely done on a voluntary and part-time basis. The large church in the chief's village was rather dilapidated at the time of our visit, and the congregation had started to make bricks for a new building. The church had a mud platform across the east end, with a flight of steps on each side. From a low wooden rail along the front of the platform fell a strip of white cloth. A well-made cross hung on the wall behind the platform; a reading desk, several chairs for the clergy and benches for the choir stood on the platform. Below it in the centre was a table and a chair for the chief steward. Crimson bougainvilia was used for decorating the table, the main entrance and the poles up the aisle supporting the roof.

While the congregation entered and sat on the built-in mud benches, the men on the left facing the pulpit, the women with the children on the right, a vestry prayer was audible. Then the choir entered in single file, singing and swinging their bodies rhythmically, two men and four girls. They wore a short white stole and black mortar boards. Two clergymen followed them, wearing clerical collars and black gowns. The visiting preacher wore a grey flannel suit. They all took seats on the platform. The Introit is sung by the choir, 'Are you ready if Jesus calls you today?' After this, and all other choir items, the congregation clapped quietly.

The liturgy followed the order of service printed in the Bemba AME Hymnbook. After the hymn 'Holy, holy, holy, Lord God Almighty', the minister called a 'sister' to lead in prayer. All knelt and one of the members of the 'Women's Missionary Society', clad in a black dress and leopard-skin hat, made the customary request for open ears, and specially thanked God for the visitors (the research workers) whom he had sent, which made them realize that Black and White are God's children. Then the congregation exclaimed 'Amen' and other words of assent.

The choir sang again, the leader alone taking the melody: 'Wake up now!' The visiting pastor read the lesson, Mark 5.1-19.

Another minister read the second part of the liturgy, the Ten Commandments sung with responses ending in a short Antiphon, a verse of 'Nearer, my God, to Thee', followed by a shortened form of the Commandment from the New Testament and the *Gloria Patri* chanted. (This was not well known by the congregation.)

The Chief Steward announced the Quarterly Conference of the Kazembe District, and asked people to bring names of delegates. He reminded the congregation that every member had to collect £1 for the building of the new church and appealed especially to the women. The local minister followed him with an exhortation relating to their failure to water the bricks, which had resulted in much loss. He also appealed to them to finish the church before the rains began. The women began to exclaim and talk, and he silenced them. A woman wearing a leopard-skin hat brought a transfer letter. She was a member of a Copperbelt congregation but had come to visit her sick daughter. After these announcements he greeted us European visitors, telling his congregation who we were, 'Do not say that all Europeans hate all Bantu people. In Christ there is no hatred.'

The choir sang 'Jesus, beloved of my heart,' The leader swung his hands like a band leader, and an old woman in a leopard-skin hat, a healed leper, came out and did a shuffle dance in time with it.

Before the sermon began, some women with small children started to go out and the preacher admonished them: 'Stay here, mothers! Give me your eyes as well as your ears. Try to quieten the children.'

The sermon centred round the words, 'Go and tell your family and your friends what great things the Lord has done for you.' 'That madman knew little of Jesus, but are we not Christ's people? Answer me!' (Reply, 'Yes, we are Christians.') 'Are we not called to work for him?' ('Yes.') The preacher made the congregation repeat the verse, to learn it by heart. He finished, 'If we fail to do Christ's work, we are like the dead men, and a legion of devils will live in us; but we are healed.'

The second of the visiting ministers led the intercessory prayers, and the people brought their gifts while the hymn 'Revive Thy work, O Lord' was sung and re-sung. Coins were put into a wooden box on the front table; some women brought cassava and others flour which was poured into a bowl. One danced for a while after presenting her gift. The hymn was continued while the money was counted and the amount announced. The choir then sang alone and jived forward in single file, circling the table three times, joined by one girl from the front row (perhaps a choir member who had come late) and one old woman. Their offering was also announced before the minister led in a prayer of consecration. We were then asked to speak. The service ended with the sung Doxology.

The congregation consisted of fourteen men, forty-eight women with six young boys and ten small children, the two men and four girls in the choir, eight members of the 'Women's Missionary Society' in their uniforms of leopard-skin hat, black gown and broad white collars, and the three ministers.

The choir sang as the people left the church; outside small groups formed to discuss news and to organize work on the building site, and the women decided who was to visit certain people known to be sick.

While the minister of Kazembe's, in his office as Presiding Elder, was touring and collecting church funds in the northern part of the district, which includes the well-to-do fishermen of Lake Mweru, the junior minister of that province took his place in the chief's township and conducted the week-day class meeting. We saw him addressing a small group outside a house at Nsensema's village. He also visited the headman, with whom he seemed to be on friendly terms. When Nsensema spoke about the AME Church members he called them BaNative, the Native Church people, and this term was also occasionally heard in the Copperbelt. Their all-African character was certainly well known in both the rural and the urban districts. A fisherman at Kazembe's told us that his grandfather made him join the Roman Catholic Church, but that he found that in their religion the Roman Catholics were 'very different from us, very European'. He married a Roman Catholic girl but they did not have a church wedding. She is still attending that church, but he left it and joined the AME Church at Kazembe's, and when his business takes him to the Copperbelt he asks for a transfer letter and goes to worship in one of the AME Copperbelt congregations.

While the up-country work of the AME is the result of individual contacts with the South African work and of the missionary zeal of those individuals after they returned from South Africa or Southern Rhodesia to their tribal homes in Northern Rhodesia, the Copperbelt AME churches are the reservoir into which many small streams of very differing origins flow. The non-Bemba-speaking members are probably in the majority, since in all the services we recorded in the Copperbelt the sermons were preached in Nyanja (a language mainly spoken in Nyasaland), Sindebele or Sotho, and either interpreted or summarized in Bemba. The Order of Service and the hymns were translations of the Sotho and Sindebele versions of the American originals. The choir showed a preference for Negro spirituals, and we did not come across any really indigenous hymns. Even the customary dancing of the women when they brought their offerings was done to European tunes, accompanied by rhythmic clapping and stamping. The members of the Nchanga congregation used their own languages in praying and singing. The choir sang occasionally in English, and many of the congregation spoke English with ease and fluency, and used it among themselves. It is interesting, however, that some of them stressed the fact that they had joined the AME congregation in Nchanga because the minister understood their southern languages. One of their most respected members said, 'I am really a Primitive Methodist. I was baptized when I was still fairly small, attending the Methodists' school in the home reserve. When I came here, I found a home in the AME church, and my wife, who used to belong to the Salvation Army Mission, goes with me simply because the minister can speak Sindebele. There is one other man of our tribe here and he is also in that church.' And, 'Here my spirit is dead because of the language difficulties. I tried preaching here with my wife but the people did not hear me. My AME minister helped me, but I was understood only by his Southern Rhodesian people and people from Bechuanaland. My wife used to preach in Bulawayo three times a week, on Tuesday, Friday and Saturday (in open-air meetings); she is now very unsatisfied.'

It was not possible to find out how many tribes were represented in the Nchanga AME church and what ratio existed between those of northern and of southern origin. The tension which was certainly unavoidable in a group of such a nature was only just noticeable and the unifying tendencies much more strongly felt. The two main forces working towards the assimilation of church members might be the well-established system of conferences on various levels above the congregations, and the drive for education, especially for higher education of the clergy. The district Quarterly Conferences were organized as meetings for all elders, ministers and evangelists. Three days of training, Bible study and discussions, as well as sessions on church busines were followed by a Sunday rally to which all the members of the congregations represented were invited. The 1958 Annual Conference was planned to bring together delegates from Northern Rhodesia and Nyasaland. This would be a most important event for all AME Churches, because fourteen candidates were to be presented for ordination. In 1957 the bishop for the Federation, Tanganyika and Portuguese East Africa ordained four ministers and three ministerial deacons at the Annual Conference.

On the local level the congregation is divided into Sunday school, Youth Work, the 'Women's Missionary Society' (which is essentially just the women's meeting of the church), and the Laymen's League (which seems to be the male counterpart of the women's meeting). All these organizations send their voluntary workers as delegates to the conferences, where they are trained, and attendance at several conferences is the precondition for holding any office in the congregation; it is also seen as part of the initial training for the ministry.

The ministers and the evangelists are responsible for the Sunday school work in their congregations. At Kazembe's the minister told us that he made up Sunday school lessons from American material, but he found these too difficult for the lay preacher-evangelists, and he told us that they had formally asked the young Copperbelt minister to write Sunday school material in Bemba for them. This young man had already started to reorganize the Sunday school work in the Copperbelt; he had a real concern not only for the children of his own congregation but also for the many who roamed in the compound every Sunday morning, whom he hoped to attract with his new Sunday School plans.

The 'Women's Missionary Society' was, as far as we could see, mainly concerned with the people of their own church. They looked after the sick and visited the bereaved and, since both congregations had just started building a new church, were very busy collecting money and helping with the labour in making bricks. In both places the minister's wife was the leader of the Women's Missionary Society.

The president of the Laymen's League, who was also responsible for the Youth Work of the African Methodist Episcopal Church in Northern Rhodesia, was a successful business man from Southern Rhodesia who lived near the Copperbelt in Ndola.

Unfortunately we missed the Quarterly Conference of the Copperbelt AME congregations, which was held in the nearby Lamba tribal area, by getting lost in the bush on our way. It is therefore difficult to assess what is the role of the lay member at such a meeting; does he participate in the government of the church, in the forming of policy, or does he mainly look for guidance, for further instruction in his faith as well as in his duties in everyday life as a member of his denomination? The ministers told us that delegates were appointed by their congregations but had on the other hand to find their own fares and hospitality fees. The layman who is keen to take an active part in the life of the church has to prove himself on the local level to be sent as a delegate, 'and those chosen for ordination have to prove themselves for a long time and attend several conferences before they are examined by a bishop.'

> 'A District Conference proposes men for the ministry. Those educated to at least Standard VI, it can send to Wilberforce for training, others it can refer to the Annual Conference. This has a Board of seven Examiners, including four elders or ministers. The candidate has to take an Admission examination, and in succeeding years a first, second, third and fourth year examination. These are based on prescribed books, and also on a report on the practical work done in the church. If he passes all five examinations, he will be ordained at the Annual Conference by a bishop supported by elders.
>
> 'The bishop, at the Annual Conference, assigns all ministers, having considered their individual requests and the recommendations of the Presiding Elders.'

This system of interaction by local congregations and the conferences drawn from wider areas produces many evangelists, or 'brothers' as they are officially called in the AME, and leads the most outstanding among them to the ordained ministry. The 'Presiding Elder' of the Lunda country told us that he worked for several years as a 'brother' before a visiting bishop from America examined him at a conference and sent him to study under the bishop of South Africa then appointed for Rhodesia. In 1951 he passed a final examination and was ordained at an Annual Conference.

This training-in-service was a definite step away from the self-appointed ministry of the old days—the men who had only very loose connections with the South African branch of the church whose servants they claimed to be. One cannot but admire the devotion and the discipline of men who, under modern conditions, have to earn their living and find time and strength to do the voluntary practical and academic work in preparation for their ordination as well. Yet, as the numbers show, the mounting difficulties have not broken their backs.

Right from the start the American mother church was concerned about the education of African mission church members, and especially the ministers who grow out of the new congregations, actively helping to establish firm links with their South African and Southern Rhodesian training schemes. The first ordained minister who was a Northern Rhodesian trained at Wilberforce reported that some mission schools in the Abercorn district, where he had collected his first congregation, refused to take the children of AME parents. He received $3,500 from the General Conference in America for African educational work. Northern Rhodesia had become a proper mission field and was visited by American church officials. One of these took a fancy to a bright schoolboy, the son of an AME school councillor and his wife, who was one of the first AME converts in the Northern Province of Rhodesia. The visitor did not take the boy with him to America but arranged that he should go for further education to Bulawayo in Southern Rhodesia, and finally to Wilberforce. After an initial training for social welfare work he offered himself for the ministry, read the three years' theological course at Wilberforce, and did one year of practical work in the congregations of Sophiatown and Port Elizabeth. Northern Rhodesian delegates appealed to the bishop because of an acute shortage of pastors in the Copperbelt, and the circle was completed: the young minister found himself charged with the work in an industrial situation in his home country, for which his South African training and experiences had prepared him well.

The AME school work ran into difficulties which have brought it, at least for a time, to a stop. The first minister founded a school at Chirwa near Abercorn, and employed two teachers who worked under his supervision. When he was transferred, his successor from South Africa did not get on well with the Rhodesian teachers, and the expenses proved to be a heavy burden for the small, young church in one of the poorer parts of the country. They failed to maintain the regular payment of the teachers' salaries and other running costs, and the school closed down. The children found places in several mission schools of another denomination, and in the meantime local authorities as well as the Missions started to manage schools. But the plan to re-open Chirwa School and take part in the much-needed expansion of African education in Northern Rhodesia was still in the minds of several members of the AME Church who spoke to us. Some of the immigrants from the South had left their children behind when they went to work in the Copperbelt. 'Education starts earlier in Southern Rhodesia, with crèche and kindergarten. My daughter in Standard I speaks good English, and the boy in Standard VI, when he came here in the holidays, was far in advance of the local Standard VI boys. Religious education is not well taught, and the school-children do not go to church or Sunday School regularly. Last year not one boy in the township school got 50 per cent in Religious Knowledge in the Standard VI examinations,' said one of the influential older men of the AME congregation in Nchanga. Even if his impressions of the local school were superficial and not based on more than hearsay, his concern for a good all-round education for his children is typical of the responsible Christian parenthood in the AME Church. It seems unlikely that they will be able to start their own schools in the near future, since most Copperbelt congregations have yet to build churches, or renew their old inadequate buildings, and that is a heavy commitment under urban building regulations, even if the help promised by their bishop is forthcoming from the General Conference in America. Nchanga AME congregation had started their church building under an African contractor, with voluntary help from men who had some knowledge of professional building work, and the organization of it put a great amount of work on the minister and the local treasurer, who had to be sure that the expenses for building materials could be met, as well as the salary of the minister. There is no fixed scale for the latter, and a minister told us that they intended to talk to the bishop at their next conference about the difficulties arising from the fact that each minister depended entirely on the voluntary giving of his congregation. Financial help from America was only used for church buildings and the bishop's salary and transport.

The present stages of development of the AME Church in Northern Rhodesia show definite trends towards conformity with the Protestant mission churches, and a certain degree of clericalism versus congregationalism which is perhaps unavoidable in the context of growing specialization in an urban industrial community. One can only hope that the church leaders will realise that they have, in their traditional strong participation of 'lay' members at all levels of the work of the church, a precious heritage and an advantage over many numerically stronger churches. The unusual lack of self-centredness, in spite of all the struggle to survive and grow, the willingness to think in ecumenical rather than parochial terms, the spirit of co-operation with other churches (pp. 216f), are all signs of grace which should be gratefully recognized in a church which rose out of one of the great problems Christians have not yet solved, the witness to unity in all diversity. An AME minister said in a sermon, 'It is not the church but only your faith which can save you.'

The link of the Northern Rhodesian AME Church with South Africa is getting more difficult to maintain, since travel restrictions make easy and frequent exchange of visitors impossible. During the study period, the Nchanga congregation delegated their minister to a conference in Cape Town, took great trouble to provide him with the necessary funds, and arranged that lay people should supply the pulpit and take over some of his other duties. After a fortnight he returned, very disappointed that he had not been able to cross the border into South Africa. Some time later a visit from the South African bishop was cancelled because he had not obtained a permit to leave the Union. This may lead to an even more rapid growing-up of the Northern Rhodesian Church, because its leaders will have to act independently. On the other hand, the supply of well-trained church officials has, in recent years, come solely from South Africa. The present bishop of the AME Church in the Federation is the son of American Negro parents, born in South Africa. Wilberforce is the only theological college for the clergy. It will be interesting to see how the church solves these problems. Is the American mother church, through the General Conference, going to assume more direct responsibility, or will the churches in the Federation try to find help on the spot, perhaps through closer co-operation with other mission churches facing the same problem of growing in self-sufficiency, though perhaps not for the same political reasons?

Persistence in its approach to the Northern Rhodesian Christian Council, which is the representative body of the European missionary enterprise, may be surprising when the AME is seen mainly as the most important church in the Ethiopian Movement of South Africa. Is not their origin in the social segregation of the Church, and their historic slogan, 'Africa for Africans'? Neither of these reasons for anti-white tendencies seemed to have any prominent place in the minds of the AME members we met in the Copperbelt and in the bush. Though Dr J. L. Dube's[7] work as the first president of the South African Native Congress must be well known to all who were trained in the South or were linked with the AME congregations there, their attention seemed to be focused on the formal and informal education of African children rather than on the political issues. One of their ministers when taking prison service found that the members of the African National Congress who were detained there refused to join in. 'Every minister is regarded as an informer.' The minister at Nchanga was well aware of the danger that nationalist feeling might bring a revival of pagan ideas, and lead to syncretism. 'Congress leaders used to come to our church, but now they try to get influence in the Lumpa church, because they say it is more African, and Lenshina is going to write her own Bible.' In the rural area the AME churches exclude members who take part in the activities or seek the help of the *ngulu* spirit movement (p. 267). All this confirms Sunkler's prognosis for the Bantu Independent Churches in the South[8] as being valid for the North as well. 'If African leadership is given a wider scope in political and civic affairs, then the energy which now flows into sectarian squabbles and seccessionist struggles will be directed to constructive and worthwhile problems.' . . . 'Leaders and masses of the Independent Bantu churches will be attracted by mission churches with episcopal authority, prestige of liturgical tradition, and a liberal attitude in social questions.' The AME in Northern Rhodesia is certainly facing that way.

NOTES

1. Minute of the Christian Council.
2. Letter to London Missionary Society.
3. B. C. M. Sundkler, *Bantu Prophets in South Africa*, Lutterworth Press, 1948, p. 40.
4. Shepperson and Price, *Independent African*, p. 92.
5. Sundkler, *op. cit.*, p. 40.
6. 'The Wilberforce Institute, near Johannesburg, with Teacher Training and Theological Departments, is aiming at becoming a South African *Tuskegee*.' Sundkler, *op. cit.*, p. 42.
7. Shepperson and Price, *op. cit.*, p. 91.
8. Sundkler, *op. cit.* pp. 298 ff.

10

The Watchtower Society or Jehovah's Witnesses

WHEN driving through a Mine African Township on an afternoon during the weekend, we noticed well-dressed young men and women standing at street corners and every hundred yards along the main roads, holding up magazines for sale. When we went visiting on another occasion, we saw a group of three or four sitting in a yard around somebody reading out of the Bible, and we found a football field crowded with people intently listening to the amplified voice of a speaker who gave a Bible reference for almost every sentence he said. We asked 'Who are those people?' In every case the answer was *Bacitawala*, or Ba Society, names which have caught on from the official title of 'The Watchtower Bible and Tract Society'—the name of the publishers, rather than the name which one finds in big letters on meeting houses all over the country, 'The Kingdom of Jehovah and His Witnesses' (*Ubufumu bwa kwa Yehovah na ba shinte bakwe*). No other church has caused so much controversy in Northern Rhodesia in the past or gets so much publicity now. Europeans in the urban communities who are easily impressed by big numbers occasionally ask the missionary if there is any other Christian church in the African Township with an equal number of adherents. In 1959 the Public Relations Officer of the Watchtower Society wrote, in an article announcing the coming of the American President, that the number of active preaching members had risen from 15,000 in 1952 to 28,000 in 1959, and that there are now 79,500 Africans and 5,000 European adherents of the Watchtower Society in Northern Rhodesia. A few days later the same newspaper published a report on the four-day assembly in Ndola in April 1959, where 30,800 had gathered and 400 had been baptized by immersion in a nearby stream. The bi-annual conference in the Luapula province, held at a remote fishing village in August 1958, gathered 17,000 to 19,000 people for each of three days, as stated by European missionaries of another denomination.[1] Cunnison reported that in 1950 he attended a district meeting, the first to be held at Chief Kazembe's village, when 'more than 7,000 people turned up from as far away as the Copperbelt and Tanganyika'.[2]

In Nchanga African Township the leaders of the three groups of the Watchtower Society attended the meetings of the Spiritual Round Table but, as the Chairman said, 'They come only because the invitations are given out by the Compound Manager. They do not really like to co-operate with other churches.' When asked to take part in the Study, their speaker was at first a bit truculent and questioned us. He had obviously not been able to understand our introductory talk. His English was not very advanced, but he promised to talk it over with others and then come up to see us, and the promise was kept. He invited us to meet a group in his house, where again we encountered a certain amount of reluctance. The young men and women there gathered, all under thirty, were busy preparing work for the next Sunday. Their monthly magazine, *Ulupungu lwa kwa Kalindi*, the Bemba for 'Watchtower', was being packed and checked against the card index. Wall maps showed the figures of membership and numbers of visits planned for each month of the year, with those actually achieved neatly filled in for comparison. But the work was stopped and all seemed to be keen to hear about the purpose of our visit and the aims of the study. One of the young men acted as interpreter. He seemed to be used to it, though his spoken English was not very fluent and he had occasional difficulty in understanding. The initial reserve gave way to friendliness more quickly than we had dared to anticipate. Our request to be permitted to attend a Sunday meeting was readily granted, once we had explained that we wanted to listen and not to preach or interfere in any way with their work. We were also taken to a choir practice which took place in the yard of a small compound house in the evening. Some of the people we had met on these occasions afterwards treated us in a very friendly way whenever they saw us in the Township. 'Their belligerent attitude has passed', said an Anglican missionary in the Luapula province.

It was somewhat more difficult to overcome the passive resistance of the few Watchtower people who lived in Nsensema's village. We were linked too much with the headman and his church and its missionaries. There were only seven members in this village, and they went for their study to the next small village, where three more members lived. The local leader was a young mechanic from Tanganyika who worked in the chief's motor launch. He had married a local girl, and the chief, being keen to attract followers who could further his development plans, had granted him permission to settle and build a house. 'In the part of Tanganyika where I was born, there were only Roman Catholics, but here I met the Watchtower Society and I joined them because they explained the Bible to me.' The African District Worker, who had been trained at the headquarters of Jehovah's Witnesses in Northern Rhodesia, visited him regularly and left him literature.

In 1951 Cunnison wrote:

> 'In the Luapula valley, Watchtower has more adherents than all the other missions put together. I estimate that more than half of the professing Christians in the area are Watchtower, in spite of the fact that the Plymouth Brethren at Johnston Falls and Kawama and the London Missionary Society at Mbereshi have been established for fifty years and the White Fathers at Lufubu for twenty. Also about half the Watchtower members originally belonged to one of the other missions.[3]

We found little evidence of their activities in the villages, but that is partly due to the fact that we concentrated our studies on a village with such a peculiar religious structure as Nsensema's, and partly to the quieter type of faith into which Watchtower has entered after its stormy period twenty-five years ago. This is not the place to discuss how far the disturbances of the Mwanalesa and the Copperbelt riots of 1935 were due to direct Watchtower influence (pp. 26-7). It may have been used as a readily available scapegoat and its name employed without discrimination by Africans with contacts in South Africa. A missionary at Mbereshi wrote in 1940, 'No direct connection seems to be established between the European leaders of the movement (in South Africa) and its African manifestations.'[4]

The most interesting part of Quick's report is the description of the early history and the special features of the Watchtower leaders and their teaching in the Kazembe country. Before 1930, 'prophets' who had mystical powers and gifts of divination attributed to them led a vehement attack on the missions because of their harsh disciplinary measures. Some of the local churches insisted on public confessions of moral lapses, and the dismissal from the church with the ostracism which followed were felt as social injustices, not only by the individuals concerned but also by their family groups. They were attracted by the possibility of being integrated into a new and all-African order. 'The watchman on the wall symbolises the hopes and aspirations of a wronged people.'[5]

The anti-mission, anti-white preachings reached their climax in the prophecy that Christ's second coming was going to happen in 1930, when Lake Mweru would boil and the Europeans of the district be cast into it. For a period enthused followers neglected their gardens in anticipation of the great event. When they were disappointed, many fell away.

Soon afterwards the numbers were again filled up with frustrated mineworkers who had lost their employment in the depression of 1932-3, and when in 1934 the Congo Government made a swoop on all non-mission religious organisations, many watchtower members crossed the Luapula river into Kazembe's Rhodesian territory. This incident is still well remembered. It was immediately followed by the purge in Northern Rhodesia. After Watchtower had been assigned part of the blame for the Copperbelt disturbances of 1935, their literature was banned as seditious, and Kazembe ordered burning of the Kingdom Halls in the villages, and for some time prohibited all gatherings.

During the war their persistent passivism, 'We are Christians', made them unpopular, and the Government kept them under suspicion because, as an official of that district said, 'Government had to watch any society which might easily depart from the original intentions of those who brought it to the country and did not supervise it closely any longer.'

After the war, however, that scrutiny could be dropped. The activities of the movement were persistently non-political and, as far as one can see, Watchtower was never cited in any Government warning regarding subversion. In 1948 the ban was lifted from the Watchtower magazine and from the second edition of some of their books.

We asked twenty District Commissioners about the activities of Watchtower, and especially if they had any evidence in court cases about their alleged promiscuity. Twelve of them replied. All said that the troubles were a matter of the past, when the movement 'was reputed inimical to civil authority and refused to pay tax at the rate set by Government at that time'. 'A primitive form of protest against Europeans.' 'Nowadays whenever there is trouble of a political nature, the Watchtower members do not only take part but actively take the side of authority.' As regards case record, there was no evidence that the custom of 'lending a wife' (*bwafwano*), which was said to have come from an old secret society in the Luapula valley, was still practised, although it had occurred among those who had camped there after the ejection from the Congo; but those people were by no means all Watchtower. Public opinion is changing slowly. 'The old slander is still repeated (p. 236).

They are accused of collecting disgruntled and excommunicated members of other churches; immorality is suspected, because Watchtower men and women definitely break with the old division of the sexes on social occasions. On the other hand, African teachers and welfare workers whose education enables them to have a more detached point of view said. 'Watchtower are very reliable people and punctual. They have good discipline and do not drink too much.' These virtues were also practised in the Nchanga groups. We found them surprisingly contrasting in this respect with most other groups. When they invited us to meet them, they were to be found in the given place, and started and closed small choir practices, as well as big Sunday meetings, exactly on time. A young African business man who had come from the Copperbelt to build a store in a village next to Nsensema's, and was looking around for a wife, told us, 'Watchtower succeeds more than other churches in keeping people to a good standard of behaviour. In this area not many girls are in Watchtower, but if you find one she is sure to be an honest girl. Watchtower parents do more to help young people in their homes. They discourage mixed marriages. Since they do not pay or receive bridal wealth they have no hesitation in getting rid of a bad son-in-law. Watchtower members do sometimes drink, but they do it privately and behave themselves. They are very orderly at their meetings.'

Their gift for mass organisation is well described by Cunnison, and by observers who visited the district meeting near Lake Mweru in 1958.

> 'The leaders, all Africans, were very friendly and ready to give information. (They knew that the visitors were missionaries of the London Missionary Society.) Boarding arrangements were made for the 17,000 to 19,000 present, and grass shelters to sleep in were provided. £5 was contributed by each of sixteen congregations and used to buy stocks of food. Delegates also brought food and whatever extra was needed. The meeting place was a very well-built enclosure with a net fence. The platform had a thatched pavilion. The gates were numbered and numerous notices were pointing the way. Seats in the enclosure were long bundles of grass. Outside was a large open space where the grass had been cut short. Bicycle sheds were provided. In front of the platform was a neat garden with whitewashed stone edges and banana trees planted. Neat whitewashed fences along the road led to the enclosure. Near the road a whitewashed wall and tower (the Watchtower symbol) advertised the meetings. Men and women sat together. During the prayers stewards enforced silence on those who were watching outside the enclosure.'

This description presents a picture which looks like an enlargement of what we saw in Nchanga and Chiwempala, the municipal African Township of Chingola. In both places the meetings were held in well-built enclosures in the open air. The pavilion platform with decorative texts, the fencing and simple seating arrangements, all showed that the people took a pride in outward appearance and devoted a considerable amount of labour to it.

The public services or meetings had the very simple design of instruction classes rather than of worship. Singing starts and finishes a meeting and fills gaps. The hymns are of the common translated pattern and some groups use the hymn-books of the Protestant mission churches. But there is no set order of service, the simple prayers are extemporary and limited to the conventional petitions for understanding Jehovah's will and for perseverance in the way of the righteous. The main purpose of the meetings is clear. It is not worship, but indoctrination. Their instruction manual states:

> 'Jehovah's Witnesses are not a sect or a cult, as men call them. Active service, not ritual, comprises their worship. They must preach. Each Witness is a minister. One not preaching is not one of Jehovah's Witnesses. Their preaching results in salvation to themselves and others.'[6]

Many of the men and women who attended a meeting on a Sunday afternoon in an enclosure on the border of Nchanga Township, had copies of the magazine in Bemba and followed the printed text of the talk, which was given with a special reference to the attached questions. Some made notes and occasionally interrupted the speaker to ask additional questions. Most of these had set answers incorporating doctrinal points and those who knew were eager to give them, and were applauded for it. Cunnison observed the same procedure at the big assembly.

A school-teacher said he could always easily discover children who belonged to Watchtower when he taught a new class. 'They are the ones who ask many questions.'

In spite of all the accusations and moral and political suspicions of the past, most people nowadays agree that the success of the Watchtower Movement is the result of its evangelism, its emphasis on teaching which is well-supported by its cheap books and magazines, and the sense of security and status it establishes among its members. Quick is right in stressing that

> 'it must not be forgotten that the African is an intensely religious person and maintains a religious attitude to life. The religious nature and vigour of the [Watchtower] movement must therefore be ascribed to the religious zeal of the African, and its manifold activities to the way in which religious, social and economic and political matters

are inseparable in indigenous culture and in the process of culture adjustment.'[7]

But one may well ask, what makes Watchtower so specially attractive, and what kind of African is found in it?

A well-educated African agricultural officer in a rather underdeveloped part of the Northern Province said, 'Watchtower is on the increase here. It is strong because it goes to other people with evangelistic zeal, preaching everywhere more than any other church. It also appeals because it teaches the Bible carefully. That is why the ex-Roman Catholics become the most ardent Watchtower members, because they are so starved of teaching.'

> 'Men want to know the reasons why things are as they are. Why is the world so full of confused ideas and shifting patterns? There are so many different beliefs, so many different religions—what should one believe in these days? who is right?—The highest authority is the Holy Bible, Jehovah's Word. This book of high authority does not ask us to accept just one statement of truth, and that blindly, but rather God's prophets say, Come now, let us reason together, says Jehovah (Isa. 1.18). That is it! Think the answer out, search for it in the Scriptures.'[8]

Cunnison rates 'the fact that in doctrine there is no room for the slightest doubt about anything'[9] as the last of the factors making for acceptability of the Watchtower in the Luapula valley. I wonder if it is not much more fundamental. The need for a new authority to depend on when old beliefs are breaking down may be only subconsciously felt, yet be all the more demanding for the minds of those who are at the same time facing the social and economic problems of their changing world. The offer of a way out of the fearful insecurity is most tempting when it promises to honour independent judgment and at the same time offers integration into a group.

The method of initiating new members by making them study the Bible with the help of printed outlines or themes, and then fix the new knowledge by repetition to others, is not only a sound teaching principle for adults, but also meets the longing for book knowledge which seems to many Africans the secret of the white man's success. The investigations regarding the educational standards of the members of various churches which were undertaken by the Christian Council in Luanshya and Mufulira in 1953 revealed that over 60 per cent of Watchtower had no form of education beyond the sub-standards, while 46 per cent of the Roman Catholics and 35 per cent of the CCAR belonged to this non-literate group. Those who had reached Standard IV and higher grades, were 10 per cent of the Watchtower, 26 per cent of the Roman Catholics and 39 per cent of the CCAR. There are those who in the past fifteen or twenty years have had no opportunity of going to a mission school, and one should not forget that even nowadays, when schools are run by Government and local authorities, only 45 per cent of the children find a place in any school, and the frustrated non-literates or half-literates are still influenced by the importance which mission education places on the Bible. Watchtower offers them a key to find the answer to any question in the Bible. Ancestor worship? see Matt. 10.37—a false practice.[10] Blood transfusion? see Ps.16.4—an unscriptural practice. Communism? claim based on Acts 2.44 that early Christian congregation was communistic is false.

The whole apparatus of encyclopaedic study helps, of quoting ten different Bible translations and Greek and Hebrew words, builds up to a pretence of scientific work; and the stress which is laid on doctrinal literature as 'a help to understand the Bible, but not a commentary' disguises the arbitrary nature of the collection of quotations, and plays on the suspicion that missionaries 'hide the true Bible'. This creates an extraordinary rationalism. Every word of the Old and the New Testaments is explainable and meaningful for the present, and since only Watchtower people have access to the full truth, it is an act of mercy to pass it on to the uninitiated and to warn them. 'If there were a great wall of water fifty feet high coming down the Luapula, what should we do, should we try to stop it by building a dam five feet high against it? No, we should warn the people to be out of the way. Thus we can show mercy not by trying to stop Armageddon but by warning others of its approach by preaching from house to house.'[11] The importance of the message which the newly instructed has to pass on sustains his self-assurance, and it is understandable that the feeling of inferiority which has troubled him in the past sometimes works itself out into a fanatic aggressiveness. 'These people don't stop anywhere, they argue even with ministers (of other denominations).' But as already said, nowadays the consciousness of being supported by a group of formidable size and considerable wealth supports the pioneer in his house-to-house visitation; and since he has been prepared to accept antagonism and even persecution as a sign of the Last Days and of his own righteousness, much of the sting is taken out of it.

Whatever the workers in his gang may say when he disputes with them in the leisure periods underground or on the building site, a Watchtower member is not dependent on the new fellowships which are formed in an urban industrial setting. He is already one of a brotherhood which is linked closer together than a clan, and which lives in firmer expectation of a glorious future than any political party or trade union can anticipate, because its fulfilment is based on some supernatural events.

'Our names are written in Lusaka' (i.e., the Watchtower headquarters), three women replied to the question of an African woman lay-preacher whether they were saved. The sense of belonging to the chosen people, the heirs of the kingdom, is especially important for the women. Watchtower teaching is radical about breaking with old social customs. 'New world living means a completely changed thinking process from that of the former course in Satan's system of things. Development of a new life pattern by daily strengthening of proper habits, leanings and mental attitude.'[12] This lack of compromise is probably most helpful to those who are most uprooted and have to venture into new behaviour. The teaching about the role of the sexes is rather naively Western. 'Marriage imposes on the husband the legal duty of supporting his wife and children, maintaining her home—the wife owes to the husband the duty of living with him where he decides—she has the duty of performing domestic services in the home.'[13] Since however so many women are already forced into such a pattern by the outward conditions of their lives, they accept these doctrines quite happily. A women who was asked how she felt having to subordinate her wishes to her husband's, answered with an old Bemba proverb, 'The woman who does not praise her husband is a fool'—*Umwanakashi ushilumba mulume cipuba.* This may sound like a rather evasive diplomatic statement, but the Watchtower families we learnt to know seem to be exceptionally well-adjusted and happy together. And the women were known for their devotion of their leisure time, which is so much greater in town life, to participation in 'Witnessing'. Some of them go around in the market and the native shops and start discussions. A Jewish shopkeeper told me how he had surprised African staff engaged in looking up references in the Book of Daniel for an old African woman who had bought a cooking pot and then asked the shop assistant to read the quotations out for her while she preached to the customers.

The leaders do not insist that all preaching members should be literate, but as the Watchtower Public Relations Officer reported, they teach those who want to learn and have about a thousand new literates every year. This statement is supported by the African Literacy Officer of the Mine Welfare Department, who once addressed a group of young catechumens in a CCAR congregation. 'Aren't you ashamed', she said, 'that none of you can read a Bible on her own, but only the Watchtower women come to my classes?' We have no evidence in numbers that women are especially attracted by Watchtower. The Copperbelt meetings we attended showed the usual fairly even numbers of men and women in any congregation, but they were more difficult to count and to compare, because they sat mixed and not in neatly divided blocks as in all other denominations. It is generally said that the women form the majority. Cunnison makes an interesting contribution on this point. He observes that some Witnesses teach that 'all women will have children in the Kingdom, in which there will be a complete absence of all the ills of this world'. When an official of the Kazembe pointed to the number of childless women at the big assembly and attributed this to the promiscuity of the Watchtower which spread disease, the Witnesses replied that those women had been ejected from other churches because of their sins, but had since repented, and Watchtower was the only church which would accept them and regard their adultery as a sin of the past. Though this is not true of the official disciplines of the other Churches, there is a sense in which it correctly describes the position. The women themselves would naturally prefer to join a new group, instead of going back in repentance to the congregation where their past would be always remembered. These women are probably one of the reasons why Watchtower morals gained such a bad name in the past.

The American headquarters put a European in charge of all African work; this official has in the last eleven years resided in Northern Rhodesia. He told us that in every congregation he appoints three to look after the morals and the money, and they are responsible to him and recommend that a lost member must be punished by 'disfellowshipping'. With him work three other European families in the districts, who visit the congregations, organize the bigger assemblies and baptize. Their colleagues are twenty-five full-time travelling African ministers, salaried by headquarters out of the gifts of the congregations. Every four to six months they return to headquarters for reporting and special training. Out of all these a governing body of 'mature, elder brothers', i.e., seven to eight appointed overseers, are taken. There is no electoral principle, no 'glorified bishop', but everybody is treated as a servant, not a servant to the church, but in the church to the world.

It is a far cry from the wild nationalism of the early beginnings, when 'in 1918-19 Watchtower prophets in Northern Rhodesia preached the sweet message of the Day when Europeans would become slaves of the Africans',[14] to the quiet refusals of the present day to take any part in Trade Union or Congress activities. We may wonder how much of this change is due to the influence of the white overseers. The European in charge of the whole organization in Northern Rhodesia told us that 'Jehovah's Witnesses are not called to change the social structure lest they attract people who are interested in social reform rather than in the Kingdom of God'. And since social segregation is widely practised in Northern Rhodesia, they do not combine African and European congregations. There are nevertheless some links, some European members almost always attending the half-yearly assemblies, but this is left to the individual. He admitted that it is difficult to know the way clearly, and that he was constantly searching his heart, so that he should not be caught in any self-deception or evasion of the call of God in this matter. One step over the racial barrier has already been taken. The large European assembly at Ndola invited the coloured (Eurafrican) members, and after the fourth day they were fully accepted and settled down well together. It would have been quite impossible to open that assembly to Africans, he added, as they are far too many.

This inequality in numbers is one of the reasons which make the picture of the movement look all-African to an outsider. The 'white' influence is exercised largely through written material, and this loses some of its foreign character by being published in the vernacular. The Bemba edition of the magazine registers forty-seven languages in which *Watchtower* is published; seven of these are Bantu languages, three West African, and there is also an Afrikaans edition, which together with the English version offer a total of twelve editions to the African market. Quick said they were the cheapest reading material, and specially attractive because they were aimed at being read in groups. Numerous secular newspapers have since entered into competition but no religious publication in Northern Rhodesia has anything near the distribution of 'Watchtower'.

The American origin of the society is well-known to its African members, but this did not seem to have any great importance for those which whom we talked. Cunnison points out that in 1950 Africans in the Luapula valley distinguished the racial attitude of the Americans who had come to speak at their assembly from that of European missionaries. They believed that in America the large African population lives in perfect harmony with white Americans. This was based on 'the free and easy manner of the American and the Canadian on the platform, showing a familiarity which they could not expect from any

Briton or Belgian'.[15] The delegation of position to Africans and the absence of the master-servant relationship in the Society, in spite of its foreign overseers and theocratic rule from above, may give as much satisfaction as the eschatological teaching that 'people overly concerned with everyday affairs of life'[16] are only another sign of the Last Days.'

Will the belief in the 'Battle of Armageddon to be fought over the Kingdom issue in this generation'[17] stand up against the increasing pressure of public opinion that freedom and happiness, i.e., political and economic advancement, can only be achieved by active participation in the struggles of National African Congress and Trade Union? People outside the Watchtower Movement have occasionally said that some of the watchmen, after looking for too long into an empty distance, have descended from their wall and entered the battle on the firm ground in front of them. The young people in secondary education are said to regard the religious fervour of Jehovah's Witnesses as 'old-fashioned and primitive'; their thinking tends to become secularised like that of most Western societies in urban settings. Their hopes and aspirations have new outlets, and Watchtower, as all other churches, is more critically scrutinized than ever before in Northern Rhodesia.

The Bamulonda ('the Watchmen'), a relic from the early Prophet movements

Although the early enthusiastic days of Jehovah's Witnesses are over, groups still remain which preserve the old spirit. We met one of these during the village study. When we discussed the aim of our investigations with the Acting Chief Councillor of Mwata Kazembe, he told us about a 'church' in which dancing and drumming 'as in old times' were used in the service. 'They meet every Sunday in a different village, and they announce their services in advance so that many people should come to attend them.' But in spite of this alleged aim at publicity, we found it difficult to track them down; the inhabitants of the Kazembe Township and their neighbours in the numerous adjoining villages were no longer interested in their activities. Finally we found their 'church' building in a village which is well known as one of the main centres of the Bangulu spirit-possession movement. It was a small house with a thatched roof, standing back from the main road at the edge of the cassava gardens. The pew blocks of sun-dried bricks could seat about 20 people, a slightly raised platform at the back was probably the place for the leaders. We had to wait a long time till these men, with cloth badges signifying their membership, arrived. They were very reluctant to talk to us, and said that the local leader was away; after a while, however, an old man arrived with two women and gave us some information, after discussing our request with the others. One of the young women was obviously a strong personality, showing herself rather aggressive and impatient with the long deliberations of the older men. We were told later by some of Nsensema's villagers that she was regarded as the most outstanding member of the Bamulonda, and that at her recent wedding all the Bamulonda of the district, even from as great a distance as the Boma at Kawambwa, had come together.

Since our discussions with the Bamulonda took place at the end of our village work, we did not have an opportunity of checking their statements. According to them, the movement did not start in the Lunda country before 1947. They knew that the first leader had been called Elliot, had lived in Nyasaland and died there. His sons had taken on the spiritual leadership. They came to preach in these parts of Northern Rhodesia, taught the first converts their language, Nyanja, and gave them the membership badges and notes on doctrine together with Nyanja Bibles. When the first members were advanced enough to go on preaching, the Nyasalanders went home; they now return only for occasional visits. Elders, who look after the business of the church, are elected by each congregation. 'There is not one European in our church. We don't tell lies.'

After the ice had been broken, we invited the leaders to visit us at Nsensema's village and went back together with some of them who lived near our way. We noticed that their houses had a big black square painted on the front wall with the inscription: *Ndi wa Yehova na Mikaeli*, 'I am of Jehovah's and Michael's', the same legend as on the badges on the men's jackets and the women's headscarves.

The very next day in the early afternoon children of Nsensema's village came running to our houses to announce that a group of Bamulonda had arrived to preach. They had planted a long bamboo with a white and red flag next to some shady mango trees in the middle of the village, and drumming called the villagers to a meeting. They had used our invitation to enter the village in which the headman had never given them permission to preach. When a fair crowd had gathered, and Nsensema been introduced, they started the meeting with a hymn; this had originally been sung in Nyanja, but they had translated it and sang in Bemba:

'Michael, start the work, the work of selection.
Darkness covered the land but now we are running to you.

'Michael, start the work. In the dry season, when sufferings are plentiful, we hide in you.

'Michael, start the work. In July, even though the people pray, the idols shall be cracked.

'Michael, start the work. Make us strong as brothers and sisters, so that we may be strong to do thy work.

'Michael, start the work. Raise our people who are bound because they themselves do not know that they are bound.'

Then a man went forward and began dancing to the drum, first saying: 'He for whom I'm dancing is Jehovah'. After a few minutes he stopped, and began his address with an explanation of his dancing by reference to David dancing before the Lord. He went on: 'The missions hid the Bible from the Africans. Elliot learned from the white people and gave the New Testament to the Africans. There is no European in our church at all. We don't tell you any lies.' Then Prov.17.18, first in Nyanja and then in Bemba, was read. (All preachers call on other members of the team to read their references.) 'A man void of understanding striketh hands . . .'

'We Africans have had many troubles, even deaths, because of shaking hands with strangers. God's Word says: "Gather not my soul with sinners, nor my life with bloody men: in whose hands is mischief" (Ps. 26. 9-10). In the hand is sin. I am not telling lies. When a child is born your hands are full of blood, and so you go quickly and look for *muti* ('medicine' in the widest sense). The Europeans have a custom that a newborn child must never be touched by hand.

'The Levites were freed from slavery and taught the Children of Israel to keep these laws. John the Baptist also taught in the wilderness. Therefore hear what we say. Ps. 149. 3: "Let (the children of Zion) praise his name in the dance".'

Then he started dancing again, shouting sentences in Nyanja, and the refrain was repeated by all with clapping.

The best dressed man, with a badge in English, came forward and said:

'I want to explain that Michael is Jesus, our Christ. John 3.19, 20: "This is the condemnation, that light is come into the world and men loved darkness rather than light, because their deeds were evil. . . ." Michael is the Light. He was sent as the Son, Christ. He created all things. You men and women are fools. You can learn it all, because the world was very bad and Michael was sent to destroy it all. Only Noah was saved. Then Sodom and Gomorrah were destroyed. God sent the Light, Jesus Christ, his Son, but the people did not accept the

Light of God. They kept clasping one another's hands in greeting. Read again John 3.20. Is it not true that adultery is going on? Therefore God sent Michael. John 1.1. Through the Word all people, white and black, are children of God always. God does not discriminate. God is here. But do you follow him? John 13.10: "... ye are clean, but not all". Isa. 40.1: "Comfort ye, comfort ye my people", and Isa. 62.10 (he pointed to the flag): Prepare a way for Jehovah, prepare a way for Jehovah. Come, come, take the stones away.

'King George had a flag and he sent it here, and wherever the flag was raised, there was his kingdom. Wherever the flag was, there was also a consul. These consuls are the same as the officers of the chief, like Lukwesa under Kazembe. In old times we were forced to approach the officers of King George humbly. We were not allowed to walk upright in Kawambwa (the Boma). Today it is easier. Look, what kingdom has come. (He pointed at their flag. The women started to ululate.) Look at the flag which is raised.'

Then followed a hymn:

'I am the Lord in Zion.
I, Michael, am the Lord.'

The third speaker wore ragged shorts. He made very clever rhythmic movements, dancing with the drum. He took up the theme of the flag and gave out Ps.60.4: 'Thou hast given a banner to them that fear thee, that it may be displayed because of the truth.'

'It is always preached that the Kingdom of God and his son Michael has come. But do people stop bad things? Have they stopped greeting each other by shaking hands or using medicine? When a child is sick does not the father go and look for medicine? He goes everywhere to find a person who knows where the right medicine is. He goes to the *ng'anga* (doctor) and the *ng'anga* tells him he must go naked at night to cut medicine from a certain tree. Does he refuse to go naked? No, he does what the *ng'anga* says to him.'

Then an older woman began a dancing song. She started by pointing at the flag.

'He has given us all things.
He gave us Elliot.
He gave us the Kingdom.
He created the sun, the moon, the water, the animals.
At last he created man.
Let us thank him.'

After every sentence that she shouted while dancing, the others cried out 'O Michael'.

A man followed with another address. Rev. 19.7: 'Let us be glad and rejoice, and give honour to him: for the marriage of the Lamb is come, and his wife has made herself ready', and v.14: 'And the armies which were in heaven followed him upon white horses, clothed in fine linen, white and clean.'

'God sent Michael. His wife is the church. The white clothes are the works of the saints. New Jerusalem is coming, but first there must be war. Armageddon will be in 1984. "There was war in heaven: Michael and his angels fought against the dragon; and the dragon fought and his angels, and they prevailed not." Rev. 12.7. Michael threw Satan down. He conquered the earth and set up his kingdom. There is no place for Satan in Heaven and there is no place of salvation in this world. This is where the London Mission is very wrong. There is no hospital on earth that can heal us, only the hospital in heaven. Mal. 4.2: "The sun of righteousness . . . with healing in his wings". God says: Fear my name. There are many missions, but they don't fear Jehovah. They don't keep his laws. Moses gave us the law of life, but we have not kept the laws of Jehovah. The children of Jehovah will be saved, not by the sacrifice of calves or sheep, but through his word, the word which came in Jesus to the Jews. From 606 until 1874, the Europeans had the blessing. The Africans are now the blessed ones, as the Jews were. Ex. 15.26: "If thou wilt diligently hearken to the voice of the Lord thy God, and wilt do that which is right in his sight, and wilt give ear to his commandments and keep all his statutes, I will put none of these diseases upon thee, which I have brought upon the Egyptians: for I am the Lord that healeth thee."

'There is no medicine which can heal, no medicine of this earth, only the medicine of heaven. Hear the Words of God, and do good, and you will not get sick like the Egyptians. It is Satan who brought sickness into this world. The Roman Catholics spoilt the ways of the Jews, but Pastor Rutherford came in 1874. Ps. 107.18: "Fools because of their transgression and because of their iniquities, are afflicted. Their soul abhorreth all manner of meat, and they drew near unto the gates of death.' The heart of man is full of worldly things, of hospitals, injections, but he shall be saved who hates these things. It is good to receive well those who bring the Word of Jehovah. The Word of God is the Medicine which will heal us all. Everyone must trust in God the Great Physician (*Shing'anga*).'

This led him into dance. He shouted a sentence and was answered by the refrain:

'God is the physician. O Jehovah.
God is the Lord. O Jehovah.
Michael was sent by Jehovah. O Jehovah.
Jehovah is good. O Jehovah.
Michael defeated Satan. O Jehovah.'

The best-dressed man came forward again, and quoted Ps. 95.1: 'O come, let us sing unto the Lord; let us make a joyful noise to the rock of our salvation,' and Ezek. 3.17: 'Son of man, I have made thee a watchman unto the house of Israel: therefore hear the word at my mouth, and give them warning from me.'

> 'The London Missionary Society brought the hospitals into this country. That was very wrong. All Europeans and Africans, great and low, must give honour to Jehovah and keep his laws. Everything is written in the Bible, about hand-shaking and about medicine, also about dancing. God says: I have made you watchmen (*bamulonda*). We have to watch all the churches, to see if they keep Jehovah's laws or use medicine or shake hands or tell lies. The London Mission teach the use of medicine: therefore, all Europeans and Africans in their church are bad. The *Bamulonda* have to watch them to stop this badness. Was it not the Europeans who brought this badness? The bad one who uses medicine, his blood is destroyed, whether he is black or white. The churches and the heathen, because they teach this, will be destroyed.'

'The Kingdom is like the owner of a house, seeking workers for his vineyard.' Matt. 20 was read at his request. He began explaining it, but people had obviously got tired and many left, so he started a hymn with a Tumbuka tune. The young woman drummer danced to it.

> 'Mighty Lord—you, Jehovah.
> Michael, our chief—you, Jehovah.
> We are of the Lord Michael's—O Jehovah.'

With this the meeting finished and the Bamulonda declared they were ready to talk to us, not just the leaders but the whole team. We offered them tea and biscuits, but they refused anything except plain water.

All the people in the group were local residents, and had been taught by Nyasaland workers who were followers of Elliot Kamwana and visited the Lunda country in 1947. Other groups had been established and still met in Mporokoso, Kalungwishi, Kawambwa, Mwinilunga and Fort Rosebery, also in Tanganyika and South Africa. (The Copperbelt was not mentioned.) The services are mainly held in the open air; Kazembe's district has only one church building. Not many people are converted to become Bamulonda, because they don't want to give up medicine and hospitals. The converts from the London Mission and the Roman Catholic mission are rebaptized, but not those who have already been baptized through total immersion by the Seventh Day Adventists and similar churches.

The Bamulonda keep the food laws of the Old Testament, for instance they don't eat water animals without scales (Lev. 11.9-10). One of Nsensema's men told us later that they do not eat any food which is cooked by a non-member. This excludes them from practically all social gatherings in their villages.

Asked about their teaching on salvation-history (*Heilsgeschichte*), they consulted a big book made out of notes handwritten on the stationery of a Nyasaland hotel.

'The first people to have the blessing were the Jews. They lost it in 606 BC. Then the Europeans had the mission to preach for 2,520 years till 1914. In 1874 Watchtower was started by Russell; Elliot Kamwana learned from an American (see p. 24, probably a reference to Booth). He was a Tonga from Nyasaland, and God made him a prophet. He prophesied that a war would break out among the Europeans, and that was what happened in 1914. Wasn't he a prophet? Elliot was put into jail by the Government for twenty-eight years, 1909-1938. Then he was allowed to preach everywhere, even at Zomba, the capital of Nyasaland. He also prophesied a trial period of thirty years in which all churches would be "mixed up". This would happen from 1955 till 1985. The Africans are now blessed, they are like the Jews in the old times. They are awakening up from their sleep.

'Christ before he came to the world was *langosi*—a Greek name which means "word" (logos), as it is mentioned in John 1. He was Michael, called to do the work of salvation, Jesus' work, as it is written in Luke 1 and in Dan. 12.1: "And at that time shall Michael stand up, the great prince which standeth for the children of thy people: and there shall be a time of trouble such as never was . . . at that time thy people shall be delivered, every one that shall be found written in the book'. Jesus is the Son of Man to do God's work, Rev. 12.7.'

The Bamulonda do not keep Watchtower rules, nor those of any other churches. They allow polygamy—didn't Abraham have two wives? They drink neither beer nor tea, tea being a medicine, but coffee and cocoa are allowed.

Three groups of people are to be saved: first sixty, then eighty, and 170,000 in the end. After giving this information, the men had a short discussion in Nyanja, and then asked the Bemba-speaking interpreter, who had not been able to follow their discussion, what church she belonged to. They recognized the name Martin Luther. 'Didn't he announce the coming of Christ in 1884? No, he is no longer alive, he is in Heaven.'

'God sent seven angels to the world:

30—70 AD	Paul
70—325	John
325—1100	Arius
1100—1518	Wyclif

1518—1874	"a German"
1874	Russell
and after him	Elliot Kamwana.

'Elliot Kamwana prophesied a *lusuba*, a hot, dry season for thirty years, 1955—1985, during which all churches would be tried. The Lord Jehovah and the Lord Michael are *Malinga*, stockades for refuge. We think this time started with Federation.

'As in Nebuchadnezzar's time, the people will not read the Bible. Christians and rich people will worship a human being, but we shall never worship in a "human" church. Rev. 3.10: "Because thou hast kept the word of my patience, I also will keep thee from the hour of temptation, which shall come upon all the world to try them that dwell upon the earth." '

Then they asked us; 'Is it your aim to join all the churches? We shall write to our president to tell him about you and what you want to do. We know that in the end all will be brought together, and in 1995-1997 a great war will be fought, Armageddon, as Elliot Kamwana has prophesied.'

After expressing our thanks for their willingness to talk with us, we asked them if we could attend one of their regular services in their little church. There was a certain reticence, but we were told that they met every Wednesday and Saturday afternoon, as well as on Sunday mornings. When we turned up at the next meeting, however, we were politely but shortly and firmly told that we were not welcome, because we did not really want to join their church.

This change of heart was somehow connected with the rumours about the Ordinance concerning the registration of societies, which at that time caused quite a lot of resentment in the smaller groups all over the country—partly because they had to pay £1 registration fee, which is still quite a considerable amount of money for villagers who have no cash crops and very few other products to sell. Most members of the Bamulonda group we met looked as if they belonged to the lowest income group; the houses which displayed their sign were small and on the outer edge of the villages. They have no air of that efficiency and assurance which come with success, as is the case with the Watchtower Movement. They were afraid that we were spies for the Government, who would trouble them with 'tax' (as they understood the registration fee).

In Nchanga the African welfare workers knew that there were a few Bamulonda in the African Township, but they were not a publicly worshipping group. In the short time at our disposal after the village study, we were not able to trace any of them, though we met quite a few of the relations of Nsensema and other former villagers of the Lunda country. None of them was much interested in their worship or their doctrine; they shared the opinion of one of the old men at Nsensema's who said: 'The Bamulonda are no use to anybody. They have no schools. They make only a lot of noise. Even with psalms they are wasting their time. Why do they refuse to go to hospital? If a child has a headache they strike it on the head with a Bible.' The Jehovah's Witnesses do not regard them as a genuine offshoot of their own movement, but rather as a collection of 'various disgruntled Christians and Adventists'. But there is definitely a connection with the followers of Elliot Kamwana in Nyasaland. The badges and the doctrinal notes were evidence of that, as well as the tradition which was retailed to us. The missionary in Livingstonia wrote at the beginning of 1959 that the district had been the birthplace of the sect: 'I am told that Elliot Chirwa Kamwana still has a following in the Nkhata Bay area of the Northern Province of Nyasaland, but that even within fifty miles of that area, his influence is virtually non-existent.'

Their importance does not lie with their numbers, or their influence on the religious life of the districts in which they still exist, but rather in the fact that they demonstrate how long the influence of a 'prophet' can persist, and how far away ideas travel. The similarities with the Zulu Zionist movements are so striking that we may ask how much of their peculiar doctrines is an import, owed by Elliot Kamwana to his spiritual fathers in South Africa, and how much is fruit grown on kindred soil, that is, the expression of Bantu religious tradition and experience. Sundkler[18] describes Zulu groups organized in the same way, with their influential women leaders, distinctive songs, eschatological messages and food taboos. The Bamulonda in Kazembe's country are only a weak shadow of their South African kindred, but who will predict whether the future will see them disappear altogether or whether they will perhaps grow as a kind of 'low' Watchtower Movement? Our short and rather superficial contact with this group did not give us sufficient insight to make any prediction based on its inner strength. More research would need to be done to reveal how widespread are the different groups which link the Bamulonda of the Luapula valley with their Nyasaland origins.

NOTES

1. *Northern News*, Ndola, N. Rhodesia, 22.iv.59 and 27.iv.59.
2. Ian Cunnison, 'A Watchtower Assembly in Central Africa,' *IRM* XL, October 1951.
3. *Ibid.*, p. 456.
4. Griffith Quick, 'Some Aspects of the African Watchtower Movement in Northern Rhodesia,' *IRM* XXIX, 1940.
5. *Ibid.*, p. 218.
6. *Make sure of all things*, Watchtower Bible and Tract Society, Brooklyn, New York, 1953.
7. Quick, *op. cit.*, p. 216.
8. *Make sure of all things*, p. 3.
9. Cunnison, *op. cit.*, p. 459.
10. *Make sure of all things*, pp. 9, 10, 47, 65.
11. Cunnison, *op. cit.*, p. 460.
12. *Make sure of all things*, p. 272.
13. *Ibid.*, p. 253.
14. B.G.M. Sundkler, *Bantu Prophets in South Africa*, p. 72.
15. Cunnison, *op. cit.*, p. 468.
16. *Make sure of all things*, p. 341.
17. *Ibid.*, pp. 235 and 27.
18. Sundkler, *op. cit.*

11

Alice Lenshina Mulenga and the Lumpa Church

AT the time when European opinion in Northern Rhodesia changed from regarding the Watchtower Movement as potentially dangerous to acknowledging the moral training and political neutrality of Jehovah's Witnesses, a new religious sect stirred public imagination and aroused even international attention. The Prophet movements of South Africa, which Sundkler studied[1] during the 1940s, and the work of the Christian leader Harris in West Africa, are well known. Missionaries and church leaders in Northern Rhodesia had, therefore, reason to expect similar occurences there, since the forces at work in their country, the cultural transition, the social tensions and the political unrest created a suitable climate for independent church movements. These, according to Sundkler, are a symptom of an inner revolt against the white man's missionary crusade, a primitive puritanism which criticizes the whites by their own standards. Since such movements show the influence of their African religious and cultural heritage in a much more uninhibited fashion than do 'mission' churches, they reveal not only what has been vital and important in the old religion, but also persisting elements of pre-Christian thinking and the real spiritual needs of the people. Africans are partly unaware of the survival of the old in their own minds, and partly shy and afraid to talk about it to their spiritual leaders, who, as they anticipate, will rebuke or ridicule these 'superstitions'.

The beginning of the Lumpa Church is best described by the African minister who was from the start deeply involved, as he was in charge of the congregation in which the prophetess entered the catechumenate and was being prepared for church membership. He wrote a report to the Presbytery of the CCAR in April 1955:

> 'In the district of Chinsali in the village of Kasomo in the country of chief Nkula a woman, Alice Mulenga Lenshina Lubusha, the wife of Petro Chintankwa, came back from the dead in September 1954.

She came back to her senses from a faint in her illness. Then she called the Christian people, women of her village, that they should come and pray for her to God. When they had prayed she got up and went outside the village to sit under a tree. People wanted to go and watch her but she stopped them. When the sun set one woman went, because, she said, she may be possessed by an *ngulu.*[2] But Alice drove her away. "Go back to the village," she said, "I do not want anybody to watch me here." She wanted her husband and he went there but nobody else.

'During that week many people heard that Lenshina Mulenga had come back from the dead. And angels had brought her books which came from heaven. And Jesus had come to speak to her. The people of Kasomo were very astonished to hear that Lenshina had died and come back from the dead; they did not know where this tale came from.

'At that time Alice started to proclaim the Good News with all her power, and telling people many things about Jesus Christ. She said that the people should stop adultery and hatred and cursing and stealing and lies and swearing. She composed a new hymn: "A man who does not repent and believe in Jesus, he cannot stand near the judgment throne of God;" a song which is good in its words and its parable.

'When the Europeans and Africans had a session of the Federal Mission Church (i.e. the UCCAR) in Lubwa Mission (the station of the Church of Scotland Mission which is nearest to Kasomo's village), Alice came to Lubwa. She carried a towel which was folded as if something was inside. She had her husband with her and came to the house of Rev. Mushindo (the local African minister), but Mushindo had gone on a journey to give the Communion of our Lord to the Christians. But at the house they found Theresa Mushindo (the minister's wife); and Petro said: "My wife has been ill and turned back from death. Therefore she has words which have been said to her by God that she should tell the minister of the church." Mushindo's wife said: "Go and speak to the elders." The elders brought her to the Europeans (i.e. the missionaries) who had the session with them; those said: "Come another morning." Alice returned to Lubwa and people from nearby villages up to twelve miles came to her and said: "Let us see the books which came from heaven." Therefore on Wednesday (at the midweek service) the church was too small for the many people who came to prayers. When Alice was on the point of lifting her parcel, a sixpence fell out, which she gave to the elders saying: "God told me that I should give gifts. The people must give gifts to God, that is what God said."

'After the service, he wanted to go and speak to the missionary in his office privately. When he came out the people asked the missionary: "She told me that angels brought her two books; then another woman came in the twilight of the evening, she clapped her hands and the books entered into the earth. But their marks can be seen clearly in the towel." When the Rev. Mushindo returned from his journey, he went to hear why she wanted him. Alice said: "When I was ill and died, I was carried by angels. Jesus said: 'Let her go back and live in the village.' But I stayed there three days and nights, and angels came and Jesus came and talked to me." Rev. Mushindo asked her about the books but she put him off. She persevered in teaching the Gospel and she brought many people to Lubwa to the services. Because she had been a catechumen preparing to be baptized, and because of her hard work and her obvious strong faith in our Lord, people believed and praised her, and worried others. In December (the beginning of the planting season) she started to give people seeds to mix with their own seeds and blessings for their seeds. And unfortunately she started to baptize people. The minister and the elders tried to stop her but she refused. She started to tell people: "Bring your magic, horns and charms, then you will be saved in God's judgment." And those who were already baptized came to be baptized by her a second time, Protestants as well as Roman Catholics, very many people from the districts of Chinsali, Kasama, Abercorn, Isoka, Lundazi and Mpika. Old and young, some made a journey of 150 miles, coming and going. Everybody had to give a penny, and the mother gave a penny to the baby on her back to throw into the gift basket.

'At night Lenshina played an instrument [a reed pipe?], and said: "Come, hear what God is telling you," and she herself interpreted what it meant.

'And the chiefs forced their people that they should bring their magic things to her. And the Africans of some congregations supported her and slandered the UCCAR. At present she is the biggest leader in the Northern and North-Eastern Provinces in respect of witchcraft and prayers.'[3]

The number of pilgrims to Lenshina increased rapidly; in the dry season of 1956, up to 1,000 a week were counted. Her fame spread from her own tribe not only to their Rhodesian neighbours and into the Copperbelt, but also into Tanganyika, where Lenshina is said to have lived with her husband some time before her vision; and people in Nyasaland who heard about her crossed through some of the wildest country in the East of Northern Rhodesia in order to be baptized by her. Those who returned built small wattle-and-daub churches in which they held services 'with a good deal of enthusiasm', in many places three times a week, singing the simple evangelical phrases which Lenshina had taught them, set to indigenous tunes, and listening to the self-appointed priests, many of whom were ex-mission catechists and teachers who had asked Lenshina's permission to pass on her message.

The District Commissioner at Chinsali had to take notice of the appearance of this prophet movement. He sent Boma messengers to fetch her, interviewed her about her vision, and in the end warned her that she would not get Government permission to establish her own church. It was difficult to find out whether Lenshina's actions were not a repetition of the witch-finding movements, like the *Bamucapi*, which had swept from Nyasaland through the Bemba country in 1934.[4] According to the Witchcraft Ordinance: 'Whoever names or indicates or threatens to accuse any person as being a wizard or witch; or imputes to any person the use of non-natural means in causing any death, injury or damage; or asserts that any person has by committing adultery caused in some non-natural way death, damage or calamity shall be liable. . . .' But it became quite obvious that the prophetess did not need to point out who used witchcraft; the masses brought their magic objects voluntarily to get rid of them, and flocked to confess their wrongdoings in order to be cleansed. A pupil of a nearby Roman Catholic school reported to the White Fathers after a holiday that he had seen a whole hut full of magic implements, including rosaries and crucifixes, which the converts had given to Lenshina before their baptism. One of the Boma clerks, an ex-mission teacher, went to investigate what was happening at Kasomo's village. He wrote a long report on his return which shows that he was convinced that Lenshina was neither a liar nor possessed by a traditional *ngulu*-spirit. He compares her doings with Christ's work on earth: 'He healed, forgave sins, fed the multitudes, proclaimed God's will and stopped people from doing what God hates —does not Lenshina do the same?'

He then argues about the accusations which he states that the Roman Catholics and the Protestants raise against her: 'They say that Lenshina plays a flute and declares that God is speaking, others say she has made an idol and says this is God. These are inventions of the spies who were sent by the missions but were quickly recognized and therefore had to leave quickly without finding the truth.' The question which really puzzled him was: Has Lenshina really been dead, and who raised her again? After hearing her own version of her vision, he is convinced that it was no hoax; the obedience which she shows in carrying out the work she has been ordered to do is proof that she did not awake again in her own power or in that of the devil. He remembers the story of the disciples opposing a self-appointed worker, and Christ's answer: 'Do nor forbid him, for he that is not against you is for you' (Luke 9.50, RSV). 'Even though Lenshina has not been empowered by the Christian ministers, she is herself a minister. John the Baptist was no priest but he called to repentance and baptized, and this is what Lenshina does. If some who have already been baptized elsewhere are baptized again, it is only because they desire it; Lenshina does not urge them.'

He finishes with a warning: 'When Noah announced that God would come and destroy the earth they said, "He is drunk." Let us not make this mistake. Lenshina is no witchfinder (*mucapi*), she is no false prophet, she is a true minister. God our Father does not want his children to perish, therefore again and again he sends a sentinel to warn us of impending danger.'[5]

The eschatological message and the promise of redemption for those who surrendered their magic objects proved far more attractive than the efforts of the mission churches to keep their flocks in orthodox ways. A missionary in Lubwa writes: 'The popularity of the proceedings at Kasomo defies belief. I should say that at least 90 per cent of the men, women and children in Chinsali district, and from one or two other districts, undertook the pilgrimage and returned 'cleansed' and often with new spiritual life.'[6] In spite of the efforts to 'give place in the Church to such special spiritual gifts as Lenshina seemed to be manifesting',[7] clashes soon occurred between Lenshina's followers and other Christians. Those who refused to make the pilgrimage were accused of being unwilling to give up witchcraft, and the African priests at the White Fathers' Mission, Ilondola, were especially threatened and assaulted. A trial of such cases led to a near riot at the Chinsali Boma; Lenshina's husband was found guilty of inciting a crowd to use violence to free the prisoners, and sentenced to three years' imprisonment.

Lenshina herself seems to have been anxious to avoid any trouble with the authorities. Her followers obeyed and tried non-violent methods after the imprisonment of Petro and other leading men. They challenged the police to lock them all up, arrived early in the mornings in the Boma grounds and started to pick up the leaves, cut the grass and clean the roads, tasks which were usually done by prisoners. The entry to Chinsali had to be guarded, and after a while the movement focused its attention on other tasks. The schism from the mission church was finalized by the end of 1958. The Government had to recognize the new 'church' as a *fait accompli*. It was presented with a declaration which showed clearly that the puritan reforming tendencies behind the message of Lenshina's vision were no deviation from the moral teachings, but rather a reinforcement of the strict rules, of the Church of Scotland Mission. The name 'Lumpa Church' now occurs for the first time, and the explanation of the name varies: The church which 'goes far', 'excels all others', 'hastens to Salvation'. As in many of the Lenshina hymns, the African White Fathers at Ilondola explained, the obvious and everyday meaning of the word makes sense, but it does not exclude the possibility of its being used with a 'hidden' meaning (*fya panshi*, literally 'below, underneath') which is, or may be, far more aggressive. The Laws of the Lumpa Church were formulated with the view of gaining the—hitherto withheld—approval of the Government after the strained relations of the trial period. They are still the basis of instruction. The Nchanga leader showed us a copy which was identical with that in the file of the District Commissioner at Chinsali:

'1. Lumpa Church is an organisation in which to worship God and his son Jesus Christ. It is not an organisation to make unruly behaviour with the laws of the country.

'2. In this organisation there shall be no racial discrimination, white and black men and women shall be Brotherhood and love each other.

'3. Every Christian must not be in the following habits: (a) Backbiting (b) insult (c) lies (d) pride (e) boasting (f) hatred (g) anger (h) harsh (i) false witness (j) selfish (k) rudeness (l) cunning (m) stealing and etc. He must be sincere, kind, trustworthy, love, patient and truthful.

'4. Every Christian must keep away from the following: coveting, witchcraft, stealing, adultery, sorcery, witches, drunkenness, bad songs and all primitive dances.

'5. Every Christian must have good manners of the public and in private, that is when eating, going to bed, getting up, starting work, at the end of his work, at happiness, at the time of sorrow, when in difficulties and when on a journey a Christian must first pray to his God.

'6. At a Christian wedding there should be no beer provided and no primitive dances to be allowed. The couple when married are bound by the Christian law that they shall never be separated until death separate them.

'7. The duties of every Christian is to see that he goes to Church for worshipping in each day that the congregation takes place.

'8. A widow must not be forced to marry another man, they must only tie a white bead on her hand. If she wishes to marry she can do so according to her own wish.

'9. A Christian must not be a polygamist.

'10. A Christian must not take part to eat food prepared for the mourner and at the mourning feast must not be prepared.

'11. During the time of prayers, there should be no smoking of cigarette, pipe or snuffing, and no one shall enter in the Church with cigarette, tobacco or snuff.

'12. If a man has taken some beer drink he shall not enter the Church for worship even if he has taken very little drink.

Who does not obey these laws is the one that God also does not like the Almighty God says do not practice witches, keep my love. Anyone who practice witches, he will at the end also suffer and be punished.

THESE ARE THE LAWS OF THE LUMPA CHURCH

LENSHINA MULENGA.'

As the rapid spread of the movement caught public attention, charges of deception, deliberate fraud and extortion of money were levelled against the leaders. Lenshina was described as a tool in the hands of radical African politicians, Christians under discipline whose grudge against the church and the mission made them active in an anti-white sectarian group. As usual, the less that was known, the wilder the interpretation. During the strained time of the emergency in 1957, the followers of Lenshina in the Copperbelt were regarded rather more as an Ethiopian, political group, than as a millennarian religious body. The most active of her priests in the Copperbelt happened to be the brother of an ANC secretary, and it was reported that Congress had declared that the Lumpa Church was the only real African church suitable for their members.

We were very glad to hear that during our study of Nchanga, Lenshina had come on one of her frequent visits to the Copperbelt and was actually staying in the camp of the railway workers in Chingola. We asked for an interview and received an invitation.

In the following five days we saw that Lenshina herself was keen to stress the rule of her church: No racial discrimination. Some of her staff, especially three or four of the leading men in Copperbelt congregations of the Lumpa Church, showed signs of uneasiness about our intrusion into the inner circle which surrounded the prophetess constantly during her public appearances and also most of the time when she rested. But no one made an attempt to hinder us in any way. Lenshina was the undisputed head of the group. 'We have to ask Mama' repeatedly proved the answer to a request. Her quiet but unmistakeably firm authority reminded me of a young woman who is the head of a Lunda village in the Luapula province. Even if the rumours are true that Lenshina had fits and other signs of spirit possession during her adolescence—and the African Roman Catholic priests of Ilondola said that they received this information from Lenshina's own mother—the prophetess, now in her early thirties, looks a healthy, rather plump and happily relaxed village matron, a chief in her own right, as other women in her cultural stratum of matrilineal Bantu are chiefs through heritage. She is certainly not a medium, or psychopath, used by ruthless and politically ambitious men, as some have described her. Her sense of vocation is the firm foundation upon which her work is built.

During the first interview she repeated several times that her message was nothing new. 'I cannot teach you anything. You know it (God's Law) just as well as I do. There is killing all over the world, and greediness and selfishness; that is the responsibility of the leaders. In the Lumpa Church the people find a special power to resist in temptation. In other churches the people, even the teachers, are weak. They still possess forbidden things. The people who follow me understand what it means to throw away charms. I want them to follow the commandments which you also know.'

The revivalist call went through all that Lenshina said, and through the sermons and prayers of her preachers: 'In my church a member must be like a small child, be born again . . . When a man wants to join the Lumpa Church, according to his own desire, he has to repent, then he can be baptized; the power of God witnesses that he has repented, not the power of a human being.'

The most important medium in the Lumpa congregations is not the spoken but the sung word. In the Copperbelt, the singing processions in the African Townships have become a feature as well-known as the Salvation Army bands in Britain, and everybody recognises the peculiar Lenshina tunes. When asked about the origin of the hymns, the local Lumpa Church secretary said: 'The One who let us have this church is the One who gives us the hymns; they come through Lenshina and she teaches them all over the country.' With a group of young choir girls and her own two women attendants, Lenshina led the singing in the processions and during the services which we attended. When we made tape-recordings, we found that even the most informal sounding texts were really set—Lenshina clapped her hand over her mouth and laughed when she made a mistake in a repetition—and one of the choir girls explained to us that all the tunes except one were old well-known Bemba ones, the odd one having been sung by the Chokwe when they visited Lenshina at Kasomo's village.

The simple type of hymn form, with the precentor introducing a short phrase which is picked up by the choir and repeated with very slight variations of the text, somewhat resembles our Western 'choruses', but is so genuinely African and wholly natural in its expression, that one cannot but regret that Western hymns, often in shockingly bad translations, fill the hymnbooks of the 'orthodox' churches in Rhodesia.

The shortest of such hymns was sung when the procession in the Buchi African township passed the newly built beerhall. It is probably one of the oldest of Lenshina's choruses, with its simple statement of the two main 'taboos', or reform rules of her movement:

'Shout to the desert, shout:
Leave beer and witchcraft.'

The call to repent is the main theme, but the sins of the lost sheep which the hymns mention are not simply the use of witchcraft and charms, or disregard for church rules on beer drinking or polygyny; although social misbehaviour is certainly termed sin, the fundamental sin, separation from God and contempt of the Saviour, is more frequently mentioned.

'God says: Come to me, my children,
Go, and find the sheep,
the lost sheep,
I will restore them.

'Look at the desert where I sent my children;
they are shouting,
Let all enemies listen to it.'

'Father, you see who is of the truth.
We have come, we show ourselves.
Cleanse us;
we are not able to do it ourselves.'

'Wash us, our Father;
wash us, our Father.
You are washed in me.'

'Teach us, Saviour;
you have shown a way of life,
it is you, O Saviour.
And he who has lost you, the way of life,
where shall he go?'

'Those who shall enter into the new Zion,
They are not the slanderers, nor those who quarrel.'

'You, my brother and my sister,
you shall not enter into the new Zion,
if you despise the Saviour, Jesus.'

'I am leading my friends;
they must see and come to my Father.
Those who stay behind,
they will be troubled,
they are lost from the Lord.'

'And we, when shall we be saved?
We who love the land of darkness,
we who love the land of slavery.'

The announcement of judgment plays on the register of eschatological imagery:

'You fool, run, the fire is coming near.
Now remember Sodom and Gomorrah.
Jesus made the fire fall down;
all were burnt.'

'The sign of the enemies,
the sign of the enemies.
If you are a sinner, you shall suffer.
You shall suffer as Satan suffered.'

'My Father, he does not look lovingly at the bad.
He sends them hardship.
He wounds the bad ones.'

'My Father, he has built his bridge;
my Father, he has built his bridge.
Those who cross it shall be blessed.
He who fails will fall into the pit.'

'You who stay behind,
you cannot follow later.
You will find
that all the space of the Lord is finished.'

The longing for redemption, and the joy of salvation, are very movingly expressed in the following, which seemed to be the favourite ones at the time of the visit of Lenshina to the Copperbelt in 1958:

'You who love the land of darkness,
let us break through, be saved.
He will help us in everything,
he will take us out of evil,
when, when?'

'Come all near,
it is my Father,
he calls us.'

'Stand all in a line!
Those who stay behind should look at us, the brothers.
Our Father stretched his arm out.
You are blessed, you who have been given.
Now shout with joy, you blessed ones.'

'Gather all together for the Lord.
We shall be spread out far and wide in the beautiful country;
We shall always roll in the dust, [*the greeting for a chief*]
hallelujah, always.'

'You, the mountain of refuge which stands in this world,
you, the highest mountain.
Those who fail to climb this mountain,
they shall be cut to pieces.
But you who have climbed the mountain,
rejoice, sing.
You are fortunate, you have found the refuge.'

The content of doctrine in the hymns is slight, but it is significant that Jesus Christ is mentioned seven times in the twenty-four hymns which we collected, the Crucifixion twice and the Second Coming once.

'Do not look for the things of this world.
God sent Noah, and he did not stop [disobey].
God sent Lot: Go and speak.
And Lot did not refuse.
At last came Jesus,
And the hostility of the world came out.'

'Great tree, a shade to make us all happy.
That is what you did long ago.
When the Lord came to this world,
someone called: Crucify him.
Take care, you murderers,
you who despised the Son of the Lord.

'We praise the Lord Jesus,
He was at the lake in a boat.
He calls us all: Come, you!
Let us go with him.
Those who stay behind are bad.
It is those who took the Lord
and crucified him.'

'You who do not believe, it is you
who cause Jesus Christ to delay his coming.
He said to his disciples: I go to heaven,
and I shall come again.'

The third person of the Trinity was mentioned in two hymns which were sung at the baptismal services:

'Welcome the Lord, the blessed Saviour.
Today comes the Spirit.
He is always descending like a dove.'

'The Word of God must shine,
it must bring light everywhere;
the Spirit brings us light.'

The prayers in the services, all of which were extempore, used the same thoughts and phrases as the hymns. One of the Copperbelt elders prayed thus after Lenshina had baptized:

'You, our Father, you, great chief,
you made heaven and earth.
You are in heaven,
we are on earth, that is trouble.
But in your mercy you came to us with love.
Our Father, we come to kneel before you
because you said:
Come near to me.
Teach us the truth.
You said: Knock and I will open.
You are a light of great honour.
We are the children of Israel in the slavery of troubles.
Strengthen us to keep your commandments.
Where else shall we look?
You said: Come to me. We are your sheep.
Bless us who have been sanctified in the pond,
we who are adulterers and sorcerers.
You are the great healer.
Go to those who are in hospital.
Strengthen them with your needle of power;
Comfort them and us.
Let us eat in heaven with our Saviour, Jesus Christ.
Amen.'

After him followed Lenshina, with this short prayer before her sermon:

'We are before you, our Father.
Teach us in your Spirit.
A blind one cannot teach a blind one.
Be with us during this time.
Give us eyes of the Spirit.
O Lord of great strength.
Amen.'

And her sermon was also rather formalized in its expressions, but delivered freely, with simple unselfconscious gestures and without excessive oratory:

> 'I cannot teach you. You must follow the Words of God which you hear and understand. The Word of God must shine (reference to one of her hymns). The Spirit gives light. The Word is also like a wound in your mind, it hurts.' Then, pointing at individuals, she said: 'I do not know you, but I know that some stand here who have not yet stopped bad things. One who kills his friend, how can he enter into God's Kingdom? God said: Stop killing and adultery. You have heard in the Book of Life that you are sinners, don't forget that.
>
> 'A minister with a clerical collar was teaching the New Testament. He taught: Don't kill. But he was always full of anger. Was he doing what he taught?
>
> 'God sent Noah to the people to say: Leave behind what is of this world. Their refusal to hear destroyed them. The Snake (Satan) is in beer. Do you want to drown like those people? They came and cried: Noah, open to us. Remember what Noah said. We are foolish people, we are concerned about things of this world.
>
> 'Point out the Word of God to your friends. Those who are lost have destroyed themselves. It is the children of God who deceived themselves, not the children of Satan.
>
> 'Lot was pulled out of Sodom. He did not want to sin. God said to him: Get out of this town. Don't look behind you. But the woman looked behind and she was lost, though she was a child of God, because she did not obey. And you, child of God, will you destroy yourself? Jesus Christ came into this world but they did not obey him. The churches of this world called themselves of Christ but they do not obey. Look at the Cross. They do not take up the cross; they hate each other, they kill.'

At this point Lenshina was interrupted by someone starting the hymn 'Great tree, a shade to make us all happy . . .' It was quickly taken up by the crowd. After six or seven repetitions, the prophetess raised her hand and went on, taking up the lines of the hymn:

> 'Look out, you murderers. A young man went out to get honey because he was hungry. He tried three times but failed. He then called a friend and they collected green wood and made a fire with much smoke under a tree which the young man climbed. His friend called: "Let me too have some." But the greedy one kept on eating till the smoke overpowered him; he fell down into the fire and was dead.
>
> 'Let us leave behind the things of this world. The Judge will judge us, we cannot do it ourselves. When we sow seeds or plant things in our gardens, we harvest what we put in. Let us pray in singing this hymn:
> "We praise the Lord Jesus,
> He was at the lake in a boat . . ." '

At the same Sunday morning service, one of her Copperbelt preachers followed with another short sermon in a very similar style. Since he spoke the Tumbuka language of Nyasaland, we could not follow him very well. He made references to Moses, who, in spite of the use of the 'desert' and the 'country of slavery' as allegories, had not been mentioned before. He described his pilgrimage to the 'new Zion', i.e., Kasomo's village, Lenshina's home. He too was interrupted by a hymn, sung in the Bemba language:

'My Father, I have built on stone,
I built on firm ground. . . .'

The preacher closed with the exhortation in Bemba: 'Praise ye the Lord,' and the congregation gave the response: 'The Lord's name be praised.'

In these and similar features that occurred during the wedding ceremony which followed, the influence of the Church of Scotland Mission was very noticeable. Tumbuka is, with Bemba, one of the main languages of that Mission, and the Scottish order of service was still an influence over the whole sequence of baptism, worship service and wedding ceremony, in spite of the fact that it was conducted without any Bible readings. It is surprising that there was no trace of Roman Catholic cult. It has been estimated that about half of Lenshina's followers come from Roman Catholic mission churches, but they have adopted her Free Church tradition, including the whole set of religious vocabulary, which in Bemba is very distinct—the name of God, words like pray, praise, read, etc., are different, and one can easily tell from a person's speech to which church his loyalty is bound.

Lenshina had told us in the first interview that only she baptized. Those who wanted baptism asked one of her preachers for instruction and then waited until her next visit. The Copperbelt men and women whose baptism we saw had been prepared by Ba Smart, an old man from Lenshina's home village who had spent six months in the towns to teach the catechumens. One of the local leaders told us that the teaching was based on the 'Laws of the Lumpa Church', not on the Bible, 'but one day soon Mama Lenshina will give us our own Bible!' Immediately before their baptism, the neophytes had to confess their previous use of black or white magic, and hand over any 'medicines' and charms which they possessed. Nobody seemed to know how these were disposed of, except that many had been collected in a hut just outside Kasomo's village.

At the beginning of each service, those who wished to be baptized were called to sit in front, and to take their hats and headscarves off—another reminiscence of Free Church practice. After introductory hymns and prayers, Ba Smart, the teacher, knelt in front of Lenshina and offered her a tin, covered with a simply embroidered white cloth. She also knelt and took it and removed the lid, which still bore the name of a well-known brand of floor polish. The water was in a glass jar in the tin. She took the jar carefully out of the carrier, wrapped it with the cloth, and proceeded to the kneeling congregation. Ba Smart asked the name of the person, then Lenshina dipped her fingers into the water and laid her hand on the head. She did not seem to say anything at all. Ba Smart also laid his hand on. The children were baptized with their mothers, most of them babies in the carry-cloth; there were also some children whose mothers, I was told, had been baptized by Lenshina in the previous year. Altogether about a hundred and twenty adults and about ninety children, far more women than men, were baptized on these two occasions. It was very moving to see the great and sincere joy which all the newly-baptized men and women showed, as of people relieved from a heavy burden who had been given a precious gift, and the way in which the congregation shared this joy in singing, ululation and shaking hands with them. One of the preachers then entered their names, addresses, home villages and Boma in a register. There was no collection or paying of fees. During the times we spent with the prophetess, we never saw anyone handling money. One of the elders came at the end of the Sunday service and whispered to Lenshina that they had forgotten to announce the collection, but she motioned him to be quiet. 'They depend too much on her leadership when she is here,' explained the Chingola leader.

After the service, eleven men stayed to be registered as preachers recognized by the prophetess; one was rejected by her, but we did not hear the reason for this. A preacher explained that most of them had made the pilgrimage to the 'new Zion', and that many of the followers, even after only some three months of instruction in the Copperbelt, went to the 'Temple' in Kasomo's village. None of the teachers and preachers are paid a fixed salary; they have to earn their own living, and therefore take turns in living in town or cultivating their village gardens. Some of them are supported by town congregations; others, as for example the Nchanga leader, are in regular employment in the Mines. Three of the Copperbelt preachers wore black gowns. Lenshina wore for the services a simple black dress, obviously made by some village tailor.

The most impressive part of Lenshina's work followed the Sunday service. After a very short interval, in which she supervised the preparation of a meal for her European visitor and also had some food herself with her children and her woman companions, she spent over five hours in receiving visitors in the small living-room of a standard two-roomed African hut. The room was crammed with people of her entourage, the nannie for her children, her chauffeur, the girl singers and several deacons. One of the black-gowned 'ministers' entered the names of the applicants in a book. I did not see anybody giving money or other presents. Small groups of twos and threes entered, knelt down to greet the prophetess and us with the polite formal clapping of their hands, others less formally shaking hands. The first was a blind man, with bad scars from smallpox, telling Lenshina how he had caught the disease in the Congo. A young man showed to her injuries on his leg caused by a fall off a bicycle. A mother handed her a baby and explained that the child had dysentery. Lenshina listened attentively, asked a few questions about the circumstances, and dismissed the patient without any promise of help or prayer, nor did she make any special gesture such as the laying-on of hands or touching the wounds. But one could clearly see the relief which the people felt when telling her about their troubles, and their gladness to be admitted to her presence. One man and two women came to speak about their matrimonial difficulties. Lenshina advised one woman who had been deserted to go back to her parents in a village. The next one explained that she preferred to stay in the Copperbelt and Lenshina left it at that. The man told her that his wife had run away from him, but received no suggestions as to how he should face his problem, yet he left quite contentedly. When the crowd became too pressing, the front and back doors were opened and the sick simply filed past and shook hands.

At one point, the recording minister brought in three young men and asked everyone else to leave the room. The men told Lenshina that during the procession back from church they had run into trouble. A Government ambulance had not slowed down but driven among the children who were running after the procession. A steward had asked him to stop, but he refused, saying he would bring a case against him. Lenshina interrupted this tale: 'Did you only speak to him?' One young man answered: 'No, Mama, I grabbed his arm on the steering-wheel, and his shirt was torn, but only a little bit.' He looked rather uncomfortable and shamed about it. Lenshina explained: 'The Government people are very many, and they are against us. We do not want trouble;

we want to live in peace.' Then dismissing the young men, she told them curtly: 'We shall see; perhaps they will not make a case of it.'

At sunset several of the leaders asked me for a lift because they had to go on night duty, and the talk during the thirty miles journey in the seclusion of the car revealed some of the awe in which Lenshina is held. With us was Ba Smart, one of the oldest of the teachers, on his way to prepare some more local adherents for baptism. He carried the wrapped-up polish tin with water for the baptisms. The secretary of the Nchanga congregation, a Mine policeman with some school education, asked if I knew what the Holy Water was. I thought they had perhaps brought it from her village, but he said emphatically, 'No, it was given to Mama Lenshina, and it does not diminish; nobody has ever filled it up, though the the people who want to be baptized are very, very many. In "Zion", you cannot drive in a car through the streets; there are too many people there. And many sick ones come. Mama Lenshina is working very hard. But she always rests on Mondays and Thursdays. Even here in the towns they cannot see her on these days.'

It was unfortunate that a few weeks later, when we visited the 'new Zion', Lenshina herself was still away with her people in the South, in Livingstone, on her way to Bulawayo in Southern Rhodesia. (The District Commissioner at Chinsali told us that he had had a query from Dar es Salaam, where a man had applied for permission to build a Lumpa church.) But though with her absence, the main attraction for the pilgrims had gone, Kasomo's village—as it is still normally called, after the headman—was clearly the centre of the movement, its devotion and its hopes. The simple shelters of the pilgrims there at that time did not house multitudes of sick and frightened folk, longing for healing of body and mind, but the grateful followers who had come to labour voluntarily on the erection of the 'Temple', a great church building which Lenshina had planned in 1956, when nobody would believe that anything might come out of these intentions. Even with our preparation for the unexpected and our experience of the deep sincerity of the Lumpa followers, we were amazed to find a great cathedral of beautiful simple lines[8] built with real craftsmanship, walls and arches perfectly laid, with wooden screens of high quality over the glass windows. The interior was just as impressive; the remarkably long nave had twenty-five pillars of alternate grey and pink courses along either side, and at the east end was a triangular arch over a canopy. Lenshina's secretary, who supervised the work in the village during her absence, told us that the interior would probably be whitewashed and curtains hung in the arch behind the platform. 'But', he said, 'Mama has not yet said what we should do.' He was a young man in his early twenties, educated and speaking fluent English, very polite and friendly when we had explained the reason for our visit and handed him some colour-prints of photos we had taken of Lenshina in the Copperbelt. The local crowd was rather more reluctant to greet the European visitors; they started singing only after we proved that we already knew some of their chants.

The plan of the building and the fine quality of work revealed the influence of the nearby Roman Catholic mission, at Ilondola. If—as a councillor at the Court of the Paramount Chief, Chitimukulu, said—Lenshina got her 'eyes' from Lubwa, the Church of Scotland Mission, she certainly got her hands from Ilondola. One of her early converts wrote in 1955 that Alice had taken on the name of Regina, the Queen of Heaven, in the Bemba version 'Lenshina', after she had been sent back to earth. I doubt whether many of her followers know this meaning of her name or placed any significance upon it. But the Roman Catholics saw it as a blasphemy, and that may have been one of the reasons why the friction between them and Lenshina's followers was much stronger, resulting in aggresiveness and assaults, than with the Protestant group.

Is Lenshina regarded as a semi-divine being? There is nothing in the so-called constitution or in any of her proclamations which indicates such a claim. Her status is in many respects similar to that of a woman chief. In her village, her simple house with its outbuildings of kitchen, grainstore and dovecot is surrounded by a stockade like a chief's; she receives the respectful greeting with kneeling and clapping, and though a young woman is called Mama, i.e., grandmother. Like any chief, she is given presents of food and money, and these must have been very considerable to make the purchase of building materials and lorries possible. Newspaper reports said that on her last Copperbelt visit, the congregation gave her a gold wrist watch. The labour which was organized to build the 'cathedral' followed the pattern of customary service for a chief; whole villages went to Kasomo's for four days at a time, bringing their own food and supplementary supplies for the sick and other pilgrims. It is not extraordinary to find a woman in such high position in the customary social organization of the Bemba, with their 'mothers of the chiefs', the princesses who are sometimes ruling chiefs in their own right, the women guardians of the *babenye*, the holy tribal relics. But these offices are inherited, whereas Lenshina's status has been acquired by vocation, the divine vision and the special power of healing inherent in her since she 'came back from the dead'. In the eyes of her people she is therefore more than a woman of customary high status. 'We know no Government, we know no chief, we only know Lenshina', shouted some Nyasaland villagers when they were told to pull down Lumpa church buildings they had erected. A District Officer wrote in 1955: 'The extent of her following—60,000 pilgrims to her village in one year—is an indication of how unsatisfying the modern missionary approach to witchcraft is for the majority of Africans. Lenshina does not say that witchcraft is nonsense, but that she has been given the power to neutralize it.'

The function of exorcizing is personal. Only she baptizes, i.e., purifies those who have used magic objects to harm others, or, probably much more frequently, obtained charms to protect themselves. Both practices, she insists, are sinful. Most other churches turn a blind eye to the use of 'white' protective magic. While it is quite usual to see charms on the infants who are brought to be baptized in other churches, people flock to her, handing over these symbols of their hidden fears. She fascinates them with her courage in bringing this evil out into the open, and in handling these potentially dangerous objects; awe for her person is, probably quite unconsciously, impressed by the knowledge that she is unafraid to keep such a collection near her village.

According to Sundkler, 'the dream and the taboo are the two backdoors through which the African past enters the church'.[9] In the Lumpa Church, it might be said that a dream and taboos were the front doors through which Christians went back into the African past. The longing for salvation, for freedom from fear, from sickness and from death, has led to a renewed emphasis on 'right' behaviour and on 'purification'—using a new powerful magic, the Holy Eternal Water. The power of the prophetess is directly related to the degree of anxiety and of ill-health in which this country lives. Her eschatological message, 'Repent now, or you may be lost,' strengthens acceptance of the old and the new taboos. In 1956 the District Commissioner at Chinsali commented on the new high sex morality in his country, under Lenshina's influence. Polygyny and adultery had from the beginning an important place in the list of taboos. It was quite astonishing to see how willingly people submitted to a minor, distinctly 'Lumpa' taboo in the Copperbelt. During the procession through the African township to the Lumpa meeting-place, an old woman limping along next to me suddenly grasped the pocket of the jacket of the man in front of her. She called one of the stewards, and the man took a small bottle of snuff out of that pocket and gave it to the woman, smiling rather embarrassedly. The old lady ran quickly into one of the neighbouring houses to leave it there, and happily rejoined the procession; the forbidden tobacco had been got rid of before we entered the place of worship. Before the sermon, a special announcement was made, 'All who have tobacco or have drunk only a little beer should go out'—and several men left. This discipline is, of course, a strong unifying force among people of such varying spiritual backgrounds.

Another link with the African past which has been repeatedly quoted by adversaries of Lenshina is her supposed connection with *ngulu*-possession, a cult which has had a recent revival in Bemba country—or it is perhaps better to say that it has come into the open again, after having been kept in secret. *Ngulu* is the name used for what the White Fathers' Dictionary terms 'secondary divinities whose abode is supposed to be in waterfalls, large trees, pythons, and is also used as a name for a person possessed by such a divinity, a "chief of spirits" (*mfumu ya mipashi*).' These *ngulu* prophesy and heal, that is, they have the power to find out under whose authority is the spirit who troubles the sick person. When this is established, the sick person is initiated, and on joining the society of the *ngulu*—'It is a kind of church', one of our informants said—his sickness will stop. 'Sometimes when a man becomes an *ngulu*, he will find that he has the power of healing, and he knows how to give people medicines which can cure them.' One of the best known *ngulu* is Mulenga. This name, however, is very common among Bemba people, and it is therefore possible that Lenshina's use of it has no connection with any former spirit possession or initiation. It is difficult to assess whether, in many peoples' minds, this name still evokes the idea of a supernatural being, whose concern is with healing. A hospital orderly who is one of the best respected church elders in the Northern Province said that the *ngulu* represent the main belief and practice which challenge the Church. It is perhaps not just a coincidence that of her four names, Alice Lenshina Mulenga Lubusha, the prophetess has chosen as the important ones, with which she signs her letters, the two middle ones, the names of two powerful 'spirits', one of the new and one of the old religion of her country.

NOTES

1. B.G.M. Sundkler, *Bantu Prophets in South Africa.*
2. *Ngulu*, a Bemba divinity, probably the spirit of a chief. See p. 267.
3. Report by Rev. Paul Mushindo to the Presbytery, 1956.
4. A. I. Richards, 'A modern movement of witchfinders,' *Africa*, Oct. 1958.
5. Sandy Rain, MS. at Boma, Chinsali, 'What I think about Lenshina.'
6. Rev. F. MacPherson, MS. at Boma, Chinsali.
7. Rev. F. MacPherson, Occasional Papers No. 1, IMC, Dept. of Missionary Studies, 1958.
8. Length 169ft. 8in., width 39ft.
9. Sundkler, *op. cit.*, p. 216.

V

THE MEANING AND VITALITY OF THE CHURCH

12

The Inward Experience

THE time available did not permit of a systematic study of the traditional religion of the African people of Northern Rhodesia, and in any case the area contains such a complexity of tribes that nothing short of a series of major works would suffice for such a theme. What little we learned was mainly incidental. But the impression that emerged was that the elements which still exercise an influence over the greatest number of people are the fear of witchcraft, with a corresponding use of protective charms, a lingering veneration of the mystical functions and insignia of the chief, and a widespread belief in possession by the *ngulu* spirits.

The effect of social change on personal faith.

The move from the villages into the Copperbelt, though for some individuals a liberating opportunity, generally proves to be a severe test of religious conviction, whatever the religion may be. Probably Christianity stands up to the transplantation a little more sturdily than paganism. One church member, reporting that there are many so-called pagans in his row of houses, commented, 'When pagans come to the towns they forget to pray; they just drink.' However, we failed to produce enough evidence to make a definite assertion. Certainly a great many give up the practice of any religion when they come to the Copperbelt, though, as we said at the end of Section I, they will on occasion still claim to belong to the particular church which predominates in their village home.

It is from the ranks of these nominal or lapsed Christians that new members, if any, are being added to the congregations on the Copperbelt. Only the Watchtower and, to a lesser degree, the Roman Catholic Church, are to any appreciable extent bringing adult pagans on the Copperbelt into the fold. The minister of the UCCAR at Chingola, who constantly has a fair number of adults attending his Hearers' class, told us that during the whole of his ministry there, he has not known one person to enter the class from a completely pagan background; every one had had some previous contact with the Church up country, either in a rural school or a village congregation.

The position is different for the children. The child of a pagan household in the Copperbelt is almost as likely as the child of Christian parents to be introduced to the Church. In the village, if a family is Christian, the children will be expected to accompany their elders to church and will grow up feeling that they are members of the congregation, until they rebel against it. But in the Copperbelt, because of the parental loss of nerve and of religious assurance, children are much less likely to be taken to church by their parents. If a child goes at all he commonly does so in company with school friends, and his church-going may bear no relation to the religion of his parents. The religious upbringing of the Copperbelt child, therefore, is much more a matter of chance than in the villages.

Yet, although so many adults abandon their religion on the Copperbelt, in times of special need there is often reversion either to pagan custom or to Christian observance or to both. There is a small but fairly constant trickle of freshly committed members into most of the Christian congregations. The minister of the UCCAR mentioned several who had entered his Hearers' class during the previous few months.

> 'One simply said: "I hear the Word of God in my heart; that is why I want to join the Church now." There was a married couple whose child had been seriously ill; the father said, "God has helped me, God loves me"; they brought a thank-offering of Shs.10 each and both started classes. A sick man whom I visited was not a church member, but when he recovered he said the prayers had made him see the love of God. Some people come on their own, others are brought by friends. Sometimes a husband and wife come back together.'

The 'materialism' of African Christianity

At first sight such cases, and a great deal of other evidence, seem to suggest that for many African Christians the function of religion is understood in terms that are largely utilitarian and materialistic. An official of the African Mineworkers' Union at Nchanga expressed a very common point of view when he said:

> 'In Nyasaland there are many ways of encouraging people to go to church, but not here. Here in the Copperbelt cases of sickness are

reported through the Union, not through the churches. While I was away in Nyasaland it was the chairman of our branch here who helped my wife, not the church, although she is a good church member. Then in the big strike in 1955 the Church had no good influence, in fact it became anti-Union. I gave up going to church then.'

Inevitably Christianity is closely associated with the concept of 'civilization', and the words commonly used to designate a non-Christian are terms of disparagement. Many people seem to regard education as the primary function of both Missions and churches, so it was symptomatic that Chief Chitimukulu answered our questions about the strength of the Church in Bemba country only with an assurance that school attendance was increasing. To be able to call oneself a church member, even though one's association is extremely tenuous, confers a certain status; and loss of status is often regarded as the greatest disadvantage in being suspended from a church or in changing from one denomination to another. As one pillar of the UCCAR said at Kansuswa:

'In my own church I am respected as a man who knows the law of this church and can be received into any congregation. But if I join another church, I become like a child again, ignorant of their ways and having to learn afresh.'

This consideration of status was evident in the disparagement of other denominations which occasionally appeared in the essays written by 194 schoolchildren of twelve to sixteen years old at Chingola. 'They pray like heathen.' 'They have very small numbers.' 'Ours is not just a church on an ant-hill' (referring to the open air meeting-places of the sects).

The 'materialism' of the African valuation of religion was most clearly apparent in these children's essays. While it would certainly be unreasonable to give undue weight to the opinions of children expressed in the context of a school essay, none the less they are of some value as reflecting the adult attitudes to which the children have become accustomed.

In the essays, those who approved of a church did so on these grounds, in order of frequency: its assistance to people moving house, entertaining visitors or facing the expense of a funeral; its provision of football clubs, hospitals, schools; its abolition of wars, slavery and witchcraft; its poor relief and sick visiting; the excellence of a particular pastor or missionary, or of church furnishings, conduct of worship and sermons. Only the Roman Catholic or Watchtower children, however, mentioned good race relations and a world-wide faith, evangelistic zeal, and spiritual benefits such as the Sacraments and knowledge of the Bible.

This apparently greater appreciation of strictly 'religious' values among the Roman Catholic children probably reflected the more thorough visitation of the schools by their priest than by any other minister. It was remarkable that the essays of the Roman Catholic children contained far more references to dogmatic Christianity than any others. Fourteen of them, it is true, only mentioned material or social advantages of Christianity, but an equal number stressed the spiritual benefits; the same balance was evident in the essays of the Watchtower children. On the other hand, five out of the six children of the DRC wrote exclusively in material terms; and nineteen children of the UCCAR did likewise, over against only two who emphasized the specifically 'religious' function of the Church.

The attitude of many African Christians towards the variety of churches is therefore surprisingly tolerant and uncommitted. A man belongs to a particular denomination for reasons of personal history and habit, but he would be quite ready to consider a change if he could see some practical advantage in it. Fairly typical of the younger generation was the youth who wrote:

> 'It is very good for a man to see the goodness and badness of a church before he joins it. As for me, I am still looking for a good church which I can join. I went to the Roman church; I found that people were praying to pictures of Jesus and his Mother Mary. Then I wanted to join it, but I thought after some minutes that it is not good for a man to pray to anything that he does not know. So I tried to go to the Church of Scotland. I found that when they go to church they must have sixpence for the church. But I was unable to pay that sixpence every Sunday. One day I went to Lenshina's Church; but I found that it is when they are drunk that they sing and dance along the streets. Is this good for a Christian to do?'

The enviable tolerance with which most Christians regard the members of other churches is partly due to the general indifference towards dogmatics. These statements from members of various denominations are not untypical: 'God alone knows which church is good' (UCCAR). 'There is no need to make a face at your friends, as if they don't know how to pray' (RC). 'Every church follows the footsteps of Jesus' (Watchtower). 'We don't know which church is correct and which is not' (Plymouth Brethren). 'We do not hate any church, for we do not know which is right. We are all in the way to find where God is' (Lumpa Church).

In contrast to this unconcern towards religious differences, there was always the strongest criticism of a church that was thought to be failing in practical helpfulness towards its members. For many Christians, indeed, the congregation seems to be regarded mainly as a friendly society existing for mutual aid. This communal care for the unfortunate is undoubtedly looked upon as an important demonstration of the power of Christ, and is watched and judged as such by non-Christians. Some of the sects are regarded with favour on account of the strong communal life which their members enjoy during the early days of the sect's existence. A staunch member of the Methodist Church, describing one break-away group he had encountered in Southern Rhodesia, said:

> 'They had a very strong fellowship. If a member wanted to cultivate and fence a field, all the members helped and it was done in a day. If another wanted to build a house, all helped to make bricks and thousands were turned out in a day. When a new member joined, all contributed to buy him a bicycle so that he could attend all the meetings. This spirit attracted many.'

Similarly a member of the Anglican congregation at Nchanga expressed admiration for the Roman Catholics, because 'they help each other in the villages with working parties'.

It would be easy to conclude from this that the religious sense of many Africans in the Copperbelt is defective and can be fostered only by more intensive instruction. Yet that would be an entirely superficial interpretation of the facts. There is certainly a rising tide of genuine materialism. Since the old African ways, in which religion and society are one, met our schizophrenic Western culture (built paradoxically, as it is, upon a materialistic technology and the Christian faith), many Africans, failing to learn the trick of holding the religious and the secular spirit in separate compartments, have abandoned themselves to a meaningless immediacy—'eat, drink and be merry, for tomorrow we die'. Nevertheless a great deal of African 'materialism' is actually accompanied by the most lively sense of a spiritual world. It is not in fact at all what it seems to Western eyes.

For, if one may be allowed a generalization, the Bantu world-view appears to contain no distinction between a natural and a supernatural order of being; even among those Africans who have adopted Western categories of thought, there are many who cannot fully accept the divorce between heaven and earth. Christian teaching, it is true, brought into greater prominence the old idea of the great God who is above and beyond all; and with this had appeared the imagery of a heavenly country which is 'somewhere else'. But these concepts have not greatly modified the belief that Nature, Man and the Unseen are inseparably involved in one another in a total community of which it might be said that all is here and all is now. A man's well-being consists in his belonging to, and being in harmony with, this totality. When things go well with him he knows he is at peace, and of a piece, with the scheme of things, and there can be no greater good than this. If things go wrong then, somehow, he has fallen out of step. He is a prey to the malice which this disharmony has released abroad in the world. He feels lost. The totality has become hostile. If misfortune persists, an acute anxiety is set up which may quickly develop into a suicidal despair.

These pre-Christian ideas were easily adapted to the first crude understanding of the Gospel. 'Often', said the leader of the Tertiaries at Kansuswa, 'I heard from the missionaries and from my parents that God would punish the wicked and reward the good. So I decided to be a Christian.' Christians faced with a run of bad luck may leave the Church; but, equally, those who have lapsed may be persuaded by a spell of misfortune to return to the Church. At a session of elders and deacons of the UCCAR at Nchanga we were told that this is probably the most common cause of reconversions.

> 'One who had fallen away found money difficulties in his life and he said "I am lost. I must go back to the Church to find peace."'
>
> 'I went to church while I was at school. But in 1948 I began work in the Northern Province police and had no time to go to church. In 1955 I said to myself, "I am not lucky; I shall be lost." So I left the police and joined the Mine and was baptized in our church after one year.'
>
> 'I was a catechumen in our village, married to a church member. But I had difficulties with my wife and came to Nchanga and took a second wife. This one refused to join the church. Afterwards I saw that she was really bad, so I divorced her and went back to my first wife. And now we are very happy as Christians together. The laws of the Church help us to be full of peace.'

Benedict Kasenga, a minister of one of the sects, the 'African Holy Spiritual Church', was trying to raise enough cash to pay the bridewealth for a wife. In two weeks he made £5 by selling bananas in the European market; then the money was stolen from his suitcase and he was thrown into extraordinary terror.

> 'These people can kill me,' he exclaimed. 'Whatever I do now it fails. I worked for three months serving in the store and in that time they cheated me and I got no pay. I leave that work and sell bananas and my money is stolen. What shall I do to buy food? They will kill me. Why does God hate me? I do not know if I have done wrong, or

if my grandfather or father did wrong, that God has now left me. I can do nothing but only suffer.' The next day, however, he was buoyant again. 'Yesterday I was unhappy, but see, now I have made a dress for a woman on my sewing machine and I have ten shillings. I have got food and I am happy again. But whether I shall get the money for my wife I do not know.'

Often, however, the run of bad luck goes on for a longer time, and then people are tempted to end their lives. An Anglican missionary at Chipili told us that attempted suicide is a fairly frequent ground for discipline cases in the Church. A Catholic priest also remarked on the number of times in the Confessional that church members mention having tried to take their lives. It is not uncommon for women to ask for the Last Sacraments, saying, 'Father, please help me in my last trouble. Set my soul free, so that I may go and hang myself.' Often, however, the act is less calculated, for fear and despair wipe out all coherent thought. As the elder of one church said:

> 'There is a time when a man so worries that he finds it is not good to live. When that feeling comes to a person, then it doesn't make any difference at all whether he is a Christian or not. It is the hour that forces a person to act. There are reasons for making a person prefer death and he has no chance of thinking whether there is a better life or a bad life ahead. He has been reading Scripture; he knows it. But in that hour his thinking vanishes away; now he thinks of nothing but a red cloth before his face. And of that hour nobody knows, not even a Christian minister. It could happen to him.'

Yet, in spite of this deep-seated tendency to equate material well-being with 'a state of grace', there is a slowly growing Christian conscience that is beginning to question this assumption and to make the ancient assertion of faith—'Though he slay me, yet will I trust him.' This is a theme that occurs from time to time in sermons. 'We deny God,' exclaimed a lay preacher at Nsensema's, 'when we meet troubles like the death of a spouse or a child. This we should not do.' Nsensema himself complained on one occasion that 'some weak Christians think that God gives them life and strength, but as soon as a person dies they say, "Where is God?"'. The minister of an African Methodist Episcopal church in the Copperbelt, describing his congregation, said:

> 'People who come to church without a complete surrender of themselves to Christ, very, very little things take them away and they walk out. But we have many members in the church, very faithful, who are used to being in great troubles. Yet they endure and say "This will not shake my faith, I know it must happen."'

It may be relevant here to recall again the meeting of some twenty young men at Kitwe, school-teachers and welfare officers, who for an hour or more poured out, one after the other, a torrent of invective against the Church because of the alleged failure of white Christians to practise the brotherhood they had preached. Suddenly they were silenced by one of their number asking, 'But are we Africans supposed to be Christians because white people have been kind to us, or because we believe that Christ is true?' The minority which can think its way to that question and have the courage to ask it openly is significant for the Church of the future.

So a closer acquaintance with some of the members of any congregation on the Copperbelt removes all doubt as to the reality of the African Christian's sense of the Unseen, though he may still divide less sharply than we do the material and the spiritual realms.

The Incalculable God

There is another feature of African spirituality which may seem paradoxical to Europeans with their more cerebral approach to religion. In the experience of many African Christians God and Christ appear to be much more incalculable and incomparable than is suggested by the theology of Western Christendom, and yet this remote God is often more vividly imagined and ardently loved than is usual in the devotion of most Europeans.

The session of elders and deacons of the UCCAR at Nchanga, when asked whether they felt in their prayers that they were speaking to one who was a friend, answered, 'The Holy One is not like a human being. We cannot speak to him as to a friend. We approach him with fear, with honour and respect.' The incomprehensibility of God is baffling to many faithful believers. One old stalwart of the congregation at Nsensema's said, 'When I pray I often say, Perhaps I am alone; but then I think, No, he is near. I am like a child in the dark.' Jesus Christ also, who so frequently in prayer or conversation is referred to as synonymous with God the Father, is dissociated from the realm of earthly experience. A minister of the UCCAR, when asked to name the person whose life most resembled Christ, was first puzzled by the question and then answered, 'I have never thought that any human being could be like Jesus.'

If God is remote and unknown some will be content with agnosticism, but others are challenged to seek and discover. The most unexpected people are constrained to the search.

An advanced underground worker at Nchanga, earning £40 a month, a melancholy middle-aged man, told how his father had died as a miner at Mufulira. Some time after that he came in contact with a visiting missionary of the Apostolic Faith Mission. 'She helped me to understand the Bible. I learned that to trust in the Blood of Jesus is everything. I decided then I must go to their Bible School in Pretoria. So I gave up my job at £35 a month. This annoyed all my friends. I left my wife and children with the missionary in Lusaka. I used £250 of my savings to support my wife and five daughters while I was away, but my family refused to help my wife and at the end of the time they were dressed in rags.' After this he returned to the Copperbelt, took a job at Nchanga, and started preaching in various churches. 'I cannot preach now, because I have to work always on Sundays, but I like to go to different churches, the Church of Central Africa, the Dutch Reformed Church and even the Roman Catholic.' Gradually as the years pass he finds the materialism of the Copperbelt life is sapping his old enthusiasm. 'When I read the Word of God in the evening I may even dream about it, but when I go to work and listen to the instructions of the shift boss, then I forget the Word of God.'

The significance of dreams

This reference to dreams sounds a theme which is constantly recurring in the spiritual histories of individual Africans. We found that people everywhere were both fascinated and terrified by dreams. One of the leading lay preachers in the Mbereshi area told us that it is generally believed that if one dreams frequently of one's dead father and this is accompanied by a string of bad luck, it certainly means that the father's ghost is a *ciwa,* or malignant spirit, that has come to torment him. Again during a discussion in the church at Nsensema's village an old man declared that 'Dreams are different from thoughts.' Nsensema himself explained, 'When I dream that I go to Kazembe's or to Luapula, my spirit is going there.' As the debate continued it became evident that many present were uncomfortable and afraid. At last a young fisherman voiced the common fear: 'If, after dreaming, my spirit fails to return, then I am dead.' Nsensema then recounted this story.

'Two hunters after a day in the bush made a bivouac and went to bed. One of them fell asleep, snoring, but the other lay awake. After some time he noticed the form of a man emerging from the crown of his sleeping friend's head. This figure took up his friend's clothing, hunting-knife and gun, and then passed out of sight through the wall of the bivouac. He lay there watching. After a while he heard a gunshot, and a little later saw the figure returning, replacing his friend's things and re-entering the corpse. Shortly after this his friend stretched and awoke, and told him that he had been dreaming and in his dream had shot an eland. So he told his friend what he had seen as he lay awake. The two of them laughed and soon fell asleep. In the morning as they went on their way they found, a short distance from the bivouac, a dead eland.'

The significance of this story is that it was recounted in unquestioning belief by the man who was not only the headman of his village but the local preacher who normally led his congregation Sunday by Sunday.

The rationalistic European has attempted to plot the chart of spiritual experience and lay down the rules of God's dealings with men. Not so the African Christian. To him God is still unpredictable, so religious experience is arbitrary and tends toward the ecstatic and visionary. If it comes upon a man it is irresistible and all-demanding; the less privileged may carry on in expectancy, but their faithfulness is tinged with scepticism. In a group of older church members at Nsensema's village on one occasion I recounted several visionary experiences that had been reported to me in Uganda. This led to the following conversation:

A: 'Yes. True believers can sometimes see God in visions.'

B: 'Those who pretend to have seen visions are not true believers, for God is invisible.'

A: 'If anyone here told such dreams as you report from Uganda, people would say, "This is nothing, they are only imagination." '

C (Sunday school teacher): 'Uganda is nearer to the country where the Disciples lived in the old days, so perhaps the people there do have such dreams.'

B: 'But if a man dreams he is in Europe, is that really true? This is nonsense. His corpse is still here.'

D: 'Believers say, "God is our father who made us,' but others answer, "Where is your God? We can see nothing of him." '

Many African Christians however, have experienced in one form or another this invasion by what a European would call the supernatural. But to them the supernatural is natural; it is strange and unaccountable, but there is no element of otherness about it, for it belongs with everything else to the here and now. So they accept it and recount it in the most matter of fact way. When such a Christian confides to a missionary his spiritual history, he initiates him into what often seems a queer world. The wise missionary will be humble enough to accept its validity even though he may not understand it. Two case histories illustrate this type of experience, which those who are concerned for the Church in Africa would do well to take more seriously into account.

The first is Benedict Kasenga, the minister of the African Holy Sprimitual Church referred to above. He is 37 years of age and very short. At the time of telling his story he was working in an African freehold Township as a salesman in one of the village shops. I have seen the red and white girdle to which he refers, at the bottom of his box of clothes.

'My grandfather was a chief of the Sena people in Portuguese East Africa. When he grew old the people wondered who should succeed him. My father refused because he was a prophet of the *ngulu* (spirits) and a medicine doctor, though he never used to accept fees. So the people imagined that one of us children would succeed. But my uncle, my father's brother, began to covet the chieftainship for himself; so he began to attack all the children with witchcraft. All were killed except me myself. I was then fifteen years old and I decided to escape. So I ran away to Umtali in Southern Rhodesia. That was in 1936. The next year my mother came to look for me and fetched me home.

'My parents were Roman Catholics and I had been taught in a Catholic school. Later I was trained in a Catholic training college to do bricklaying, carpentry and tailoring.

'But in 1942 I again became afraid of my uncle and ran away to Umtali. Again my mother came and fetched me. Now I saw that my grandfather was likely to die. People told me that I would be the next chief, and my grandfather called me and gave me his stick and his long staff. So I saw I was in great danger and after only six months I ran away for good. Just after that my grandfather died. I shall never go back. Once or twice my mother has come looking for me, but I hid from seeing her and dare not write to her in case she comes and finds me.

'I found in Southern Rhodesia that there are separate black and white churches. There was no colour bar in our church at home. When, later, I moved to Livingstone, Father Coleman wanted me to become a church worker. I started taking my Bible to church. But in that church they study only the catechism, very little Bible. So after a time I joined the Watchtower at Marandellas. I was there for three and a half years. The Watchtower law was very difficult. I did not like to be a witness in Zulu after only two or three days as a member of that church, because I knew nothing. I wanted a chance to speak in my own language.

'In 1947 my father died. After that I came to Northern Rhodesia, to Livingstone. Once while I was working at a small lathe a chip flew into my left eye and cut it so that I cannot see well with that eye.

'During this time I was well known as a dancer and a saxophone player. I began to live very hard, a very bad life, and for three years and eight months I never went to any church. I also became a good boxer. One time when I was back at Marandellas I had a very fierce quarrel with Tom, a very tall and good-looking boxer. We fought and it seemed as if I had killed him. I was arrested and bound up by the police. This made me have a great fear and I thought I must do something to save my life. Tom got well and the police dismissed the case and let me go. So I began looking for a church that could really help me. I tried the Salvation Army and then the Anglican Church but I found they were just like other churches I had seen. I knew I could be a member of them and still have a bad life.

'One day I went to the African Methodist Episcopal Church and heard an African preaching the Gospel. He preached as I have never heard. Every word he said in his story was as if he was pointing to me. I wanted to call out, "Yes, that is true. How do you know me?" But I did not like to trouble the preacher and other people. Yet after that day I found that I could strip off all my dancing and saxophone and boxing. In the old days if I heard a drum playing and refused to dance, my hands and arms would begin soon to swell up because of the great thing in me wanting to dance. But now I found it had gone from me. I loved Jesus Christ and for some time I was attending that church eagerly and began studying Bible doctrine.

'But after some time I met the bishop of the African Holy Spiritual Church in Livingstone and joined him, and in 1951 I was chosen to be a deacon. That year I met my wife there and married her. But then I was transferred to preach in Bechuanaland for one year and a half.

'After this my eyes became very, very bad. I was in hospital in Livingstone for three months and during that time my wife never visited me. The doctor failed to cure me and then he wanted to do an operation. The pain was then so fierce I agreed with him. But that night my father spoke to me. He was very tall and had a long beard and he was white, not black. Yet I knew it was my father. He gave me a long white robe with red cuffs, and a red girdle such as I had often dreamed about as a child.

'And he said to me: "There is no cure for you in this place, but African medicines will cure you."

'The next morning the doctor came and wanted to syringe my eyes and do the operation the day after. But now I refused. So I was discharged.

'I came then to my wife's house and lay there for a week. I managed to make a robe and girdle exactly as I had dreamed. Then my wife persuaded me to go to her brother's home for two days, for she said she had left our second boy, ten months old, with the grandmother and must go and fetch him. She also said she wanted to brew beer to get money to buy medicines that would cure me. But when she came back she found me very ill, unconscious, so she became frightened and ran away.

'After two weeks they tried African medicines but the pain was terrible. Then I began to dream. At first I knew nothing, only pain. But then my father came and said,

' "My son, Benedict, wake up. Go over to that side, and cut down the tree standing by the road. Then come home and burn it and look at it as it burns. Burn it also with a castor oil bean."

'When I awoke I felt the pain was much less and for the first time since I became unconscious I was able to get out of bed. I dressed myself in the white and red robe and went up the road in the direction I had seen in my dream. There I found the *tuntulwa* tree exactly where I expected. I cut out a piece of the root and brought it home. I sent someone to get a castor oil pod. I burned them together and gazed at the red, burning wood, once in the morning and again in the evening. Then I went to sleep.

'The next morning I awoke and found all pain was gone. No weakness. I could use my eyes as before, except that the left eye is still damaged and can see not far. The people in that house were greatly surprised, especially when I got up and brought water and did my work in that home. I stayed with them for two months, digging a large food garden which I left for my wife's mother and brother.

'When my wife heard of this story she called me to come back to her house.

'But I said, "No. It is better you leave me alone. You ran away when I was so ill and never came near me. You were leaving me to die.'

'So I left her in 1956. In January 1957 the African Holy Spiritual Church sent me to come to Kansuswa to be the preacher of the Gospel in these towns. That year I sent £6 to help my wife and children, but her brothers wrote to inform me that she had already married another man. They wanted to bring the case and sue for me because they were angry with her. But I wrote to the chief and to the brothers to say, Let the matter go. The chief again said he wanted to make a case, but I said that if I did this, I could not keep my heart peaceful, so I must let it finish.

'But the congregation here do not want me to stay in the work without a wife. Now I have promised them to get a wife. But I do not know; she may leave me like my other wife if ever I am ill. I have found a Tokaleya girl whose parents live here. Her father is a Christian, a New Apostolic; but there is something not right in his heart. I have paid him £5 to have her; so now they have sent her to her brother at Lusaka so that I am not tempted to play with her before I marry her. They have agreed on £15 for bridewealth. I have asked for a public marriage in the rules of my church. I sent a letter to the headquarters in Johannesburg and they have agreed that I must be free to marry again. So now I am working to get that money. I don't want to divorce my wife who bore my children, but she did that wrong to me and now the church says I must be married again.

'If I say I am a holy man, why have I got children? I don't find it that Jesus Christ had a wife. But then he was the Son of God. We want to follow him but we are like his workmen; he is the Bwana. I am only a boy for this Bwana. I want benefit for this work that many may say I am a Christian. But what about Jesus?"

What, indeed?

It was interesting that at the London Missionary Society's station at Mbereshi an African teacher also assured us that cures are from time to time revealed in dreams. He knew of a man who had been partly paralysed. His friends dreamed of a certain medicine and when this was applied he was healed.

The second history appears, to Western eyes at least, less syncretistic than the first and more clearly lit up by the experience of Christ. Sammy Ntara, a man of Matebeleland, was between forty and fifty years of age. At the time he told his story, in three separate interviews, he was a driver working in the open pit of the Nchanga Mine.

> 'My great-grandfather was alive with Lobengula. My grandfather's land was in the place where Bulawayo stands today, but he moved further to the West when the Europeans came and fought. Later he was made a chief, but by that time Lobengula was dead. My father had 180 cattle and mealie fields as big as the whole compound of this mine. He never was a Christian but he had only one wife. He died in 1933.
>
> 'Until I was about twelve years old, I was still herding my father's cattle. My father wore skins instead of trousers, very soft and beautiful, and bracelets on his arms. The women also wore only very fine skins, and all had skins to cover them at night. But I wanted to go to school, so I had my name written down by the teacher of the Wesleyan Methodist School without my parents knowing. I began to attend school. When my parents stopped me the headmaster showed them the boys' names in his book and mine also, and he threatened to call the Government. So they were frightened and let me attend school. I was baptized when I was still rather young, attending school. Afterwards I went to Johannesburg from 1936 to 1938 and did leather work, but I ended my time there after I had typhoid fever.
>
> 'My wife's parents were both of the Salvation Army. We were married first in the High Court (by Ordinance). Then the Minister went to the Native Commissioner and got a permission to marry us in church. We have four children who are left in the Reserve in Southern Rhodesia in boarding school.
>
> 'It is difficult in these days in Southern Rhodesia because Europeans chase us and we have not enough land for ploughing. For such reasons I decided to leave that land. I got a job in Bulawayo. I have three brothers and four sisters. One brother is a chef at Johannesburg and two sisters are married there. Another brother is driving-instructor at Potchefstoom. He is very much drinking. The third brother is in Capetown but I do not know what he is doing. But he is a great dancer. In 1957 when my wife returned here from visiting our children she brought another of my sisters. But she became ill and died here after three months in hospital, while her husband was in Capetown

and sent no word. None of my brothers or sisters is Christian, although I have often persuaded them. But my mother listened to me and my wife, and she became Christian; and when she died on the third of September 1956 she was believing.'

In Bulawayo he ran a truck carrying firewood into the town. Later he left his wife in the Bulawayo location to look after this business for him while he went north to Broken Hill, following up the advertisement of a bus company. On arrival he found no job; and after a period of great suffering as a foreigner out of work, sleeping often in the open bush, he was put in touch with the Nchanga Mine.

'I was taken on as a driver and I thanked the God. After two months my wife came also and after three months I was made a driving instructor.

'Even when I was young I understood the Christian way. I believed then. But later on something happened which made me believe more deep. In 1948 when we were still at Bulawayo I became ill in my house. I walked out of the door but fell down. I stood up again and walked but I fell over a second time. When I woke up I was in hospital. I grew worse and then I died for three days. I was in a certain country and there was a man with me. He looked like a shadow but he had a voice like a man's voice.

'He asked me what was my name. Then he said, "Did you hear the name of Jesus? Do you believe?"

'I said, "I believe."

'But this one said, "No, you do not believe. I have known you since you were born and I know you have not believed deeply."

'Then he said, "Look behind you."

'I turned round and saw a big river and on the other side a very beautiful house and it was full of people who were singing "Hallelujah, Hallelujah, Hallelujah!' I wanted to jump into that river and cross over although it was so wide. Then I saw it was full of animals—dogs, lions, snakes and many others. But even then I still wanted to go in and cross over.

'But this man had a long stick, very thin, and he flipped me over although it was so thin. Then he said to me. "I want you to go back."

'I said, "Nkosi (Lord)! I don't want to go back to that work where there is too much suffering, and people fighting each other, and paying taxes."

'Although the man was like a shadow the stick was a real stick but very thin, yet it knocked me over.

'The man said, "You must go back in deep believing."

'I was now knocked over so that my feet were above my head. And in that position I fell through a hole in the sky which closed up behind me. So I went on falling down until I returned into that room in the hospital. There I saw my own body lying in the bed. All round there were people wearing long robes like Indians. I knew that they were various ancestors although I did not recognize them. One was my grandfather's mother. One of them I did know: she was my grandmother, who bore my mother.

'They said to me, "You must go back now and sleep in that body."

'I said, "No, I don't want to go back in that body. I don't want to even touch that body. I want to remain in this body of spirit and I want to go and live in that village over the river."

'But they said, "No, you must go back and preach and believe; and then sometime you will go over the river to that kraal."

'Then they took me and made me return into that body on the bed.

'It is hard here because I cannot preach as I used to preach in Bulawayo, in the Government compound called Matapos. Here my spirit is dead because of the difficulty of language. I tried to preach here, and my wife also, but the people did not hear me. My African Methodist Episcopal minister helped me, but I was understood only by his Southern Rhodesian people and people from Bechuanaland. My wife used to preach in Bulawayo three times a week, on Tuesday, Friday and Saturday. She is now very unsatisfied.'

A few months later he told us, 'Last week I dreamed that the Government was allowing me to go in any train freely to preach the Word of God.'

Sammy Ntara was a very normal African mineworker in a higher income group. It is remarkable that his own experience should so closely resemble the more famous visionary experience of Alice Lenshina, and, in a more Roman Catholic idiom, Emilio Mulolani, the leader of the 'Children of the Sacred Heart', who have broken away from the Roman Catholics. The 'return from death' with a message for the living is indeed a not uncommon feature of African spiritual histories. African ministers of Copperbelt churches, meeting in conference, recounted with complete conviction, and with apparently no trace of scepticism among their hearers, stories of such resuscitations in their own pastoral experience:

'He died in the morning at four o'clock and he got up again between three and four in the afternoon, and said he had not paid his church dues. He said to his father "You must pay them". I tried to pay for him, but he refused and said it must be his father. So he did so. In this particular place we have the strongest Christians because many of them are still living who saw these things.'

'We said prayers and then we took them both to the graveyard. After some long time they sent a message to me that I must come and see him. Then I rushed down there and found that he was still living, and we sang and prayed, for we found he was still living but very sick. I went to bed between midnight and one a.m. and they came again and called me. And he said, "I have been away and saw a lot of things, and I came back and I must tell the people that God is there." Then I called all the people and he went on preaching to them that they should believe, that they should not think it is a lie that there is any other world.'

The call, in a dream, to be a messenger is frequently quoted as the origin of a Christian's vocation to the Ministry. A young hospital orderly of the Anglican Mission at Chipili dreamed that God was calling him to the priesthood. Nothing could shake this conviction and he is now serving in Orders at Msoro.

This irrational, Dionysian element in the African experience of God presents the missionary with a perpetual dilemma. His own understanding of religion is systematic and, while admitting the ultimate mystery, he believes that God is essentially rational and predictable in his dealings with men. Even if he can recognize the validity of an utterly different experience he cannot share it and is predisposed to distrust it. How can he foster and guide the spiritual life of his African fellow-Christian? The difficulty is typified in the story of a pupil in an Anglican Mission who later joined the Seventh Day Adventists.

> 'I had been baptized "Benedict" and I tried to be like him, even fasting many times. But when I asked them about the Bible they would not give me true answers. I was very much puzzled about Daniel and Revelation. But they said, "Those are only dreams. You need not read those books. They are very hard and nobody can understand those books. It is better to read the Gospel." But there was a great demand in my mind to understand these. I saw the beast coming out of the sea. I saw the beast with ten horns. I wanted to know.'

In the light of those words it is not hard to understand the appeal of the Jehovah's Witnesses and of the 'Alice' movement.

The sense of vocation

Dreams are not the only means by which African Christians receive a vocation. This often comes along what Europeans would call more normal channels, but even then there is a strong sense of being in the grip of an inescapable constraint. Sometimes it arises when a man recognizes the hand of God in the past vicissitudes of his life. 'I remembered how I had received a full education and been helped to travel to so many places in the Union, all without money of my own. So I felt that God who had done this for me had a purpose in it.' 'I thought, what must I do to show gratitude to Jesus Christ, my Lord, who has made me what I am? I must serve him as a minister in my declining years.'

A recognition of some specific need may constitute a call. 'I wanted to be a social worker, but I began to see the spiritual need of my people.' 'All the time, even when I had become a teacher, it was hammering in my heart: Why no young men as ministers? Why?'

The following two cases illustrate the ordinary Christian's sense of Providence, and the persistence with which a person who believes himself to be under the summons of God will search for an opportunity to obey.

The first is a woman orderly in a European hospital on the Copperbelt. Her father came from Nyasaland to Tanganyika, where he married a woman near Karanga, and had twelve children, seven of whom survived. The youngest of these he called Martha, for he and his wife were officially Christian. But they left the Church because of their love of beer, when Martha was still small. In spite of parental opposition she attended a mission school as far as Standard III. She was so keen on education that she decided that she would change her name to Fastness when she had reached puberty, 'because I wanted to learn fast'. When she was about eight years old her elder sister's husband complained because his wife was barren and demanded another girl as compensation for the cattle he had given. So her father agreed that Martha should join that household. For a while she managed to remain at school, but when the missionaries heard that she was a second wife they refused to baptize her. Eventually her husband insisted on her living with him and took her away from school; but she was so unhappy that in the end her father freed her by paying back the bridewealth.

After this her brother fell dangerously ill and Fastness, as she now was, was sent to be with him in the Moravian hospital. While she was there the German doctor and two sisters—'Margrit the old one and Margrit the good—we called her that because of her beautiful manners'—encouraged her to learn nursing. But she disliked that and worked for them for five years as a housemaid. Then she returned to her mother and married her present husband, a Nyakyusa. He wanted a church marriage, so Fastness was baptized in the Moravian Church. She also was barren like her sister and very much troubled. She tried 'nearly thirty doctors and also African medicine'; she was operated on, but to no avail. In 1951 her husband found work as a shop assistant on the Copperbelt and Fastness came with him. Some of her brothers' children lived with them. She asked for work in the Mine European hospital and was accepted as an orderly in spite of her low educational qualifications. But the Matron did not approve of the name Fastness, so in the hospital she is named Florence, 'after Florence Nightingale'. After two years she entered, with a number of male orderlies, for the Chamber of Mines' efficiency test and was the first woman ever to pass this examination.

When her husband went on long leave to Tanganyika, Fastness sent in her resignation.

> 'But Matron said to me: "Go home on leave but think again about resignation. God has given you work in this place and the strength to do it. You should not easily leave it." And I knew that she was right. I got my heart-prayer when I was very young. I know that God does not speak directly to us as he spoke to the prophets and other people in the old times. He speaks to us through other people. I knew that Matron told me what was really God's will. And I came back to my job.'

The second case is that of a Nyasalander, who, so far from coming back to any job, had moved rapidly from one employment to another in the way that often exasperates the European. But underlying all the restlessness was a sense of vocation frustrated until it found fulfilment. He had become a Christian while at school and had then done some teacher-training. In 1934, shortly after his marriage at the age of twenty-four, he felt a call to the ministry and offered himself to the Livingstonia Mission. He was turned down as being too young. From that point the stone began to roll. Ten months teaching for the Salvation Army in Northern Rhodesia; three years teaching for the Dutch Reformed Mission in Southern Rhodesia, followed by a two-year course in their Teacher-Training Centre at Morginster; one year in the Methodist 'Railway school' at Selukwe; one year as a clerk; six months teaching for the Dutch Reformed Mission in Salisbury; two years as a clerk again at Queque; six months as a court interpreter in Nyasaland; eighteen months as filing clerk for the Bata Shoe Company at Gwelo in Southern Rhodesia; four years teaching at Bulawayo; one year's course at the Jeanes School near Zomba, Nyasaland. Then, searching for a girl cousin whose maternal relatives had abducted her, he came late in 1951 to the Copperbelt and there he worked for seven years as a clerk in an African Personnel Office. And now at last the wheel has come full circle: in 1958 he offered again and was accepted into training for the ministry.

The frustration of this sense of vocation can lead not only to restlessness but to a deep melancholia. This is noticeable in a considerable proportion of the rejects from the Senior Seminaries of the Roman

Catholic Church, though the Church does its best to place all such men as teachers or in some other post.

Insecurity and Joy

Perhaps it is because God is felt to be incalculable, and the deepest religious experience something impulsive which comes upon a man and possesses him, that many of the Christians we met in the Copperbelt, did not seem to have the assurance of an inalienable salvation. In spite of his visionary experience and his desire to preach the Gospel, Sammy Ntara at our last interview with him said:

> 'When I read the Bible I come to Moses. He tried to make people follow God; he even talked to God. But Moses failed. So it was even when the Son of God came. Of course he did not fail, but we failed him. Unless I give myself to stand fast and not to move, I will fail. But I must stand fast so that he may receive me. The Son of God fought very hard, and we should fight to stand firm.'

He then showed us a small tract, translated by the South African Baptist Mission, with rather crude illustrations showing the spiritual progress of a man who after his conversion fell away into sin. Though in the last pages the man is reconciled to Christ on his death-bed, yet Sammy was obsessed with the possibility of being ultimately lost. 'When I read this book I think, Why do I not die now, so that I do not have a lot of sins?'

Even in the prayers of the faithful and the sermons of lay preachers, this lack of Christian certainty was sometimes evident. 'If I am blessed in 1956 or 1957 and sin in 1958, what will save me? The judgment will come!' 'They are lost, as we too shall be lost if we do not stay being your people.'

Some of this spiritual insecurity may derive from the deep physical insecurity caused by the shadow of mortality. Earlier in the same conversation Sammy had remarked, 'My flesh is smelling. One day they will put me into the grave.' Similarly Benedict Kasenga, the minister of the African Holy Spiritual Church, exclaimed once,

> 'This my life is a very nice life. I can eat and drink and sleep. But shall I live for ever? No, I can die. When I think much on that question I can cry. What people can bring death? Sometimes I feel weak and I am heavy. But God sends this as a witness that this body is not to live for ever.'

So faith ebbs and flows with the sense of psychic well-being; and if one way more than another can produce the assurance of being right with God, a man will turn to it. Benedict said one day to the Jehovah's

Witnesses, 'If you can tell me something to give me Life, I can leave my clerical collar and follow you.'

But when it is present the sense of the benediction of God produces an intense joy and courage. The group of older Christians at Nsensema's, when asked, 'What is God like?', first gave these answers. 'When I am sick, before I ask anyone else for help, I pray, saying, "Lesa, help me"; for I know he is more powerful than all others to help me.' 'If a man falls from a tree and is paralysed, at first he thinks, Today my life is ended; but then he says, No, God help me. Or he meets a lion and thinks, It is all over with me; but then he says, No, with God's power I may be saved. So he takes courage to defend himself.'

The sheer joy in the favour of God finds expression in African worship whenever it is not inhibited by European ideas of decorum. A schoolboy, explaining why people go to Church, said, 'They want to come and sit together with God and sing for the Creator.'

A minister of the AME Church, asked whether it was true that his congregation danced in their worship, replied, 'We do not dance any African or customary dances. It is happiness only and nothing else.' He then shuffled and beat his feet on the floor. 'It is only happiness, but you people do not understand it.'

At this a minister of the UCCAR added (his pronouns perhaps show his uncertainty of his hearers' reactions), 'Yes, among my people we think—they feel they are very happy when they are singing, so they shake themselves and that kind of thing. We are happy to worship God. They are happy and excited. We are in the presence of God and we are not fearing; we are approaching God with happiness. That makes people to remember the old days and the African customs. Bad ones we should leave out, but the good ones which connect with the Christian way, we should take them for the Church.'

13

Worship, Doctrine and Ethics

The Significance of Worship

THIS sense of grateful exultation in the presence of God is more often a communal than a private experience. Being in good standing with God is for this reason very closely linked, if not identified, with church attendance. A preacher at Kansuswa, dealing with the story of Zacchaeus, said, 'We cannot see Jesus when we are in the crowd with everybody around us, but the church is like that tree; we come to church to get a chance to see him.' In many sermons there were exhortations to church attendance, couched in the terms of evangelical appeal. 'Let us rise up quickly when we hear the drum for Sundays or for other meetings. Come back quickly from the swamp, you women.' Prayers at the beginning of a service often expressed the same conviction. 'Since you have said, Come, all who are heavy laden, we have followed you and we ask, Be with us now.' 'Many have failed to come; look after them.'

A minister of the AME Church showed how a man's inner sense of his own standing with God is reflected in his presence or absence from the church services:

> 'It sometimes happens that one comes out of the church to do a thing that he cannot do in the church. There is something forcing him to do it, he is just blinded by it. He may realize his mistake in a week's time, but it takes him two or three years to come back to church, because he is thinking, "Perhaps when I go back, they will not allow me." Until one day he forces himself to come back, saying, "It doesn't matter if they refuse me." If you question him, he will not tell you what has changed him; he just says he wants to come back to church because of the Table.'

Nevertheless the distinction between church-going and a personal prayer life is occasionally made both by the more sophisticated and the more spiritually mature. Nsensema himself, when preaching to his people one Sunday, asked, 'What is our nature, we Christians? Coming to class on Tuesdays and Thursdays, but otherwise seeing only what is in front of us?' Many of the more educated young men on the Copperbelt, calling themselves 'undenominational Christians', have ceased going to church, though they claim to say their prayers and read their Bible at home. In most cases this is probably an excuse only. Schoolteachers and other Christian laymen all agreed that very few Christians read the Bible in their homes, and only in rare cases are regular 'family prayers' observed. There are, however, exceptions. A few years ago, when daily Evensong was discontinued at Chipili boys' school, a small group of scholars sought permission to continue to say the office together voluntarily. Later these boys asked the missionary in charge to guide them in forming a simple rule of life. Their own proposal was to pray every day and to refrain from shaking hands with girls! But eventually they agreed to keep half-an-hour daily for Bible reading and prayer and to spend one day in retreat each year. Several of them have maintained this rule long after leaving school.

Generally speaking, however, communal worship is supremely the means, and the expression, of the realization of the presence and benediction of God. But it is primarily an emotional experience. The one significant exception is Jehovah's Witnesses. Though we found at Nchanga that they enjoy a hymn-singing session on Friday evenings similar to those of other congregations of the Free Church tradition, yet in their Sunday assemblies there is the minimum of singing and prayer, and almost the whole of the two-hour session is devoted to the exposition of Scripture contained in the current Watchtower magazine. Yet even here we are dealing not so much with an intellectual activity as with a deep psychic re-orientation effected over a long period (see pp. 232-3). Several converts to the movement made this clear in their accounts to us of their own experience. 'First I believed without knowledge, then I was learning; but when I believed *and* had learned, then I was strong to go forward.' 'I am still going further and preaching until I shall be saved and have the everlasting New World.' 'Salvation means to understand the Bible, with the whole heart and to follow it.' 'When a man really learns the Bible, then a man is able to stop the bad thinking.' 'Many people have weak hearts till they find the way of Jehovah's Witnesses. They know how to make people strong.'

In all other congregations, however, worship seems to be supremely a renewal of the sense of the presence of God through sharing in a communal experience. To say that emotionalism is paramount would be entirely misleading, yet the fundamental emphasis of their worship is emotive rather than rational. An analysis of a number of services in the church at Nsensema's village showed that the time (75 minutes on average) was spent as follows: 50 per cent sermon; 32 per cent singing (18 per cent congregational, 14 per cent choir only); 7 per cent prayer; 6 per cent Bible reading; 5 per cent notices. In the town, services were rather longer, but the distribution of the time was similar, with slightly more given to Bible reading.

The significance of these figures is only apparent when one remembers that the preaching, like the singing, is more often than not emotive. There are, of course, some whose sermons are expository and discursive in the European manner, but these are the exception. The theme of most preachers is biblical, and the appeal is moralistic, but the effect is cathartic rather than rational. Even normally soft-spoken men seem to prefer in the pulpit a monotonous high-pitched singing tone, repeating a phrase in spasmodic bursts of sound which have the effect of wearing down resistance in an almost hypnotic way. In some traditions, notably that of the Tumbuka from Nyasaland, it is customary for a congregation to break into a hymn at certain points during the sermon; on the occasion when we saw this, it noticeably stimulated the preacher to more vigorous bodily movements. Such preaching may sometimes be called for among a group of Christians in a private house. Benedict Kasenga once told how

> 'the week before last, when that child died of smallpox, I went to the funeral and preached the Gospel many minutes at the cemetery. Many people started crying and thinking much. But people don't understand. But they came to ask me to preach again, so at night time I preached again for them. They never slept, but spent the night talking to me and singing songs.'

In her brilliant study of one aspect of church life in South Africa, Mrs Brandel Syrier has this penetrating comparison of European and African preaching:

> 'That the subject matter and manner of presentation of a religious sermon is carefully prepared by a European priest is wholly unsuspected by his African audience, and they do not like his sermon. "A European sermon has too many different thoughts," they say. It usually takes two or three or even four different ideas or Bible verses, explains these in a new light or a deeper sense, and links them together logically in a coherent pattern. An African preacher prepares his mood; he takes one leading idea or image or sentence or story and turns this over and over again, savours it this way and that way, describes it in various emotional terms and metaphors, and repeats it *ad*

infinitum. Gradually the audience imbibes it; they become possessed of it and it becomes part of them. They feel it and act it in sounds and gestures; they absorb it by identification.'[1]

Hymn-singing has a similar function. The constant repetition of a phrase by a congregation enables the individual to 'absorb by identification' the idea that it expresses. For this reason a congregation has no objection to singing the same hymn, or verse of a hymn, several times in succession, and the most popular hymns are those with a chorus.

The trance condition that can be induced by hymn-singing, which is actually encouraged in some churches in the Congo and South Africa, seems generally to be suspect and feared in Northern Rhodesia because it is associated with the old *ngulu* possession. In Kansuswa township, I found that adherents of the New Apostolic Church met regularly for hymn-singing in the home of one of their members; but the mother of the household used to beg them not to sing for a great length of time because, as a child, she had been subject to attacks of *ngulu* possession, and now, if the singing was prolonged, she felt herself on the verge of a similar state. The congregations appear to be aware of the danger that lies beyond a certain limit; but this does not mean that they abandon the paramountcy of the communal emotional experience in worship. It is of the utmost importance that the leaders in Missions and Church should recognize that Christian Africa is awakening from the tamed, classroom religion of respectable good behaviour and reaching out her hands to the ecstasy, the terror and the beauty of the Lord. Canon Fison's words about the Holy Spirit are most relevant here:

'There can be no knowledge in experience of the Holy Spirit without a willingness to expose to him the unplumbed depths of the subconscious and unconscious. The risk of a relapse to the primitive and elemental condition of the past has got to be taken, if the chance of pushing on towards the creative possibilities of the future is to be seized.... Nothing is as futile as the condemnation by respectable established churches of the excesses of revivalist, prophetic and Pentecostal sects. It is the fire the latter so manifestly exhibit that the former so woefully lack. A church merely conducted decently and in order, in the face of communism, nationalism and rock 'n roll, has no gospel for today. There is no possibility of contact with the divine without running the risk of being destroyed by the demonic. That is why biblical religion ... is always either bliss or perdition, salvation or damnation, the greatest curse or the most wonderful blessing in life. It cannot be the one without running the risk of the other: promise and peril must always co-exist.'[2]

The Emphases of the Teaching

It must be clearly understood that what is said above concerning sermons refers to the manner rather than the matter of preaching. Though the congregation may learn by 'absorption' rather than by a train of reasoning, there is none the less a theological content to the teaching. The number of services that we attended is too small for any reliable generalization; yet a study of the most common themes in the prayers and sermons does give some indication of what might be called the *leit-motifs* of popular Christian belief.

Most frequent of all is the concept of the Way. Christianity is seen as a new, good road. 'We bow our heads in shame because we have sinned and gone away from the true way. Keep us, great Lesa, lead us the right way.' 'Teach us, Saviour', says one of Lenshina's hymns, 'You have shown a way, the way of life, and he who has lost you, the way of life, where shall he go?' A favourite text is the Baptist's quotation of Isaiah. 'Prepare the way of the Lord. Make a straight way in your heart. Satan wants to destroy our ways. ' 'Prepare a way for Jehovah. Come, come, clear the stones away.' 'In the deserts and on the great rivers many people are lost, but we shall be saved.' Lenshina's hymns and prayers make much of this desert road. 'Look at the desert where I send my children. They are shouting; let all the enemies listen to it.' 'We who stay in the desert, we do not want the things of this world, nor do we long for them.' The road is Christ and his laws. 'Let us follow the way; he who walks in the spoor of the Lord, he shall be forgiven.' After telling a version of the Atalanta story, a preacher at Nchanga said, 'This girl who ran is Jesus—Have you caught him in your heart? He is running in front of you. Are you set to run after him? He is the way, we must follow his laws.' Faith is following: 'The hunter heard and because he followed he was successful.' 'You who stay behind, you cannot follow later.'

Almost as common is the imagery of the Light, which is often linked with that of the Way. 'Let your light shine on us, your witnesses, let us see the way.' 'Others live in darkness, let them hear your word; others are going in bad ways, let them return to the good way.' 'Let us be in the light of the world, your light.' 'Our Father, let all the land see your light and know your Kingdom has come.' The light also brings judgment. 'The great light shows all badness in us. When Jesus said, "I am the light," the king was afraid—"Perhaps he will take my kingdom."' 'Death will come like a thief. Then God's light will show what we are like.' 'The Word of God must shine', said Alice Lenshina in a sermon,

'His Spirit gives light. The Word is also like a wound in your soul; it hurts.'

In general, however, a sense of sin seems to be felt not so much as guilt before God, but as being lost, cut off and destroyed. 'Soon we shall be scattered; why do we not all keep together, why do we love death?' 'Why should we always be committing suicide?' 'Our sins shall be murderers and kill us.' 'Rule our hearts, let us not be wild.' In the list of sins, anger and hatred rank very high. 'The Son of God preached: Stop sin, hatred, greed, adultery.' 'Tomorrow there will be disputes. We shall hate Christ, which is to love death, crying and gnashing of teeth. Let us follow Christ who said "Forgive". Let us look at Stephen who conquered death. Don't love bad people, but don't just say, "Kantwa is bad," for we are bad ourselves.'

Closely linked with the admission of human lostness is the conviction that God alone can help. 'Nobody has strength unless God stretches out his arms to him.' 'Nothing can heal us, no medicine of this world, but only your power.' 'We have the Cross, where else can we be saved? We have nothing else, nothing else, nothing else.'

God is still the incalculable, but here, in the context of the Christian community, the emphasis is placed upon his pity. 'You are in heaven, we on earth: that is trouble. But in your mercy you come to us with love.' Sometimes, but by no means always, God's pardon is associated with the work of Christ. 'There is no way to God except through Jesus Christ. We can't enter the house of a noble unless we find a resident who knows the owner.' 'Great tree, a shade to make us all happy. That is what you did long ago when the Lord came into this world.' Sometimes Christ and the Father are unwittingly identified: 'Father, cleanse us with your blood.' The Gospel, on the whole, seems to consist not in a scheme of salvation, but in the news of a welcoming and merciful God. 'Everyone is welcomed by him, however bad they are.'

Often the members of a congregation are encouraged to see themselves as God's poor. 'Jesus said, "Blessed are the poor", because they have Christ in their hearts.' 'Send us your Holy Spirit. You promised him to the poor, not to the rich, big people.' 'If you find a rich and a poor man, which is blessed? The poor man will save his threepence or sixpence; but when the Lord comes the rich man will say, "I have spent all my money."' So there is a special poignancy in this Gospel which welcomes the poor into the aristocracy of the 'royal village' of God. We noted several times the use of an idiomatic word, *bantungwa*, 'Chief's children', not commoners, in place of the usual 'sons of God'.

God also was often addressed as *Mulopwe*, the term of respect for a people's chief. 'It is dark, let your name be the light, *Tata*. Make light in your *musumba* (royal village).' 'Jesus is among us to try to bring us to his home.' 'We shall be spread out far and wide in the beautiful country; there we shall always roll in the dust (traditional obeisance to a chief), Hallelujah, always!' This image of the homecoming is associated with the return of the 'mine-boy' to his tribal area: 'Do we long for the sight of Jesus as the old people in the village long to see us, their people?'

It was a surprise to discover the frequency of the call to bear witness before the non-Christians. 'Many in the compounds are hungry for the Word of God. Go and feed them.' 'Many people here at Kazembe's are not Christians; if we fail to do Christ's work here, we are like the dead man.' 'Receive these small gifts from our hands to make more people believe in Jesus Christ.' The need to present a good example to the world was an important factor in the very common complaint that baptized members were not yet living in accordance with their profession of Christianity. 'Our Christianity is only in this house; when we come outside we are separated from it. Don't complain about the doings of the heathen before we have cleaned our own house.' 'Even baptized people have many devils in their hearts.' 'We are called Christians; we are baptized. But how does that help us if we are not saved?' 'If our elders ask, "Do you agree to stop drinking beer and committing adultery?", you always answer, "Yes". And two weeks later you say, "Give me a cup." You are like the hyena—you, the children of God!'

Ethics—official and felt

Sooner or later every sermon seems to turn into an exhortation to morality; the Way becomes a way of behaviour, the Gospel becomes the new law. 'These laws rule the work of God. These words of God are very old but they still remain. They are still true laws.' 'We know the laws—don't drink beer, don't commit adultery, don't tell lies. If we break these, do you think Christ will recognize us? The Word of God is not something that can be ignored again and again; it is very powerful.' These prohibitions, and a few others, can be heard in many sermons. They are, as it were, the official negative *mores* of the Church. It comes as a surprise, therefore, to learn in conversation with even devout pillars of the congregation, that these are not, in fact, the sins which they actually feel to be most wrong. In a prolonged conversation with the leaders of the local church at Nsensema's, we tried to discover what behaviour they considered particularly bad or good, and what accusations would make a person feel ashamed. These were their answers:

> 'If we go and discuss private matters with a person and afterwards he tells it to someone else, he is bad.'
>
> 'The good man is not quarrelsome or abusive.'
>
> 'If someone passes by who is hungry and any man refuses to give him food, that is sin.'
>
> 'To call a man a thief makes a man so ashamed that he cannot lift up his eyes even though he is innocent. He may say, "It is not true," but he will not speak again.'
>
> 'To call a man a liar is not an important thing: he may shout back some abuse, but he will not be troubled inwardly.'
>
> 'An adulterer will feel ashamed in the presence of the woman's husband even if he is not found out.' 'Two people, both married, who had committed adultery together, would feel an equal shame; they would hate each other afterwards.' 'Fornication between unmarried people is no cause for shame, unless the girl becomes pregnant.'
>
> 'A man could be a heavy drinker and still be considered a good person.'
>
> 'If you drink and then go home and sleep it off, this is no trouble at all; but if you become quarrelsome, then you are bad.'

These leaders of the Christian community in the village, when they revealed what they *felt* to be right and wrong, as distinct from what they said in their sermons, still regarded morality almost entirely as a function of society. Ministers and leading laymen on the Copperbelt, however, showed a clearer awareness of a distinctive Christian ethic, though they were hard put to define what it was.

> 'There is a distinction,' said a minister of the African Methodist Episcopal Church, 'between a good man who is a Christian and a good man who is not a Christian. This man shows it in one way, but the Christian shows it in many ways. In the villages goodness is based on kindness; but even if the Christian is very kind to other people, he must also avoid things that show he is not a Christian. A person who is not a Christian can do them and it does not worry people very much. But the same thing, if a Christian does it, will be a very big thing. So besides kindness, helping people, visiting the sick, he must also show good living.'

But what are the 'things that show he is not a Christian' and what does 'good living' consist of? The answer to such questions is not generally given with much certainty or conviction.

Two reasons may be tentatively advanced for this 'ethical agnosticism'. The first is the sense, already mentioned, that God is fundamentally incalculable. In the moral realm, therefore, there can be no absolutes. Believing in God's tolerance rather than God's forgiveness, preachers and pastors tend to take an empirical and accommodating line in matters of church discipline or else to condemn purely by rule of thumb. A Roman Catholic girl who had entered a religious order was found to be pregnant only a few months before she was to have taken her vows. Thinking herself an outcast she fell into despair and loose behaviour. The local Actio's and the Tertiaries tried to help her pastorally and, as one of them pointed out, 'she was not the first girl to have done this: it is one of the things that often happens in the lives of Christians. But it is up to her to repent.' A lay-preacher at Nsensema's said in his sermon: 'Is it written, "Do not drink"? No, you can have a cup if you are wise, but drinking can be the way to destruction.' A preacher's forbearance is sometimes based on an admission of his own sinfulness; it is, as it were, the obverse of the lack of Christian assurance which was noted earlier. 'I myself was baptized in 1940, but I am not yet completely Christian.'

The second reason for this lack of conviction regarding the Christian ethic is the dichotomy that exists between the demands of the pulpit and the demands of conscience. If the Christian elders in a village feel that 'to call a man a liar is not an important thing,' and that 'a man could be a heavy drinker and still be considered a good person,' then to continue to proclaim in the little church, 'We know the laws—don't drink beer, don't tell lies,' is not only ineffectual but positively prevents the growth of a Christian conscience with regard to lying and drunkenness. For spiritual growth seems to take place not through hearing and submitting to an extraneous demand, but by following a traditional pattern of thought and behaviour until the moment when a disconcerted conscience begins to question it. Where Christians are still thinking in pagan ways, there may be the danger of reversion, but there is also the opportunity for a spiritual stride forward. The Christian ethic emerges at the point where pagan lines of thinking are brought up against Christ. This is the true pattern of a Church's growth, for it is at the point of deviation from convention that decision is made.

This is apparent in several of the examples already given in this section. The many Christians whose faith is shaken by misfortune are following the pagan concept of religion; the few who, in trouble, endure, saying 'This will not shake my faith', have deviated from the norm and taken a great step forward.

The many who have implicit faith in their dreams are in line with traditional thought; as long as they are uninhibited in this, they are free to make a further, Christian discovery. The hospital orderly was rightly allowed to regard his dream as a call to the ministry; but the school-teacher who dreamed that his dead wife told him that his second wife was no good and was calling him to leave her, decided on his own account that such a dream was a temptation to be resisted! This was a thorough deviation from the conventional response.

The popular idea of prayer is essentially pagan still. One night in Kansuswa a young man was explaining how he was losing his faith.

> 'In the old days men who were in need mentioned God's name under a tree or in the bush. I have heard of a man who was on a journey and suffered greatly from hunger. So he knelt and prayed for food. When he rose and turned round he saw a buffalo lying dead on the ground, but there was no wound in it. So he got meat from God. But I have been praying in church since 1948, yet I have never seen anything happening to help people who were suffering. But if I tried to do what our grandfathers used to do, I could get no help from that either. So I can honestly say there is no use for us in praying. If I am hungry and faint in church, God will not kill any buffalo to feed me. Now we are lost. The people who brought the churches are those who made God angry with Africans.'

Out of that tradition it is a great step of spiritual discovery to say as another man, also at Kansuswa, said: 'When I am fishing I do not pray that I may be given a very big catch of fish. I see that if Jesus wants to give that to me he can do so, as he did to his disciples. But I should be greedy if I asked for it.'

Such points of Christian deviation must be innumerable; but there are one or two which constitute the most crucial moral battlegrounds for many Christians.

When Nsensema himself was asked the question 'What is the temptation with which Christians have to wrestle most painfully?' he answered without hesitation: 'Fear'. For the majority of African Christians, in town as well as country, the conviction that an enemy's witchcraft will do no harm is an act of faith precisely similar to believing that one will be protected from his poison also. We were told that in 1957 during a campaign of witch-finding in Chief Kazembe's district it was often Christians who were accused because they refused to allow the *mucape*, or witch-finder, to investigate in their houses. Numbers of Christian leaders told us how in times of sickness their relatives had tried to urge them to consult the *ng'anga* doctor because they were sure the sickness was caused by spirit-possession; sometimes the pressure of the family, combined with the fears of the Christian, prove too strong. The same applies to the use of protective medicine and good-luck charms. One white-collar worker at Nchanga, for example, had recently been offered for £15 medicine that would ensure a long life. The death of a relative or neighbour is almost always a point at which Christians feel called to deviate from conventional behaviour. Many, under the stress of bereavement, conform. As Sammy Ntara put it, 'When they reach the mortuary they forget about Christianity and join another thing.' Or, as one of the deacons said at Nsensema's, 'At funerals strong Christians do not wail, only the close relatives naturally weep, but others sing hymns. But some Christians fail to understand; they say: "Yes, we are full of hope; but death is still here and we may die tomorrow." So they go back to the old things.' Christians know that their attitude can be misconstrued —'Once a person is buried you forget him, like taking off your glasses from your eyes'—or, much more seriously, 'If you don't go and mourn, people will say that you are a witch and have caused the death. If you stop wailing at the place of the funeral wake, people turn round and say, *Muloshi!* (witch).' Bereaved Christians are put under great pressure from relatives to seek help from a *ng'anga* doctor to discover who is responsible for the death, for it is commonly believed that, apart from witchcraft, the unfaithfulness of one spouse may cause the death of the other, or of the children. A welfare officer at Nchanga reported that quite frequently when a man is killed in the mine, the wife is blamed and punished; or if a wife dies in the African Mine Township, men may begin beating up the bereaved husband even at the mortuary. In some tribes also, where it is customary for a widow to 'get rid of death' by having intercourse with a close relative of her dead husband, a Christian woman may be put under great pressure to conform, since all believe they are endangered by her refusal.

The whole world of magic is difficult to leave, particularly as the Christian faith appears often to offer nothing in its place. Many are bewildered by the loss of all disciplines once the old sanctions of fear have been removed. One member of the Urban Advisory Council at Mufulira, a man carrying great responsibility, said. 'Playing with girls used to be thought dangerous as a razor blade; we regarded it as the most malicious danger to our boyhood. The fear of *ecifuba* (the chest disease that is believed to follow sexual irregularity) was the key to good behaviour. If I could go to my village and pray to the older gods, I would be a better man. We had no Jesus, because that never happened to us. But Christianity now had destroyed all those things.'

Such nostalgia for the past is often only a stereotyped excuse. As

Benedict Kasenga pointed out, 'They won't go back to the old way and they won't go the Gospel way. They are in between, with no God.' Being 'in between', however, often means that, in an emergency, when one way seems to fail, the other may be tried. Sammy Ntara said,

> 'Even when a person is full of proper belief that Jesus Christ is the Son of God, he may still trust in spells and charms because these are only a small thing. When the shortest way to my house is blocked by snakes, then I may go a roundabout way to my house. Christian people know that the old way can kill them, yet they still follow that way. They believe Christianity, but not very deep; they still think what their parents taught them to do.'

Then he added—and his words spotlight all the naked, lonely wrestlers by whose response, under the lordship of the Holy Spirit, the young Church must grow—

> 'You people received Christianity long before us. Your parents are praying for you, so God must give you the Spirit and make you strong. But it is not so with us. We have to stand alone with no one behind us.'

Did he but know it, the weakness of the Church in the Anglo-Saxon West is a good deal due to the fact that we so rarely stand alone with no one behind us. Our Christianity also is 'not very deep', because it consists so largely of thinking what our parents taught us. The great peril for any Church is to be satisfied with taking over ready-made patterns from the past and so escaping the real decisions. This is the danger of emphasizing the once-for-all and universal aspect of Christianity, at the expense of the immediate and unique call and response.

This constitutes the supreme challenge to the imagination, faith and patience of the modern missionary. It is questionable whether he should ever insist on anything in his own spiritual inheritance which does not compel the conscience of the Church he goes to serve. For when people do not develop step by step from their point of departure by a series of choices, but jump over into an apparently Christian new pattern without growth by decision then, sooner or later, old pagan patterns reassert themselves. But the missionary, by the very nature of his calling, is always being tempted to seek acknowledgement rather than decision; and that is what the Church for its part is always too prone to give. It is infinitely harder for all concerned 'in making clear the truth, to commend ourselves to every man's conscience in the sight of God.'[3]

NOTES

1. Mrs Mia Brandel Syrier has kindly allowed me to quote from the MS. of her absorbing and most significant study of Women's Church organizations in the Union, which is shortly to be published under the title *Manyano*.
2. J. E. Fison, *Fire upon the Earth*, Edinburgh House Press, 1958, pp. 2, 8, 9.
3. II Cor. 4.2.

INDEX

of persons, Churches and Organisations, and some places

INDEX OF SUBJECTS

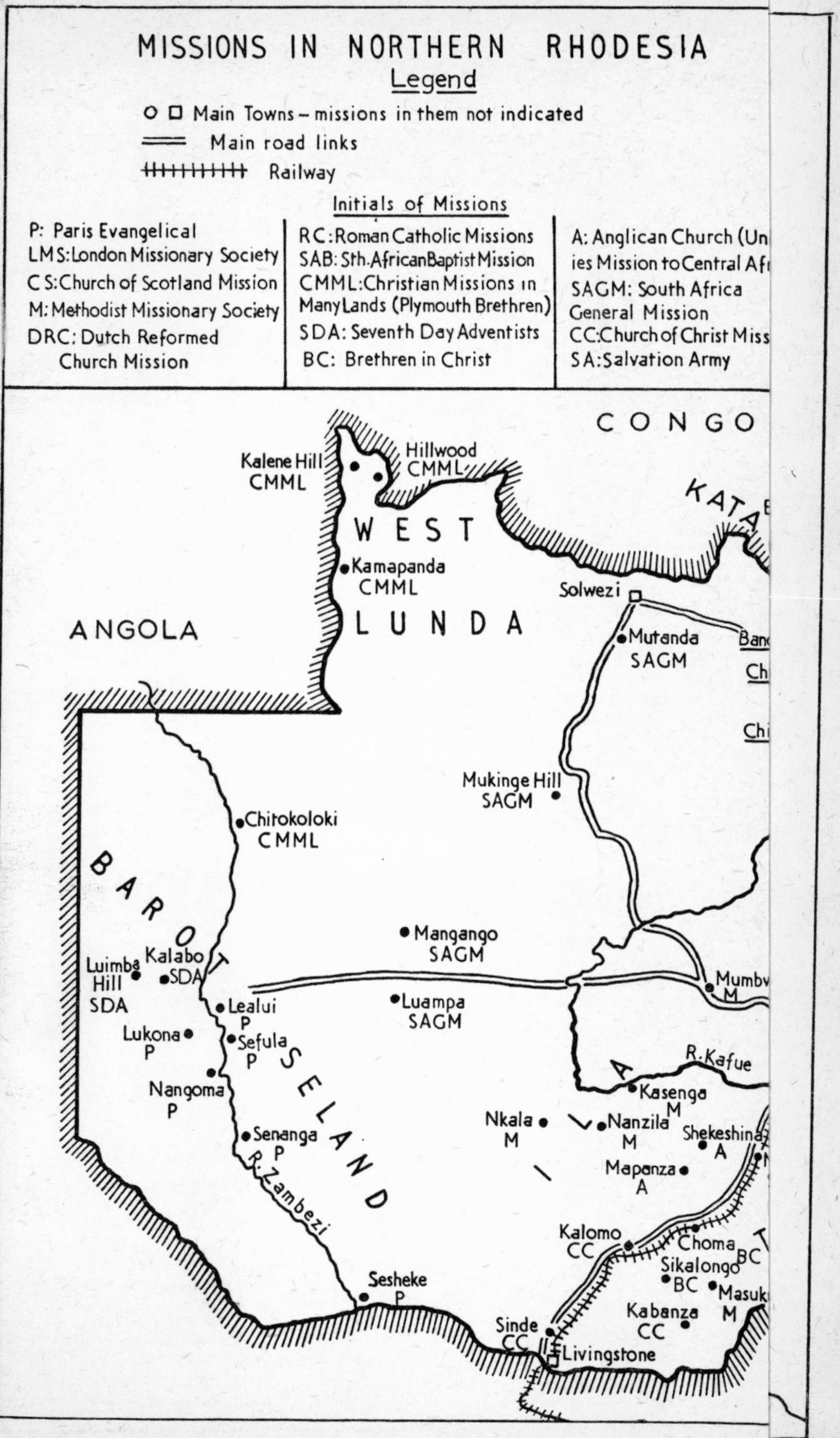
MISSIONS IN NORTHERN RHODESIA
Legend
Main Towns – missions in them not indicated
Main road links
Railway
Initials of Missions
P: Paris Evangelical
LMS: London Missionary Society
C S: Church of Scotland Mission
M: Methodist Missionary Society
DRC: Dutch Reformed Church Mission
RC: Roman Catholic Missions
SAB: Sth. African Baptist Mission
CMML: Christian Missions in Many Lands (Plymouth Brethren)
SDA: Seventh Day Adventists
BC: Brethren in Christ
A: Anglican Church (Un
ies Mission to Central Af
SAGM: South Africa General Mission
CC: Church of Christ Miss
SA: Salvation Army
CONGO
Kalene Hill CMML
Hillwood CMML
WEST LUNDA
Kamapanda CMML
Solwezi
Mutanda SAGM
ANGOLA
Mukinge Hill SAGM
Chitokoloki CMML
BAROTSELAND
Mangango SAGM
Luimba Hill SDA
Kalabo SDA
Lealui P
Luampa SAGM
Mumbw
M
Lukona P
Sefula P
R. Kafue
Nangoma P
Kasenga M
Nkala M
Nanzila M
Shekeshina A
Senanga P
Mapanza A
R. Zambezi
Kalomo CC
Choma BC
Sikalongo BC
Sesheke P
Masuk
M
Kabanza CC
Sinde CC
Livingstone

[4]